The Meeting of Religions and the Trinity

FAITH MEETS FAITH

An Orbis Series in Interreligious Dialogue
Paul F. Knitter, General Editor
Editorial Advisors
John Berthrong
Julia Ching
Diana Eck
Karl-Josef Kuschel
Lamin Sanneh
George E. Tinker
Felix Wilfred

In the contemporary world, the many religions and spiritualities stand in need of greater communication and cooperation. More than ever before, they must speak to, learn from, and work with each other in order to maintain their vital identities and to contribute to fashioning a better world.

The FAITH MEETS FAITH Series seeks to promote interreligious dialogue by providing an open forum for exchange among followers of different religious paths. While the Series wants to encourage creative and bold responses to questions arising from contemporary appreciations of religious plurality, it also recognizes the multiplicity of basic perspectives concerning the methods and content of interreligious dialogue.

Although rooted in a Christian theological perspective, the Series does not limit itself to endorsing any single school of thought or approach. By making available to both the scholarly community and the general public works that represent a variety of religious and methodological viewpoints, FAITH MEETS FAITH seeks to foster an encounter among followers of the religions of the world on matters of common concern.

FAITH MEETS FAITH SERIES

The Meeting of Religions and the Trinity

Gavin D'Costa

Maryknoll, New York 10545

The Catholic Foreign Mission Society of America (Maryknoll) recruits and trains people for overseas missionary service. Through Orbis Books, Maryknoll aims to foster the international dialogue that is essential to mission. The books published, however, reflect the opinions of their authors and are not meant to represent the official position of the society. To obtain more information about Maryknoll and Orbis Books, please visit our website at www.maryknoll.org.

Published by Orbis Books, Maryknoll, New York, U.S.A.

Manufactured in the United States of America.

The Revised Standard Version Bible (Oxford University Press, Oxford, 1971 edition) is used throughout. All citations of Vatican II documents are from Walter M. Abbott, ed., *The Documents of Vatican II*, Guild Press, New York, 1966.

Library of Congress Cataloging-in-Publication Data

D'Costa, Gavin, 1958-
The meeting of religions and the Trinity / Gavin D'Costa.
p. cm. -- (Faith meets faith)
Includes bibliographical references and index.
ISBN 1-57075-303-2 (pbk.)
1. Christianity and other religions. 2. Religious pluralism. 3. Trinity. 4. Catholic Church--Doctrines. 5. Religious pluralism--Catholic Church. I. Title. II. Series.

BR127 .D39 2000
261.2—dc21

00-026620

For
Beryl

Contents

Acknowledgments

There are numerous people who have helped me write this book. For those who explicitly read chapters in draft form or listened to them being delivered and responded so generously and critically, my sincere thanks. I list their names alphabetically: Mr. Nik Ansell, Professor Paul Badham, Fr. Michael Barnes S.J., Dr. Tina Beattie, Mr. Hugh Boulter, Dr. Bill Burrows, Mr. Peter Byrne, Rabbi Professor Dan Cohn-Sherbok, Dr. Jane Compson, Rev. Dr. John Daniels, Mrs. Beryl De Stone, Rev. Yves Dubouis, Dr. Robert Forrest, Miss Margaret Fraser, Professor Paul Helm, Professor John Hick, Rev. Dr. Philip Jenson, Dr. Richard Johnson, Professor Paul Knitter, Canon Rev. Dr. Christopher Lamb, Dr. Julius Lipner, Dr. Gerard Loughlin, Professor Ian Markham, Rev. Dr. David Marshall, Dr. Christopher Sinkinson, Rev. Professor Keith Ward, Professor Paul Williams, and Dr. John Zavos. I am also especially grateful to my two postgraduate students Daniel Strange and Tessa Kuin who looked through the entire manuscript and made many helpful suggestions and corrected numerous typographical mistakes. Dr. Gerard Loughlin saw the entire manuscript in various draft versions. I remain indebted to his humor, patience, wisdom, and friendship. None of the above bear responsibility for what I have written.

I am also blessed in working in a department with some wonderful colleagues who provide encouragement and support. Too many students remain unnamed above, but in my teaching I have often been the one taught. I am also grateful to the University of Bristol for a University Research Fellowship, that allowed me a year off (1997-98) from teaching and administration to complete this and another book. My thanks also to Clifton Cathedral, Bristol, and especially the choir and the children's liturgy group. I would also like to thank the Dean, and Rev. Professors Gerry O'Collins and Jacques Dupuis, and the inspiring students in my class at the Pontifical Gregorian University in Rome, at the Faculty of Theology, where I was the Visiting McCarthy Professor while completing this book in 1998. I am also grateful to the Rector, Vice-Rector, and students of the Irish College, Rome, where my family and I stayed during this period.

Finally, special thanks to Dr. Bill Burrows of Orbis and Professor Paul Knitter, who were more than patient with a manuscript that changed its name constantly, and also failed to arrive at expected times. Their critical comments on an earlier draft saved this book from being much worse than it is.

Finally, my thanks to my wife, Beryl, and children, Sachin and Roshan, who sustained me over the years of writing with special relations of love, healthy criticism, and lots of fun. I dedicate this book to Beryl.

This book gestated over a number of years. I sometimes tested ideas out in the form of published papers, all of which have been substantially reworked for inclusion into this book. I thank the following for copyright permission: part of chapter 1: "The Impossibility of a Pluralist View of Religions," *Religious Studies*, 32, 1996, 223-32; section III of chapter 4: "The Resurrection, the Holy Spirit and the World Religions," in Gavin D'Costa, ed., *Resurrection Reconsidered*, Oneworld, Oxford, 1996, 150-67.

Technical Notes

In my discussion of different religions, various languages have been employed, such as Greek, Hebrew, Latin, Sanskrit, Pali, and Arabic. In all instances I have given an English translation after a word has been used for the first time, or it is explained in the text. The use of diacritical marks is consistent within the text. There is no single manner in which diacritical marks are employed within the entire academic community, but those familiar with them will recognize the word immediately and those who are not will not be affected by the conventions I have employed.

When texts are cited frequently the page numbers of the citation will be kept in the main body of the chapter, rather than in the endnotes. When this is done, it will be clear from the main text, and full bibliographical details of the work being cited will be found in the accompanying endnote. In the endnotes for each chapter, after the first full citation of a title, subsequent references to that title within the notes will be abbreviated.

Introduction

There has been much recent discussion on Christianity's relation to other religions.[1] One interesting feature of this debate is the emergence of a dominant model within which to construe the discussion, and the growing influence of one of the three types within the dominant model. The model contains the threefold typology of pluralism, inclusivism, and exclusivism; and the growing influence of pluralism can be seen in the literature after the second world war. Roughly speaking, pluralism is the position which claims that all religions, more or less, are equally valid ways in helping men and women find their way to God. Pluralists are usually critical of exclusivists, who hold that only Christianity (and often, a particular denominational version) is true, and exclusively capable of helping men and women to a full relationship with God. Pluralists usually argue that exclusivists have no grounds for real openness and tolerance toward other religions, nor have they anything to learn from these religions. The resultant attitude is politically translated into empire, imperialism, and aggressive mission.[2] Of course, biblical, theological, and philosophical arguments are also employed by all groups. Inclusivism is often characterized as holding to the definitive truth of Christianity, but recognizing that other religions may be "lawful religions" (Rahner), even if in a provisional manner.[3]

A further interesting feature within this area of the debate (the threefold typology, and the growth of pluralism) is the critique mounted against pluralism by some authors (for example, Kenneth Surin, John Milbank, and Gerard Loughlin) that Christian pluralism is in fact Enlightenment modernity.[4] This is the point within the debate at which I hope to make my intervention. Following Alasdair MacIntyre, I am as convinced as the writers just cited that Christian pluralism is a species of Enlightenment modernity. If this is the case, and I shall be trying to further demonstrate that it is, then two further interesting questions arise.

First, what of pluralists within other religious communities in the modern world? Are they also covert modernists? Second, are these forms of pluralism successful—by their own criteria? As far as I know there has been very little research in this area. There have been a number of excellent collections of essays on those from the religions outlining their views on religions other than their own, and there have been some historical overviews of the matter.[5] However, I know of no sustained analysis of "pluralism" within differing religions. This then is what I shall offer in Part I, where I explore the meeting of religions as theorized by pluralists from Christianity, Judaism, Hinduism, and Buddhism.

I shall be arguing that not all pluralists are modernists, but those who are, hold positions that fail. Despite their intentions to encourage openness, tolerance, and equality they fail to attain these goals (on their own definition) because of the tradition-specific nature of their positions. Their particular shaping tradition is the Enlightenment. While this complex historical movement had many positive aspects, I shall be focusing selectively on the negative aspects in what follows. The Enlightenment, in granting a type of equality to all religions, ended up denying public truth to any and all of them. This is the unintended outcome of the Christian and Jewish pluralist positions that I examine—John Hick and Paul Knitter, and Dan Cohn-Sherbok respectively. Their god is modernity's god.

The neo-Hindu pluralism advanced by Sarvapelli Radhakrishnan provides an interesting variation. It too fails. In being neo-Hindu, that is modern, it sometimes tries to advance a positionless pluralism that is not dependent on Hinduism. This maneuver is doomed, for it attempts to erase the historicity of all positions. It is also doomed for it cannot find any particular authority for its claims, and if it evokes Hindu authority at the crucial moment in the argument, then it fails by prioritizing Hinduism's claims over the others. However, it is different from Enlightenment pluralism as it finally affirms the truth of the tradition-specific Advaita understanding of Brahman. In so much as it does this, then it fails to be pluralist in the way it intends, and also displays a lack of real historical interest in the difference, or challenge, that other religions may present. Like modernity's pluralism, it has slotted the religions into a theoretical framework which has *a priori* domesticated them before real historical engagement.

In turning to my Tibetan Buddhist pluralist, His Holiness the Dalai Lama, I find that his pluralism is entirely pragmatic, which is in keeping with various premodern features of Buddhism. However, it too fails to be the type of thing that pluralism is supposed to be: open, tolerant, and granting equality. In one sense, my Buddhist pluralist is quite aware of his Tibetan Buddhist exclusivism, but I argue that on Tibetan Buddhist grounds some of the claims he advances regarding other religions cannot be sustained.

I do not claim that my own study in this area is comprehensive, for I do not deal with Islam, New Age movements, Confucianism and many other traditions, nor do I deal with the diverse forms of pluralism within the religions that I do address. I leave the further exploration of this to those who may find the arguments presented here convincing or contentious. I have confined my study to the twentieth century, given my yet to be proven assumption that pluralism is entirely novel. This is not surprising if pluralism is a child of modernity, be it through direct birth (Hick, Knitter, and Cohn-Sherbok), or secondary influence (Radhakrishnan and the Dalai

Lama). Nevertheless, I would suggest that this study is still novel in developing this particular line of argument with regard to two questions generated at a certain point of the debate.

Are all pluralists covert modernists? How successful are their projects? In tandem with these two questions, I raise and answer a third. I want to ask whether the typology that has sustained and formed much of the debate is coherent, and whether all forms of pluralism inevitably collapse into different tradition-specific forms of exclusivism, and could not do otherwise? If this is the case, and I shall argue that it is, then a number of further interesting avenues emerge.

One regards the fate of inclusivism. Is it a middle position if there is no middle in this particular typology? I shall be suggesting that inclusivism also collapses into differing types of exclusivism. Second, if pluralism cannot deliver on its attractive and populist promises of openness, tolerance, and equality in its attitude to other religions, can any position do so? "Rhetorically," I shall be suggesting that a form of Roman Catholic trinitarianism can better deliver on the goals desired by pluralists, even if these "goals" are thus transformed in my rendering of them. I shall return to this in a moment for it forms Part II of my book. Third, if the typology evaporates, it allows us to develop a more historically oriented sensibility toward the debate. It allows us to see that all positions, religious or otherwise, are historically contingent tradition-specific forms of enquiry and practice that are therefore irreducibly different. There may be important overlaps, although the extent of this cannot be predicted. Furthermore, there may be possibilities of mutual political action, but none can be predicted *a priori*.

However, before proceeding to outline the trinitarian theology of Part II, I need to pause. There is much in the above account that calls for further justification, especially my assessment of modernity, and structuring of the book as a type of dialectical debate against pluralism so as to commend my own form of Roman Catholic trinitarianism. I will try to attend to this task by narrating the project of Alasdair MacIntyre, upon whom I am greatly dependent, and John Milbank's critique of MacIntyre. I am indebted to both writers and see my book as a modest critical development of aspects of both their achievements. I only touch on some highlights within both writers to illuminate aspects of the present book.

In brief, MacIntyre's *After Virtue* (1981) helps to highlight the problems and pervasiveness of modernity, or as he calls it, the Enlightenment project.[6] MacIntyre persuasively argues that the Enlightenment project was doomed to failure. John Horton and Susan Mendus provide a good summary of that book's argument:

> The Enlightenment project which has dominated philosophy during the past three hundred years promised a conception of rationality independent of historical and social context, and independent of any specific understanding of man's nature or purpose. But not only has

> that promise in fact been unfulfilled, the project is itself fundamentally flawed and the promise could never be fulfilled. In consequence, modern moral and political thought are in a state of disarray from which they can be rescued only if we revert to an Aristotelian paradigm, with its essential commitment to teleology, and construct an account of practical reason premised on that commitment.[7]

The Enlightenment project, in so much as it has dominated philosophy and moral and political thought, has inevitably affected religious thought, primarily Christian, but also other religions in differing ways. Milbank's work is particularly helpful in charting the impact of modernity on Christian theology and practice. It is worth noting two features of this impact. First, the Enlightenment trajectory in part accounts for the demise of trinitarian theology and Christian practice in rendering and reconstructing the world within the grand-narratives of philosophy (Kant, Hobbes, Locke, and Rousseau, and eventually Marx and Hegel), sociology (Comte, Durkheim, and Weber) and science. Within these narratives the world is best understood and analyzed without God, who is always positioned as moral authorizer, social cement, and expedient but ultimately redundant explanatory principle. Deism was the initial home for this unemployed god, but agnosticism, atheism, and secularism were the inevitable trajectories, such that unemployment eventually led to redundancy and liquidation.[8]

Second, the relationship between morality and deity underwent a radical shift. The Christian telos was ousted, such that universal reason and freedom became both the ethical means and ends. The Kantian move toward a universal ethics which could be grounded in pure reason and fleshed out in practical reason was inevitable. Kant could view the religions, with Christianity as the unsurpassable best, as more or less embodying the ethical universals he was able to arrive at through reason alone. This form of ethical thinking required an impartial state to arbitrate political, social, and ethical matters. Christianity would have to align itself with these ethical universals or lose social credibility and privilege.

The pervasiveness of the Enlightenment project has special consequences for my argument. It sets the context for my search in Part I to examine the relationship of pluralism to the Enlightenment. Second, in finding forms of pluralism that are not entirely reducible to Enlightenment ideology, but nevertheless generated by religions engaging with the modern west, I critically inspect the relationship of modernity to Hinduism and Buddhism in regard to my specific question of how religions view each other. Admittedly, the pervasiveness of modernity means that "religious traditions" today are far from a seamless narrative. However, precisely because of this, John Milbank suggests that if we dialogue with living articulate exponents of, say, Hinduism, we are more likely to be engaged as liberal moderns talking with other liberal moderns. Milbank's point is important, but he pushes the argument too far in then suggesting that such Hindu speakers, in their

> very willingness to speak will probably betray an alienation from the seamless narrative succession of a tradition which never felt the need for dialogical self-justification. . . . Rather, it is we ourselves who have to conjure up this difference, not by listening to the most articulate of the living, but by an attentive reading of "dead" texts pre-dating Western intrusion and practices relatively uncontaminated by Western influence.[9]

Milbank assumes that all religious traditions are constructed out of a "seamless narrative succession," which is a profoundly (and uncharacteristic) ahistorical judgment. Hinduism has been far from a "seamless narrative succession," such that it historically exemplifies some traditions in which caste is central to social organization, and traditions (less successful) in which caste has been contested; it exemplifies profound devotional theism (Madhva) and an austere philosophical monism that also incorporates a vibrant devotionalism (Śankara); it conducts sophisticated philosophical "dialogical self-justification" against the Buddhists, and in turn those self-justifications are called into question—witness the debate between Śankara and Rāmānuja.[10]

Furthermore, one might ask how it is that Milbank can adjudicate between what might be "legitimate" Hindu developments, without any recourse to the complex symphony of Hindu voices, or differing notions of authority within the traditions of Hinduism, and deem himself ("we ourselves have to conjure up . . . ") the arbiter of pristine Hinduism? However, I am not concerned to pursue this argument with Milbank, and am quite sympathetic to the main point he is making. Rather, I want to highlight that one task in my own project is to actually uncover the extent of modernity's influence upon the religions in their meeting, and to analyze, case by case, the way in which modernity (in its different forms) internally coheres with, or grates against, the premodern forms of religious thinking upon which it has been grafted.

Consequently, I have chosen modern thinkers, in part because they have engaged with questions that their predecessors did not have to face, precisely because their predecessors were not moderns. Furthermore, I am interested in engaging with such thinkers, not simply to out-narrate them and convert them, as Milbank suggests, but also following MacIntyre, to engage in dialectics.[11] To flush out the meaning and significance of Milbank's rhetorical out-narration (conversion by faith) and MacIntyre's dialectics (historically contextualized rational argument), let me follow MacIntyre into his second book: *Whose Justice? Which Rationality?* (1988).

In this book, MacIntyre defends himself from relativism, the charge aimed at *After Virtue*, and tries instead to show that different positions might be able to engage in rational debate such that there may be a successful outcome. His example is the debate that takes place in twelfth-century Paris between Aquinas and the Aristotelian and Augustinian traditions, with Thomism emerging the victor. Hauerwas and Pinches summarize the argument succinctly:

> Crucial to [MacIntyre's] project is the possibility that the Christian account of the virtues can be successfully grafted onto the Greek heritage. Hence, he attempts to demonstrate how Augustine was able to resolve antinomies intrinsic to and yet unresolvable within the Greek account of virtue, and how Aquinas, revising and extending Augustine's insights, did the same, producing the most satisfactory version of morality we have had so far.[12]

The notion of dialectic that emerges in this account is closely tied to the Thomism that MacIntyre finds so persuasive. It has three features that I want to highlight because they are so important to Part I of this present book. First, it involves the learning of a second language, which we learn to speak almost as fluently as our first. Otherwise, we are always in danger of assimilating difference and otherness, imagining that the Other can be understood purely within our own terms of reference. We must be intellectually well-prepared to engage with other traditions and practices. Second, it involves locating the internal problems within that tradition, by that tradition's own standards and criteria, and showing why those problems and the questions they seek to address are possibly irresolvable within those traditions on their own terms. Traditionally this is called "apologetics." Third, it requires that our tradition is able to address both the lacunae within the other tradition and more satisfactorily resolve the problems that exercised that tradition. This conception of dialectics operates in *Whose Justice?* and is extended and developed in his next book, *Three Rival Versions of Moral Enquiry* (1990) to consider the debate between the Enlightenment project, postmodernism, and Roman Catholic Thomism.

MacIntyre's signaling toward "an Aristotelian paradigm" at the end of *After Virtue* has been seen as "little more than whistling in the dark to keep the spirits up when set against his coruscating critique of modernity."[13] This judgment is only half correcth. The weakness of MacIntyre's early position is not, as such critics would have it, that he has nowhere to stand since he has so relentlessly demolished the Enlightenment, but rather that his virtue ethics lacks substantial teleological specification to provide a credible social alternative. It is impossible to see how, and from where, MacIntyre opposes the Enlightenment project, other than from gesturing toward the antique *polis* of Aristotle. Even if this is remedied to some extent in *Whose Justice?* where MacIntyre's vague Aristotelianism is given more specification in terms of Roman Catholic Thomism, it is an underdeveloped remedy. We have to await the next book to see his Thomism coming of age, for only there does it find itself actually located within a community of practice—Roman Catholicism.

Milbank's critique of *Whose Justice?* is particularly helpful in two respects. First, Milbank rightly notes of MacIntyre's book that "at the *philosophic* level, an air of non-commitment hovers over MacIntyre's position."[14] Second, Milbank also notes that the Aristotelian virtue advocated by MacIntyre should be sharply contrasted with Christian virtue. There is no simple continuity established by dialectical reasoning. After showing the important ways in which Aristotle's magnanimous man, the highest embodiment of virtue, differs significantly from Aquinas's understanding of the virtuous person, especially in so much as the former is established through heroism in war, Milbank concludes: "the main consideration here is that antiquity failed really to arrive at the ontological priority of peace to conflict and therefore failed . . . to break with the heroic conception of virtue and arrive at a genuinely ethical good."[15]

In one sense, Milbank's criticisms are vindicated by MacIntyre himself, in so much as MacIntyre's next book becomes profoundly more Thomist and also coincides with MacIntyre's becoming a Roman Catholic. However, one of Milbank's further criticisms of MacIntyre is less convincing. He charges MacIntyre with a return to foundationalism:

> [MacIntyre] also believes that the dialectical questioning of the starting points establishes them more securely in their relationship to reality, if they constantly withstand skeptical interrogation. Thus, perfectly contingent starting points progressively but negatively struggle free of the historical chrysalis and float upwards to universality. This "securing" of virtue, I shall argue, is a new mode of foundationalism. Likewise I shall reject MacIntyre's dialectical rendering of the modification of tradition, and the abandonment of one tradition for another. This is particularly apparent in his account of the grafting of the Christian onto the Greek inheritance; Augustine's and Aquinas's ethical thought is *validated primarily because* they give better answers than the Greeks to Greek problems, according to Greek criteria. Such a perspective may not, however, do justice to the fact that the Fathers and scholastics understood the beliefs grounding their ethics as matters of persuasion, or of faith. These positions of faith could not be dialectically inferred or called into question but were, rather, "rhetorically" instilled.[16]

Milbank's charge is both specific and general. The specific relates to whether MacIntyre is right about Thomism as dialectically constituted, rather than rhetorically instilled. The general charge is that MacIntyre operates with a foundational belief in rational dialectics as the means to truth. On the specific charge, it seems unnecessary to stage the question in either/or terms. Thomism is surely rhetorically constituted (and in this sense Milbank is correct), but also at the same time, not without dialectics, precisely because of Thomism's confidence in reason, which is always, of course, traditioned reason (and in this sense MacIntyre is correct). Milbank's reading of MacIntyre as presenting Aquinas's ethical thought as "validated primarily because" it gives "better answers than the Greeks to Greek problems, according to Greek criteria" is no where substantiated. It is surely a case of reading into MacIntyre, and forcing an argument on the materials. The arguments employed by Aquinas were used to persuade the "opponent" that they were incoherent or inconsistent in holding their position, and that their problems would be better dealt with from Thomas's position. Neither Aquinas nor MacIntyre believed that this would simply lead to opponents' abandoning their position, nor do either present these as grounds for "validating" their own position. Milbank pushes too hard at the process of dialectics as reconstructed by MacIntyre and is therefore led to his second general charge, which I also find unconvincing. It is unconvincing because MacIntyre is not advancing dialectics as a universal method, but showing that specifically in this historical instance, it did important work to resolve contesting arguments. Furthermore, he also shows in his next book that rival traditions in our own age might be argued against on their own grounds to commend the vitality of Thomism. In both instances the specific case illustrates not the general law of dialectics, but the possible triumph of Thomism in particular engagements with different and rival traditions when they have enough of a shared sense of rational argument. I find Milbank's resort to rhetorically out-narrating different traditions quite persuasive in some instances. Nevertheless, to assume that rhetorical out-narration, in place of dialectics, is *the* method of engagement, is to replace one form of foundationalism, if that were indeed MacIntyre's position, with another.

If Milbank's point is that different positions are different, all the way down, and cannot simply be seen as leading rationally from one to another, then I think MacIntyre cannot be assimilated into his critique of Hegelianism. Nowhere does MacIntyre make such a broad claim. In fact, one might turn the argument against Milbank and note that his own position is continuously established by showing why other positions fail on their own criteria (Plato and Aristotle), and on an alien criterion: that they are not founded on an ontology of peace as is Christianity.[17] The latter move is rhetorical, by Milbank's definition, and has a legitimate place in engagement with other positions. The former strategy is dialectical, by MacIntyre's definition, and also seems to have a legitimate role as long as it is not confused with rhetoric. Milbank thinks that MacIntyre has conflated one with the other, and I have been suggesting otherwise.

One point I want to make is that if history and contingency are taken seriously, then neither dialectics nor rhetoric can assume a methodological *a priorism*, but one must simply work in an *ad hoc* fashion. Both strategies might be employed as and when they seem appropriate. Dialectics may be appropriate depending on the traditioned understanding of rationality held by the Other, and the particular historical context of engagement. For example, when people do change traditions, both dialectical and rhetorical consideration might operate, and there is no need to insist on the priority of one over the other, nor limit our analysis to these two ways of construing the matter.

I have attended to this difference between Milbank and MacIntyre for a number of reasons. Part I of my book is straightforward apologetics. I am trying to show that pluralism does not work by its own criteria. This apologetic or dialectical task is directed at four religious traditions in so much as they advance pluralism, and a hidden fifth tradition—modernity. Part II of my book can be understood in terms of both rhetoric and dialectics, for I try to show that the most important aspirations of pluralists (openness, tolerance, and equality toward other religions) are actually better embodied, more coherently justified, and fully articulated within modern Roman Catholic trinitarianism. However, dialectics must concede to rhetoric in so much as the "goals" of pluralists are renarrated within my own position such that they might be unrecognizable to the pluralist. Furthermore, these are hardly the "goals" of my own position, but contingent outcomes of worshiping a trinitarian God within the context of religious pluralism.

A further reason for attending to these two authors, is to suggest in contrast, that one need not construe the other as "rival" (MacIntyre), nor as the object of out-narration (Milbank). Within a Roman Catholic trinitarian orientation, the other is always interesting in their difference and may be the possible face of God, or the face of violence, greed, and death. Furthermore, the other may teach Christians to know and worship their own trinitarian God more truthfully and richly. Trinitarian theology provides the context for a critical, reverent, and open engagement with otherness, without any predictable outcome. Finally, there is one further reason for attending to these two authors. Both have confined their projects to Christianity and its parasitic off-springs: modernity and postmodernity. I hope to move a step further. However, to show why and how, let me return to MacIntyre's third book.

MacIntyre's third book, *Three Rival Versions of Moral Enquiry* (1990), continues his project and also forms a vital bridge to my own. In it he argues that western European society is confronted by three rival versions of moral enquiry, each with its own epistemological, ontological, ethical, and methodological assumptions. While they may seem incommensurable, MacIntyre also seeks to show that there may be the possibility of a historically narrated rational debate between them, such that one might emerge the superior.[18] What are the three rival versions? There is of course the Enlightenment project, which MacIntyre here calls the "Encyclopedic," for he characterizes it in its embodiment in the ninth edition of the *Encyclopedia Britannica*. The second tradition, which has always been on the horizons of MacIntyre's work, is that of the "Genealogical," or the postmodern, typified by Nietzsche's *Genealogy of Morals*. The postmodern is parasitic upon the Enlightenment. To understand how, we must briefly return to MacIntyre's critique of Enlightenment morality.

In the words of Kelvin Knight, MacIntyre argues that despite all their important differences, what

> united Hume, Kant and others in a single project was . . . their agreement that the prerequisite for enlightenment was the rejection of their Aristotelian heritage. A central part of what they thereby rejected was a syllogistic way of justifying the rules of morality on the basis not only of an apprehension of "man-as-he-happens-to-be" but also of "human-nature-as-it-could-be-if-it-realized-its-*telos*." In so doing, claims MacIntyre, they [such enlightenment thinkers] rejected the only way of coherently moving from an apprehension of what is to an apprehension of what ought to be. Only when apprehended as the only means by which to move from one's present self to one's *telos*, to one's true good in society with others, can it be concluded that the rules of morality are categorical. What followed from Enlightenment philosophers' rejection of teleology was their interminable disagreement about how the rules of morality might be justified, insoluble problems in the proposals of each being identified by others.[19]

Eventually all that could be agreed was that people ought to be free to agree or disagree, and the birth of the modern nation state and liberal democracy was its social and political counterpart. However, with no common *telos* even this minimal consensus would eventually come into question. Nietzsche was inevitable, given the unresolvable lacunae within the Enlightenment project which replaced the *telos* of the common good with the formal requirement of human freedom. Nietzsche saw that there could be no real foundation for ethics in this stance and consequently celebrated the will to power, which was always the repressed truth within the Enlightenment matrix. For MacIntyre's own argument to work, he develops a further critique of the postmodern or Nietzschian Genealogical "tradition" which is not my concern here. However, I do believe that MacIntyre is fundamentally right in calling into question the nihilism of (some) postmodern philosophy and practice.

The position which allows him to reveal and to narrate the shortcomings of both the Encyclopedic and the Genealogical is Thomism, mediated by Pope Leo XIII's *Aeterni Patris*. While distorting Thomism, it nevertheless presents the most satisfactory alternative to the others, even by their own criteria. I find MacIntyre's arguments persuasive, and I see my own book as a kind of footnote critically developing certain trajectories out of his project, and with a more theological orientation that reflects my own training. I do not locate myself as a Roman Catholic Thomist as such, but write out of a fluid and complex Roman Catholic "tradition." While MacIntyre has been both criticized for working, on the one hand, with too rigid a definition of tradition, and, on the other hand, with too ambiguous a notion of tradition, I do not find him guilty on either of these counts. Admittedly, it doesn't help his case when he linguistically conflates the "Thomist" with "tradition," and pits "Tradition against Encyclopedia" and "Tradition against Genealogy" in chapters eight and nine respectively of *Three Rival Versions*. However, MacIntyre is unambiguous in this same book that liberal Enlightenment constitutes a tradition even if it is paradoxically an anti-tradition, as does Genealogy, even if it is doubly paradoxically, as an anti-anti-tradition. He is clear at the outset of his project in *After Virtue* that "a living tradition then is a historically extended, socially embodied argument, and an argument precisely in part about the good which constitute that tradition."[20] Traditions change and develop and will constitute complex sets of internal debates and differences. There is no pristine tradition, either in Roman Catholicism or in Hinduism, as Milbank seems to assume.

I see my book as developing MacIntyre's project in two particular directions. First, MacIntyre is rather selective (necessarily so) in his assessment of western culture. There are only three rival versions of moral enquiry, and as Milbank has correctly argued, the Enlightenment and the Genealogical are both generated out of the Christian tradition. But what of those distinctly Other western cultural forces: Judaism and Islam? Why are they not part of MacIntyre's geography, since both, and especially Islam, have drawn so heavily from Aristotle? Furthermore, given the real religious plurality within the west, what of Hindu and Buddhist forms of social practice and metaphysical thought—not to mention many others? The complexity of disagreements and debate are obscured by MacIntyre's limited cartography.

To be fair, MacIntyre is well aware of this, and has more recently addressed Confucianism on this very score.[21] One cannot criticize MacIntyre for not carrying out a project he never intended to address. But it is a project that is required if Christian thought and practice is engaged with other religions, both in the west and elsewhere. Let me give one example from a Muslim critic of MacIntyre, Muhammad Legenhausen. He notes Islam's relationship to the Aristotelian tradition upon which MacIntyre is so dependent, and therefore criticizes the omission of Islam in MacIntyre's discussion. Furthermore, Legenhausen, writing in Iran, suggests that Islam can account for the aporia within MacIntyre's argument whereby MacIntyre's espousal of small sectarian communities, after the order of St. Benedict, fails entirely to engage with the problem of the nation state which MacIntyre identifies as one of the roots of the contemporary malaise. According to Legenhausen, Islam is able to deal with precisely this question and offers a theocratic solution, allegedly avoiding both "nationalism and liberalism," an alternative that is "not taken seriously by Western theorists."[22] These are precisely the further conflicts that need to be addressed, which are somewhat obscured by MacIntyre's present cartography, but also made available through his perspective.

The second direction in which I wish to develop a new path within MacIntyre's project is in terms of staging a form of both dialectical argument and rhetorical persuasion in regard to the religious traditions with which I engage. In doing so I focus on a trinitarian form of Christianity, rather than a predominantly philosophical form of Thomism. I see these as complementary rather than opposing approaches, and I view Milbank's development of an Augustinian trinitarian rhetoric as yet another complementary project, even if Milbank sees his own as calling MacIntyre's into question. I would not wish to compare this small book with the scope and depth of both these writers, but as a development out of the paths they have opened up. Milbank, like MacIntyre, has stayed within the orbit of the Enlightenment and Genealogical, and this book extends the discussion.[23] My method of dealing with the trinity and the question of interreligious prayer in the final chapters further distinguishes a complementary difference between myself and these two authors.

My entire discussion is firmly rooted in ecclesial documents from Vatican II to the present day. This is taking tradition-specificity seriously. This inevitable contingent point of departure means that any Christian position advanced on these questions must be rooted in, and accountable to, an ecclesial community. I find this aspect sometimes overlooked in Milbank and MacIntyre. I certainly do not want to suggest that the Bible, philosophy, and other disciplines are unimportant. My position is advanced with careful attention to biblical witness. However, strategically intrachurch dialectics is more important to me in Part II than the dialectical conversation with other religions and modernity. This alone justifies my method. However, while this justification suffices on its own, it highlights one of the arguments that shapes Part II: the doctrine of the trinity is a community-forming doctrine. Hence, to use the community's own authoritative documents is theologically necessary, even though one should not be limited to these documents alone, or for that matter to literary documentary sources.

In the chapter on my trinitarian orientation, I hope to show three things. First, that Vatican II and post-Vatican II documents do not legitimate pluralism or inclusivism. This is the bridge between Parts I and II of the book. Second, I try to show that since Vatican II the Roman Catholic church advances a position on other religions that is highly trinitarian and allows for the active sanctifying role of the Holy Spirit to be present within other religions that cannot be predicted by the church. Given the Johannine understanding of the Holy Spirit's function as forming the body of Christ and leading it into ever greater truth, I argue that the church must begin to learn the ecclesial significance of the presence of other religions. Hence, it is both an extremely traditional and conservative approach as well as deeply radical. Third, I then try to show how modern Roman Catholicism has worked out the implications of its own position by analyzing Vatican II's *Declaration on Religious Freedom* (*Dignitatis Humanae* in Latin). Here

I want to suggest that pluralism's goals are best met within Roman Catholicism, but in the process are renarrated intelligibly. "Openness" becomes "taking history seriously"; "tolerance" becomes the "qualified establishment of civic religious freedom for all on the basis of Christian revelation and natural law"; "equality" becomes the "equal and inviolable dignity of all persons."

In the final chapter I take up just one theme regarding the Spirit: how She leads us into prayer. This is a particularly important theme as it provides a test case by which to see if this type of trinitarian approach is able to illuminate a pressing pastoral question raised in interreligious dialogue: that of interreligious prayer. I wanted to focus on this question since, as I have argued elsewhere, all theology should originate and end in prayer.[24] Hence in a book dealing with the meeting of religions, there is no more suitable place to end than in the question of the possibility of shared prayer. I can also admit that when I began researching this final chapter I could not have imagined ever coming to the conclusion that I now advance. In this, I rejoice. There are so many more questions and issues to be addressed, but this book is only a very small start in trying to struggle free from some of the ways both questions and answers have been put in this field.[25]

Notes

1. For very good theological summaries and overviews see Alan Race, *Christians and Religious Pluralism*, SCM, London, 1983; 2nd ed., 1994; Paul F. Knitter, *No Other Name? A Critical Study of Christian Attitudes toward the World Religions*, Orbis, Maryknoll, N.Y., 1985; and Jacques Dupuis, *Toward a Christian Theology of Religious Pluralism*, Orbis, Maryknoll, N.Y., 1997. For more historically oriented presentations, see Carl F. Hallencreutz, *New Approaches to Men of Other Faith*, World Council of Churches, Geneva, 1970; Eric Sharpe, *Not to Destroy but to Fulfil*, Gleerups, Lund, 1965; and Francis Sullivan, *Salvation outside the Church?* Geoffrey Chapman, London, 1992; and Dupuis, *Toward a Christian Theology*, 1997.

2. John Hick makes this argument most clearly in "The Non-Absoluteness of Christianity," in John H. Hick and Paul F. Knitter, eds., *The Myth of Christian Uniqueness: Toward a Pluralistic Theology of Religions*, Orbis, Maryknoll, N.Y., 1987, 16-36; and see also Marjorie Hewitt Suchocki, "In Search of Justice," in the same collection, 149-61. Many other pluralists are agreed on this.

3. See my study of Rahner, and my defense of his position in *Theology and Religious Pluralism*, Blackwell, Oxford, 1986, 80-117.

4. See John Milbank and Kenneth Surin in their essays in Gavin D'Costa, ed., *Christian Uniqueness Reconsidered*, Orbis, Maryknoll, N.Y., 1990, 174-91, 192-212 respectively; and Gerard Loughlin, "Prefacing Pluralism: John Hick and the Mystery of Religion," *Modern Theology*, 7, 1990, 29-55.

5. For edited collections see: John Hick and Hasan Askari, eds., *Religious Diversity*, Gower, Aldershot, 1985; and Paul J. Griffiths, ed., *Christianity through Non-Christian Eyes*, Orbis, Maryknoll, N.Y., 1990; Moses Jung, et al., eds., *Relations*

among Religions Today, E. J. Brill, Leiden, 1963; David W. McKain, ed., *Christianity: Some Non-Christian Approaches*, Greenwood Press, London, 1964. For overviews, see the survey provided by Griffiths, ed., *Christianity through Non-Christian Eyes*; and Harold Coward, *Pluralism: Challenge to World Religions*, Orbis, Maryknoll, N.Y., 1985.

6. *After Virtue*, Duckworth, London, 1985, 2nd. ed.; and then his subsequent books: *Whose Justice? Which Rationality?*, Duckworth, London, 1988; *Three Rival Versions of Moral Enquiry*, Duckworth, London, 1990.

7. John Horton and Susan Mendus, eds., *After MacIntyre: Critical Perspectives on the Work of Alasdair MacIntyre*, Polity Press, Oxford, 1994, 3.

8. Besides Milbank, *Theology and Social Theory*, Blackwell, Oxford, 1990, Michael J. Buckley traces the origins of modern atheism to pre-Enlightenment theology, in the thirteenth century, whereas Hans Frei locates it in the eighteenth century. See Michael Buckley, *At the Origins of Modern Atheism*, Yale University Press, New Haven, 1987; Hans W. Frei, *The Eclipse of Biblical Narrative: A Study in Eighteenth and Nineteenth Century Hermeneutics*, Yale University Press, New Haven, 1974. Prudence Allen goes right back to Aristotle and his eventual employment within thirteenth-century Paris for the structuring of the Faculties in the newly emerging Universities. Prudence Allen, *The Concept of Woman: The Aristotelian Revolution 750 BC – AD 1250*, Eden Press, Quebec, 1985, ch. 5. The historical origins of modern atheism are complex, but this does not detract from the sociopolitical consolidation of atheism in the institutions of the Enlightenment.

9. John Milbank, "The End of Dialogue," in D'Costa, ed., *Christian Uniqueness*, 178.

10. See Sarvapelli Radhakrishnan, *Indian Philosophy*, Vol. 2, George, Allen & Unwin, London, 1923, chs. 8, 9; and Milton Singer, *When a Great Tradition Modernizes*, Pacific Press, Mount View, California, 1980. Wilhelm Halbfass, *India and Europe: An Essay in Understanding*, State University Press of New York, Albany, 1988, whom Milbank cites, does not actually support Milbank on this particular point.

11. See Milbank in D'Costa, ed., *Christian Uniqueness*, 19; and *Theology and Social Theory*, ch. 11.

12. See Stanley Hauerwas and Charles Pinches, *Christians among the Virtues: Theological Conversations with Ancient and Modern Ethics*, University of Notre Dame Press, Notre Dame, Indiana, 1997, 62.

13. Horton and Mendus, eds., *After MacIntyre*, 3.

14. Milbank, *Theology and Social Theory*, 329.

15. Milbank, *Theology and Social Theory*, 363-64.

16. Milbank, *Theology and Social Theory*, 328, my added emphasis.

17. For Milbank's admission of his carrying out MacIntyrean dialectics, see Milbank, *Theology and Social Theory*, 329ff, although he tries to defend himself from being read in this manner.

18. *Three Rival Versions*, 5.

19. Kelvin Knight, "Editor's Introduction," *The MacIntyre Reader*, Polity Press, Oxford, 1998, 8.

20. MacIntyre, *After Virtue*, 207.

21. See his "Incommensurability, truth, and the conversation between Confucians and Aristotelians about the virtues," in Eliot Deutsch, ed., *Culture and Modernity: East-West Philosophic Perspectives*, University of Hawaii Press, Honolulu, 1991, 104-22.

22. Muhammad Legenhausen, extended book review of *Whose Justice?* in *Al-Twid*, 14, 2, 1997, 158-76, 169.
23. An important exception in Milbank is his excursus into Hinduism in D'Costa, ed., *Christian Uniqueness*, 174-91.
24. "On cultivating the disciplined habits of a love affair *or* on how to do theology on your knees," *New Blackfriars*, 79, 925, 1998, 116-36.
25. I continue this struggle in *The Trinity and the Murder of the Mother*, SCM, London, 2000.

PART I

Whose God, Which Tradition?

1

Modernity's Hidden God within Christian and Jewish Pluralism

WHOSE "GOD," WHICH TRADITION?

In this chapter I want to analyze two influential "pluralist" Christian theologians who suggest overlapping strategies for engaging with other religions. I look at two Christians rather than one for three reasons. First, I am particularly interested in Christian theology on this matter, as I am a Christian theologian. Second, both John Hick and Paul Knitter are increasingly influential, so much so that a senior Roman Catholic cardinal has spoken out against both within one lecture—and given that Hick is a Presbyterian, this is quite an honor! Knitter is Roman Catholic. Third, I think they represent two very different forms of pluralism: Hick's orientation is basically philosophical; and Knitter's is theological, with a special emphasis on ethics. In this sense I want to show that despite important differences of approach and orientation, they can both be analyzed in terms of the Enlightenment tradition.

By "pluralist" I mean a range of features, shared by writers who use this term of self-description, to indicate the broad assumption that: all religions (with qualifications) lead to the same divine reality; there is no privileged self-manifestation of the divine; and finally, religious harmony will follow if tradition-specific (exclusivist) approaches which allegedly claim monopoly over the truth are abandoned in favor of pluralist approaches which recognize that all religions display the truth in differing ways. One of my arguments will be that no non-tradition-specific approach can exist, and such an apparently neutral disembodied location is in fact the tradition-specific starting point of liberal modernity, what MacIntyre calls the Encyclopedic tradition.

If my argument is persuasive then a number of consequences should follow in relation to such pluralist claims. First, one should find that they do not work. Logically, pluralists simply present themselves as honest brokers to disputing parties, while concealing the fact that they represent yet another party which invites the disputants actually to leave their parties and join the pluralist one: then, of course, interreligious harmony will be attained. Ironically, there would be no religions left when such harmony was attained, for the disputants are invited to leave their traditions (which constituted the original points of disagreement), so as to join a common and new one: liberal modernity. Second, if they do not work, then we shall find that our Christian pluralists (and later, a Jewish pluralist) in fact espouse one of the "gods" of modernity: unitarian, deistic or agnostic. The trinitarian God can find no place within such "Christian" approaches, except as the alleged cause of obstructing good interreligious relations. Third, if the two above suppositions are true, we will be able to claim properly that "pluralists" are really "exclusivists," the category type which they constantly criticize. Related to this polarity of pluralism and exclusivism, we also find the middle-ground term, inclusivism. I shall suggest that the term inclusivism is unhelpful. Before testing my arguments against two Christian theologians (John Hick and Paul Knitter), and then in regard to one Jewish theologian (Dan Cohn-Sherbok), I need to attend briefly to the genesis of this influential typology which I once defended and now wish to deconstruct.

In 1983 Alan Race put the typology of pluralism, inclusivism, and exclusivism firmly on the map in his influential book, *Christians and Religious Pluralism*.[1] Race acknowledged his debt regarding the threefold typology to the European nineteenth-century Christian missionary, John Farquhar. In 1986, I, among many other writers, followed suit in adopting and developing this threefold typology which is now found in many works dealing with Christian attitudes to other religions. The types have also been used as logical categories to analyze other religions' attitudes to each other, for example, Hindu attitudes to other religions, or Jewish attitudes to religious diversity.[2] Hence, my concern is in part with the logical form of the typology in so much as it serves to mask the "god" behind "pluralism." The process of unmasking will allow the debate to move out beyond the typologies into richer and more rewarding fields of enquiry.

First, let me define the three types more carefully before deconstructing them. The distinctions between the three positions of exclusivism, pluralism, and inclusivism are as follows. On one extreme of the spectrum there is exclusivism. This type is defined as holding that only one single revelation is true or one single religion is true and all other revelations or religions are ultimately false. Truth, revelation, and salvation are tightly and explicitly connected. In its most strict logical form, it will mean that, for example, when proposed by certain Southern Baptists, all those who are not Southern Baptists will be lost to the fires of hell.[3] In various softer versions it will allow for possibilities such as a general postmortem confrontation with Christ which gives everyone the chance to choose for or against Christian truth, so as to allow for the possibility of salvation for all. (Already, one of the dividing lines between the types becomes thin and blurred, for an alleged exclusivist like Karl Barth can also coherently be a universalist just like the pluralist, John Hick.[4]) In Buddhist and Hindu versions of exclusivism, a person in a future life will have the opportunity to come to liberation through the process of reincarnation and *karma* when they return as, for example, a *bodhisattva* or *jīvanmuktī*. Such softer versions still keep the basic exclusivist insight intact: that fundamentally only one single revelation or one single religion is true and all other revelations or religions alike are finally false.

On the opposite end of the spectrum is pluralism. This type is defined as holding that all the major religions have true revelations in part, while no single revelation or religion can claim final and definitive truth. This means that all religions are viewed as more or less equally true, and more or less as equally valid paths to salvation. The advantage of this position, argue its supporters, is that it renders genuine respect and autonomy to the various different religions and facilitates good interreligious harmony. In their opinion, this is one of their chief strengths. There are no adherents to this position that I know of who imply uncritical endorsement of every phenomenon that might present itself as religious, such as the People's Temple (of the 1978 Jonestown mass suicide), or the Branch Davidians (of the 1993 Waco massacre), or the Order of the Solar Temple (of the 1994 Swiss mass suicide). Hence, pluralists usually differentiate between very corrupt minor religious cults and the major world religions. Pluralists usually criticize exclusivist positions from their own traditions on two principal points: exclusivists are committed to denying the significance of good, holy, or compassionate people (or whatever sort of description is apt) in other religions; and, further, that exclusivists have incorrect readings of their own sacred texts which misguidedly lead them to exclusivism. The question of the interpretation of texts and experience are the two main points which pluralists usually employ in their revisionary strategies. The order in which these criticisms are developed is sometimes reversible and the details of the argument will, of course, vary.

In the middle of the spectrum are those called inclusivist, who, as is often the case with those in the middle, try to have it both ways. They are committed to claiming that one revelation or religion (sometimes in a specific denominational form) is the only one true and definitive one, but that truth, and therefore salvation, can be found in various, though incomplete, forms within other religions and within their different structures. It is always the case that such different and sometimes rival claims are judged by the criteria arising from the one true revelation or religion, and in fact true rival claims must conform to the true revelation or religion. The traditional implication of this position is that Christianity (or Hinduism, or whichever religion) is regarded as the fulfillment of other religions.

There are important variations within all these types, but this is not relevant to my concern, for I want to suggest that "pluralism" represents a tradition-specific approach that bears all the same features as exclusivism—except that it is western liberal modernity's exclusivism. I will be suggesting later that liberal modernity's response to the fact of diversity is less promising than the form of trinitarian Christianity I am advancing. In this chapter, both Christian and Jewish pluralists will be seen to be Enlightenment exclusivists. (The same cannot be said of the Hindu and Buddhist pluralists.) In so much as they are Enlightenment exclusivists, I shall argue they fail in terms of their own stated intentions: to facilitate better interreligious conversation. Unwittingly, they stifle religious differences within the grand narrative of liberal modernity so that no religion, even their own, is allowed to speak with its full force. One might say, polemically, that they are hard-line exclusivists.

And what of inclusivism? I want to suggest that inclusivism logically collapses into exclusivism in three particular ways. First, inclusivists, like exclusivists, hold that their tradition finally contains the truth regarding ontological, epistemological, and ethical claims. This particular narrative helps to narrate all creation. While inclusivists acknowledge truth elsewhere, it is always mitigated in some form or other, in its own right, such that it cannot be on the same logical level as the truth of, for example, Christianity. This view can be held by both inclusivists and exclusivists, while also acknowledging that the tradition is reformable and capable of a certain erring. In this fundamentally important sense, there is no difference between the two. Second, both inclusivists and exclusivists hold to the inseparability of ontology, epistemology, and ethics such that truth cannot be separated from the mediator: Christ and his church. In so much as a separability is conceded, inclusivists tend toward pluralism. Third, both inclusivists and exclusivists recognize the tradition-specific nature of their enquiry, such that they are committed to defend their position and engage in argument with rival or alternative traditions. The claims they make are taken to be important, for they concern questions of truth. Hence, in the most important logical sense, it is difficult to see what separates these two positions, except for one very important point: inclusivists seek to affirm religions other than Christianity as the means to salvation. (They both, as we have seen, have no problem about the possibility that non-Christians can be saved.)

However, I want to call this inclusivist point into question, not because I do not think non-Christians will be saved, but because I do not think inclusivism is able logically to make this claim for two reasons. If religious traditions are properly to be considered in their unity of practice and theory, and in their organic interrelatedness, then such "totalities" cannot simply be dismembered into parts (be they doctrines, practices, images, or music) which are then taken up and "affirmed" by inclusivists, for the parts will always relate to the whole and will only take their meaning in this organic context. Hence, what is thus included from a religion being engaged with, is not really that religion *per se*, but a reinterpretation of that tradition in so much as that which is included is now included within a different paradigm, such that its meanings and utilization within that new paradigm can only perhaps bear some analogical resemblance to its meaning and utilization within its original paradigm.

One might substantiate this claim with various historical examples which can be easily furnished from the history of Christianity—and from the histories of most other religions. Interestingly, these various histories are replete with examples of inclusion which are in fact radical transformations of the original. Sikhism is one prime example, where its inclusion of the best of Hinduism and Islam produced a transformation into an entirely new religious tradition. Likewise, Christianity's "inclusion" of Judaism and Islam's "inclusion" of Christianity and Judaism are other examples of this process.

In the preface I noted how MacIntyre traced the emergence of Thomism as the resolution of the tension between Aristotelianism and Augustinianism and various Greek philosophical problems. While Aquinas made much use of Aristotle, it would be odd to think that Aquinas thought that there was any final teleological truth within Aristotelianism *on its own terms*. In fact, his very utilization of Aristotle was to show that while Aristotle discerned much that was good, true, and noble, his was a vision that did not finally grasp the truth which is presented in the gospels. One might say there is both continuity (which is what traditional inclusivism has sought to stress) *and* discontinuity (which is the watchword of exclusivism) in Aquinas's appropriation of Aristotle. And any continuity must always also be framed within a greater discontinuity to be truthful to the realities being understood. Thomism is not Aristotle perfected, but Aristotle reinterpreted and transformed. Aristotle and Aristotelians might well find that they wish to resist Thomism. Dialectics may persuade Thomists, but not necessarily Aristotelians. The basic shift from Aristotle to Aquinas requires both dialectics and faith (rhetoric), an entire paradigm shift.

The point I am making is that inclusivism does not describe well the actual process of historical engagement that takes place when two traditions meet. In affirming something from another tradition, the significance of this affirmation for the affirmer might well be quite different from that given in its original home. In this sense I contest that the other religion as it understands itself is never the object of affirmation by the inclusivist; rather what we have is the inclusivist affirming those elements within another religion that it tends to prize—usually as being reflections of the best parts of itself. This cannot be said really to affirm, both because it is a part and not the whole, and because what is being affirmed is not that tradition as it understands itself, but what the alien theologian chooses to prioritize and select. Here is a simple example: a westerner's affirmation of vegetarianism within Hinduism, and their own subsequent adoption of vegetarian practice. Nevertheless, a westerner's practice might be connected with ecological motives that are foreign to the Hindu context of vegetarianism that involves concepts of reincarnation, the Sāṃkhya cosmology which associates certain negative spiritual properties with red meats, and so on. Or, take another example. Were Greek concepts of substance simply and uncritically used by Christians to say what they wanted to about God in Christ, or did they actually employ, develop, and modify these concepts in a novel and unique manner? I think the latter, and in this sense, Greek philosophy was not being celebrated in its own right, nor seen as a legitimate salvific structure.

I will return to this part of the overall argument in chapter two to show how a pluralist unveiled will himself resist the title of inclusivism—and rightly so. This will provide a good test case for my argument. So let me now turn to the first of my two representative Christian pluralists, the Presbyterian theologian-philosopher John Hick.

JOHN HICK'S LIBERAL INTOLERANCE

John Hick is one of the most influential and highly developed pluralists. His writings on the subject span nearly two decades and his position has developed over this time. His current position is to be found in its magisterial entirety in *An Interpretation of Religions* (1990). This huge book is based on Hick's Gifford Lectures of 1986-87. It contains considerable indological, philosophical, and theological arguments, but in what follows I shall be dealing with one aspect only—his argument for pluralism. Initially, Hick tells us that he began as a conservative exclusivist Christian. Over the years he made a pilgrimage through to pluralism, which itself has undergone considerable development, culminating in his recent book.[5]

To put Hick's radical pluralism into perspective, it will be helpful to trace briefly its genesis. In 1973, using an astronomical analogy, Hick suggested a Copernican revolution in the Christian theology of religions whereby Christians should "shift from the dogma that Christianity is at the center to the realization that it is *God* who is at center, and that all religions . . . including our own, serve and revolve around him."[6] The earlier "Ptolemaic" dogmas placed the Church and Christ as the source of and means to salvation. According to Hick, these dogmas became increasingly implausible in the light of the truth and holiness evident in other religions. They also contradict the Christian belief in a God who loves all people. Hence the Copernican revolution marked a shift from *ecclesio*centrism and *Christo*centrism to *theo*centrism, analogous to the monumental paradigm shift in astronomy precipitated by Copernicus. Hick never defined theocentrism in terms of trinitarianism, which indicates that the problem I shall locate in his work was well in place, even in these earliest stages. To return to the exposition: God, not Christ or the Church, should be the center of the universe of faiths. Hick suggested that this paradigmatic shift would facilitate a new understanding of religions whereby claims to superiority and exclusivity would dissolve. A new era of interreligious ecumenism would dawn.

To facilitate this theocentric move Hick had to decenter the incarnation. Basically, Hick's argument is that Jesus should not be seen as God incarnate. Instead, the divinity of Christ should be viewed mythologically. Hick's definition of myth is important and plays a major role in his later thinking. He defined myth as:

> a story which is told but which is not literally true, or an idea or image which is applied to something or someone but which does not literally apply, but which invites a particular attitude in its hearers. Thus the truth of a myth is a kind of practical truth consisting in the appropriateness of the attitude which it evokes.[7]

Hence, Jesus' divinity is a mythological construct that expresses the literal truth that "God has been encountered through Jesus" which is "not an assertion of unique saving effectiveness in human life, but a particular redemption-myth attached to one great historical way of salvation."[8] Hick seems to employ a purely instrumentalist view of religious discourse, by which language is seen as an expression of intentions, attitudes, or particular programs, but not concerned with making cognitive claims about any ontological reality, analogically or otherwise. This instrumentalist view is a child of modernity, in so much as the ontological claims of religions are negated, and religion's only usefulness lies in its ethical force, which is possible to replicate without the particular trappings of religion. The latter was Kant's argument. Hick seems untroubled by the literal statements that he uses, such as "God has been encountered through Jesus." What is significant at this stage is Hick's maintaining the reality of God at the center of salvation—although whose "god" remains unclear.

Hick's latest writings signal a radical shift away from *theo*centrism to what he calls *Reality*centeredness. (All subsequent page references in the text are to *An Interpretation of Religion*). He argues that all religions are salvific paths to the one Divine "Real," none being better or worse and none with a privileged or exclusive revelation, despite what some of their adherents may claim. The word "Real" or "Reality" better expresses the fact that the Divine cannot be ultimately regarded as personal (theistic) or impersonal (non-theistic). This crucial move occurred in Hick's pilgrimage as a result of dealing with the objection that Hick was a covert theist, for his Copernican revolution did not accommodate non-theistic religions. How could it, if he contended that all religions represented different paths to the one all-loving *God*?

To overcome this difficulty, Hick developed a Kantian-type distinction between the noumenal, which exists independently and outside of human perception, and the phenomenal world, which is that world as it appears to our human consciousness (246 ff.). The varying phenomenal responses within the different religious traditions, both theistic and non-theistic, are to be viewed as authentic but different responses to the noumenal Real. Hence, according to Hick, we cannot say that the "Real *an sich* (in itself) has the characteristics displayed by its manifestations, such as (in the case of the heavenly Father) love and justice or (in the case of Brahman) consciousness and bliss" (247). So just what does this talk about a "heavenly Father" amount to? Once again, the notion of myth is utilized to deal with the problem, but now it is applied not only to the incarnation, but to the very idea of God; and is further extended to the ultimate realities designated by the various religions, such as the Hindu Brahman, or Allāh in Islam, Yahweh in Judaism, and so on (343-61). Therefore, in Hick's view, speech about our "heavenly Father" is:

> mythological speech about the Real. I define a myth as a story or statement which is not literally true but which tends to evoke an appropriate dispositional attitude to its subject matter. Thus the truth of a myth is a practical truthfulness: a true myth is one which rightly relates us to a reality about which we cannot speak in non-mythological terms (248).

With this Kantian distinction in place Hick effectively severs any ontological connection between our human language and the divine reality, and introduces an entirely instrumental use of religious language. Some critics rightly note the establishment of Hick's Kantian epistemology well before his dealing with the questions of religious pluralism.[9] According to Hick all the world religions encourage us to turn away from the Self toward the Divine Reality, engendering love and compassion toward all people. The common soteriological goal is thereby matched by a common ethical goal which therefore confirms the pluralistic thesis.

Hick's "pluralism" masks the advocation of liberal modernity's "god," in this case a form of ethical agnosticism. If ethical agnostics were to suggest that the conflict between religions would be best dealt with by everyone becoming an ethical agnostic, not only would this fail to deal with plurality, in so much as it fails to take plurality seriously, it would also fail to take religious cultures seriously by dissolving them into instrumental mythical configurations best understood within modernity's mastercode. This mythologizing hermeneutic bears the marks of what Roland Barthes, in his important book, *Mythologies*, has called the "rhetorical forms" of "bourgeois myth."[10] (All subsequent page references in the text are to *Mythologies*.) Barthes sees this hermeneutic as one of the marks of liberal modernity, and using Barthes's analysis helps to reinforce and illuminate my overall argument. Underlying this myth, according to Barthes, is the attempt to turn history into "Essences," a restless drive which will not cease until modernity has "fixated this world into an object which can be forever possessed, catalogued its riches, embalmed it, and injected into reality some purifying essence which will stop its transformation" (155). This tendency toward essentialism in the theology of religions ironically hastens the closure of dialogue rather than offering a new beginning. Hick's system has already begun the process of cataloging history and making religions conform to the schema of pluralism so that they can be possessed by the mythologizer.

The notion of myth is first applied to the incarnation to decenter it so as to facilitate Hick's move to theocentrism. But now Hick has to decenter theocentrism (God) in order to facilitate his move to "the Real." All theistic traditions must undergo Hick's mythologizing hermeneutic, as well as the non-theistic traditions, for they, too, cannot claim any privileged access to reality, except on the terms stipulated by the pluralist framework. This deprivileging of the particular is a major theme within modernity's reinterpretation of Christianity. If the adherents of world religions are not allowed to make fundamental ontological claims with their full force and implications, then harmony is arrived at through the destruction and neutralizing of the Other. Barthes writes that one rhetorical form of bourgeois mythology is that it is "unable to imagine the Other." If the pluralist mythographer comes face to face with the Other, "he blinds himself, ignores and denies him, or else transforms him into himself . . . all experiences of confrontation are reverberating, any otherness is reduced to sameness" (151).

This is indeed the effect of Hick's mythologizing hermeneutic: it seems to ignore or deny the really difficult conflicting truth claims by, in effect, reducing them to sameness: i.e., they are all mythological assertions. All religious people should view their religions as does the mythographer. If they do not, then they cannot be accounted for in this schema and are seen as holding false views about the nature of their doctrines and truth claims.[11] Underlying this form of pluralism is an implicit epistemology (that God cannot choose to reveal God's self in the particular), and its concomitant ontology (God cannot be known in history, with its attendant deism or agnosticism), and its espousal of a universal ethic that should be followed by all rational men and women. The golden rule, do unto others as you would have them do to you, claimed by Hick to operate in all religions (325), is of course an empty formal injunction. It specifies no *telos*, only the formal requirement that free subjects should be allowed to act freely. The *telos*, what is good for you and me, and the habits of virtue required to inhabit such a role, as well as the type of social organization that might support these roles, such that we might participate in the good, is left ambiguous. The point is: how does each person actually understand and practice the various "goals" that are formulated within their different traditions? MacIntyre, as we saw earlier, has argued that once "goals" are detached from their narrative contexts, as was the Kantian procedure, they cannot properly be justified, so that emotivism is the inevitable outcome.

Barthes also notes that this type of myth "consists of stating two opposites and balancing the one by the other so as to reject them both" (153). Here again the analogy is clear. One can see the way in which reifications such as theism (as if this were one "thing" in Judaism, Christianity, and Islam) and non-theism are balanced in Hick's schema only, in fact, by rejecting them both. The balance in Hick's schema amounts to something quite different from theism or non-theism; it amounts to agnosticism. Hick is led into agnosticism when he presses the distinction, and severs the link, between the Real *in itself* and its various phenomenal manifestations *in relation* to humankind. He writes: "It follows from this distinction between the Real as it is in itself and as it is thought and experienced through our religious concepts that we cannot apply to the Real *an sich* (in itself) the characteristics encountered in its various manifestations" (246). The outcome leaves Hick with no real access to "the Real." The ways of analogy and metaphor, for example, are rendered impotent. This inability to speak of the Real *or* even allow "it" the possibility of self-utterance leads to the Real's redundancy. Ironically, any detailed and serious interest in the religions of the world is subverted as they are unable to furnish clues about the Real. The color, diversity, difference, and detail are bleached of their meaning, for the Real apparently resists all description and is incapable of self-utterance.

This outcome has a close analogue with Barthes's description of yet another rhetorical form of mythology. It is that "the accidental failure of language is magically identified with what one decides is a natural resistance of the object" (151). This maneuver, which Barthes calls tautology, "creates a dead, a motionless world." Hick's system does this precisely because it has decided all things in advance; every form of religion is cataloged and encoded into modernity's narrative of time, space, and history. The history and particularities of the various traditions are just icing on a cake, already tasted, known, and digested. The many intractable particularities of the religions with their unique histories and traditions are drained of their power.

It is precisely this absolute incomprehensibility regarding the nature of Reality that genealogically locates Hick's pluralist project. It mystifies, rather than illuminates, the nature of the Real. Similarly, Kant had to face the question of how he could claim to know that there is a correspondence between phenomena and things in themselves, and to know that the latter acts upon our consciousness. Agnosticism is the inevitable outcome of the trajectory of Hick's flight from particularity, first from the particularity of the incarnation, then from the particularity of a theistic God, and then from the particularity of any religious claim, be it Christian or non-Christian. The outcome of the escape from particularity can only be into nothing in particular, or in Barthes's words, "history evaporates" under the power of the myth (151).

It would seem then that the Real's invulnerability leads also to its redundancy. Only the moral human activity of turning away from self is left, although with less and less tradition-specific narration regarding what this turning away from self might involve. Here, finally, we arrive at the ethical counterpart to Kant's ontological agnosticism. In the same way that all religions are seen as ultimately related to one and the same "Real," despite their considerable differences and intractable particularities, so, too, there is an ethical counterpart to this claim. We are told that despite all the differences in injunctions to act and follow specific ways of life enjoined by each particular tradition, the religions are ultimately united in putting forward the same ethical principles that will provide the basis to unite them in a new harmony. Hick finds that all the great traditions teach "love, compassion, self-sacrificing, concern for the good of others, generous kindness and forgiveness" (325). It is perhaps not surprising that Hick has to sever these values from their tradition-specific narrative contexts. He writes tellingly that the above ideal "is not an alien ideal imposed by supernatural authority but one arising out of our human nature" (325), and which happens to concur with the "modern liberal moral outlook" (330). This latter alignment, the "coincidental" relation between the way things are (nature) and modern liberalism (the transparent description of that "nature"), even more clearly reveals Hick's tradition-specific starting point. The basic criterion for judging salvific religions is, therefore, a commonly accepted set of values which are rooted in human nature and modern liberalism, not in any authority within differing religious constructions of "what is."

There are two points that should be made about this ethical turn in Hick's work, which I shall develop in relation to Paul Knitter's work in the next section. The first is that the system, in Barthes's words, "continuously transforms the products of history into essential types" and when it has done this, deems them to be "Nature" (155). One then proceeds to call in Nature to adjudicate matters of controversy (e.g., as to which are salvific religions) and impartiality is apparently achieved at the same time. This maneuver continues the process of essentialism first noticed in ontology and now found in ethics, a maneuver which seeks to occlude and erase the particularities of history and the uniqueness of religious traditions. For example, those religions where ethics is viewed as intrinsically related to the life of the community, in response to a particular revelation, and which, therefore, place a significant emphasis on the precise narrative context of ethics rather than its instrumental outcome, such as Thomistic virtue ethics, are marginalized and occluded within Hick's system.

Second, the specificity of the ethical agenda and its political and social baggage go unnoticed, for it is claimed that this ethical approach is impartial and favors all equally. I have been trying to show that it does not, and that it masks a highly specified form of liberal modernity. Others have also noted these same features and accused Hick of bourgeois politics.[12] In using Barthes I have tried to indicate that it is not by chance that Hick's mythologizing program shares the characteristics of modernity in what Barthes calls the "bourgeois myth." Hick's Enlightenment exclusivism stems from his Kantian epistemology and establishes his ontological agnosticism. This eventually drives him into a foundational turn toward ethics. Knitter, in contrast, wants to start with ethics. If we see the emergence of modernity over Christianity in Hick's work, does the Roman Catholic eco-liberation theologian, Paul Knitter, fare any better?

PAUL KNITTER'S ECO-LIBERATION APPROACH

Paul Knitter, a good friend and general editor of the *Faith Meets Faith Series*, like John Hick, went through a pilgrimage from exclusivism and inclusivism to pluralism. He has also gone on a further excursion within pluralism, from a theocentrism, of Hick's Copernican type with "God" at the center of the different religions, to a liberation-eco-theological form of pluralism. In this last stage, the divine is to be found in socio-political-ecological emancipatory movements and "mother-earth" affirms and guides this process. While I find Knitter's stress on the poor and the environment absolutely important, I shall be showing why his form of theology actually hinders his political intentions. I shall be arguing that Knitter's proposal is wedded to the Enlightenment project begun by Kant, such that a universal ethical imperative is prioritized over metaphysics and religion—not unlike Hick's project.[13] All people are subject to this ethical "ought," prior to their formation within religious communities, and the value of their formation within such communities is judged by their ability to respond to this ethical imperative. The alleged attractiveness of this Kantian path, when originally developed by Kant, was its appeal to common universals, beyond the petty sectarian interests of religious groups. Jesus Christ, within this schema, became a representative of truths already known and not, as in most orthodox forms of Christianity, constitutive of truth. Knitter adds an ecological twist to this story but never really departs from it, as his ecological argument is closely allied to modernity's sacralization of science as the determinative master-code. Knitter's project therefore fails, in my opinion, for it appears as an appeal to the religions to band together to fight a common enemy, but this maneuver conceals the real nature of Knitter's Trojan Horse; the presuppositions of the project are corrosive to the religions, or to be specific, to trinitarian Christianity which resists Kant and the secular authoritarianism of modernity. Interestingly, those from other religions have expressed analogous misgivings.[14]

First, let me outline the argument Knitter presents in his important two volume work: (Volume 1) *One Earth Many Religions. Multifaith Dialogue and Global Responsibility* (1995), and (Volume 2) *Jesus and the Other Names* (1996).[15] (Page references in the text; the 1 or 2 prefacing the page number indicates the volume number.) *One Earth* opens with a moving and interesting autobiography in which Knitter plots his pilgrimage and conversions in the theology of religions. He started as an exclusivist wanting to convert heathens and bring them to the light of the gospel (1:3). Very soon, through experience and reflection he became a Rahnerian inclusivist (1:5), but this turned into a bridge that led him into pluralism, initially of a Hickian type. In *No Other Name?* (1985) Knitter was defending theocentrism against ecclesiocentrism or Christocentrism (which had marked his early stages), arguing that God was greater than any one mediator, including Jesus, and that "other religions may have their own valid views of and responses to this Mystery" (1:8). Soon he was deeply immersed in liberation theology and began developing a liberation theology of religions in his contribution to *The Myth of Christian Uniqueness: Toward a Pluralistic Theology of Religions* (1987), which he felt steered away from John Hick's position in one important respect: rather than arguing that there was a common core to the religions, he began to argue that all religions are to be judged as to their salvific efficacy in so far as they promote the "kingdom," characterized by justice, peace, and goodness in both personal relations and socio-economic structures.[16]

Knitter's two volumes mark a new stage in his odyssey, extending his version of liberation theology to include ecological justice:

> I will be urging that religious persons seek to understand and speak with each other on the *basis of a common commitment* to human and ecological well-being. Global responsibility therefore includes the notion of liberation intended by traditional liberation theologians but goes beyond it in seeking not just social justice but eco-human justice and well-being; it does so aware that such a project, in order truly to attend to the needs of all the globe, *must* be an effort by the entire globe and all its nations and religions (1:15, my emphasis).

The argument of the first book is that *suffering* and *eco-balance* are unmediated and primary universals, prior to religious and cultural formation, that call for global cooperative action. If the religions and the nations of the earth cannot respond to these two universally felt problems, together and in cooperation, then we will face extinction. In so much as the religions alleviate suffering personally and socio-economically, and tend to the earth's well being (which is also our well being), they are channels of salvation. However, one needs critically to examine these two universals, for the notion that they are unmediated should immediately remind us that they probably belong to an Encyclopedic genealogy. Knitter argues that suffering is universally experienced: "Suffering has a universality and immediacy that makes it the most suitable, and necessary, site for establishing common ground for interreligious encounter" (1:89). Hence, there is a prior universal experience more primary than any interpretation which forms a common human experience/essence.[17]

This attempt to provide a foundational narrative within which all religions can find their place is even more strongly stated when it comes to eco-well-being. Here we see the exaltation of science as the mastercode within which religions will find themselves interpreted. According to Knitter, the story of the universe related by science acts as a "transcultural religious story," "providing all religions with a *common creation myth*" (1:119). Furthermore, this new mastercode, or as Knitter calls it "a shared religious story," generates a "common ethical story":

> This Earth provides the religions not only with a religious community in which they can share myths of origin, but also with an ethical community in which they can identify and defend common criteria of truth. In their basic content, such criteria will probably be something like those being worked out by international ecological groups, especially non-governmental (1:123).

Non-governmental environmental groups become the new guardians of common truth, and their lack of partisanship (in being non-governmental) is in keeping with this refusal of tradition-specific forms of enquiry and description. Speaking of the interreligious earth summit in Rio de Janeiro (1992) where it was declared that "For the first time in our history, we have empirical evidence for a common creation story," Knitter does not question this highly contentious statement, but instead comments:

> They were announcing on the international level what some theologians have been saying among themselves and their communities: science, in what it tells us about how the universe originated and how it works, is providing all religions with a *common creation myth*. What Thomas Berry and Brian Swimme call the universe story can function as a transcultural religious story[18] (1:119).

Volume 1 ends on this prophetic note, echoing Hans Küng's call for a global ethics. Before outlining volume 2, *Jesus and the Other Names*, I would like to make three observations. First, the fact that Knitter can relegate Christology to the second volume such that the main task there will be to offer a Christology that responds to a predefined crisis and a solution that is already known, such that Christ becomes a resource to support the solution, rather than ever challenging the articulation of the crisis and its alleged solution, suggests that Knitter's Christology serves an ideological cause. This is betrayed in his assumption that one can analyze the world and its problems apart from theological and ecclesiological categories. Hence, Knitter is able to state the problems and partial solutions, and only then asks: does Jesus fit into this schema? This suggests that the Kantian project is well in place, an intuition that is further confirmed when we turn to Knitter's *representative* Christology in volume 2, where Jesus represents precisely the global values of peace, justice, and love that are required by Knitter's global analysis carried out in volume 1; and these values are detachable from Jesus' person and his church. To bring into relief this pattern of modernity I need to locate the foundational ethical universals that steer the Kantian motor—which leads to my second observation.

The main argument of volume 1 is an appeal to universals ("suffering" and the "earth") that are unmediated by cultural construction which lead to ethical obligations that are universally binding. This structure mirrors the Kantian attempt to cut through particularity, and to found ethics (and therefore religion) on a universal foundational site. It is worth noting that Knitter's new ecologism, the second of his universals, is not a departure from this Kantian project but a reiteration of it, in privileging scientific discourse as establishing modern cultural hegemony. That is why Knitter fails to recognize modernity's imperialism when he writes with a sense of liberation: "science, in what it tells us about how the universe originated and how it works, is providing all religions with a *common creation myth*" (1:119). This fails to recognize that the scientific story is also a culturally constructed one which cannot claim uncontested mastercode status (providing all religions with their story) unless it denies its historical situatedness; which it does, when it appears as "the Earth itself" (note the capital letter for Earth) narrating a "common cosmological story" (1:119)—even if it is through the particular mouths of Thomas Berry and Brian Swimme. John Milbank criticizes this form of scientific modernity in the following manner:

> After the collapse of the medieval consensus, faced with the difficulties of containing the conflicts amongst communities of diverse belief, the early modern age already fled to the arms of nature as support for a new objectivity. . . . Displacement towards nature was therefore in place from the outset of modernity, although "nature" was also from the outset a cultural construct: initially a disguised projection of a new mode of human power.[19]

The danger of divinizing the Earth coupled with claiming the Earth's unitary and authoritative voice is always at the margins of Knitter's project. A further feature of this tendency is either to gloss over the chaotic and bloody destruction present in nature, or alternatively, to see this as intrinsic to the process, thereby legitimating violence as required by or as necessary to the sacred. This sacralizing of violence runs counter to the explicit intentions of groups usually holding such theories and is certainly not Knitter's intention, but is inevitable in so much as there is an endorsement of "the human" and "nature" without any reference to sin. Furthermore, such a strategy fails to recognize that nature is culturally constructed, and therefore constructed very differently by different traditions at various times in their history. Compare for example, the Christian *ex nihilo* doctrine with the cosmic dualism in Zoroastrianism, and *māyā* within Śankara and Rāmānuja in Vedāntic Hinduism.[20] Furthermore, such constructions suggest differing patterns of relationship to the natural and cultural world which cannot always be theoretically predicted in advance.[21] Knitter unwittingly perpetuates modernity's project in employing unmediated foundational ethical universals, and he is driven to this in trying to find a universal site for interreligious agreement. The problem is that he constructs such a site, rather than naturally finds it. This leads to my third observation.

Concomitant with the apparent discovery of such universal ethical "oughts" regarding suffering and the earth, there are co-related *right actions.* And such right actions become a new foundational and universal site, so that religion and metaphysics serve an already organized practice. Knitter often calls this the "priority of praxis" and my point here relates to my earlier one regarding Knitter's Christology serving a hidden ideology. Knitter knows what is required, even if outlined at a very low level of specification. He does not examine in any detail the various non-governmental environmental groups that form the vanguard of truth. Hence, the job for theologians is to find models and theologies that will support this already endorsed praxis. Kant envisaged a similar job for historical religions, and some forms of liberation theology are often in danger of replicating this same pattern.[22] Take the following quotation, for example:

> If followers of various religious traditions can agree *in the beginning* that *whatever else* their experience of truth or of the Divine or of Enlightenment may *bring about*, it *must* always promote greater eco-human well-being and help remove the sufferings of our world, then they have a shared reference point from which to affirm or criticize each other's claims (1:127, my emphases).

The logic here is that regardless of what each religion believes and practices as a result of its beliefs and practices, it must nevertheless, first and foremost, believe and practice eco-human justice! Right practice is self-evident. It is not surprising that one main theological challenge to this view derives from an Aristotelian virtue ethics approach in which the relationship of action, theory, and goods is very differently construed. Here the *telos* of action is understood in terms of the goods that are internal to particular types of activity, not in their outcome—consequentialism and pragmatism. And this *telos*, in Aquinas's utilization of Aristotle, is fundamentally part of the human-divine drama, not prior to it, for there could be no "prior." Whether my suspicions regarding Knitter's ethics are misplaced will in part be answered as I now turn to his Christology in volume 2, *Jesus and the Other Names*.

In volume 2, Knitter's basic argument is already in place: those religions that promote socio-ecological justice are channels of salvation. Christianity needs to rethink itself to conform to this view. Hence, this second volume maintains the pluralist case that Christians must stop claiming that salvation is from Christ and recognize multinormed sources of salvation. Typically of Knitter, he scrupulously outlines the many criticisms made of his Christology (chapter 3) before embarking on a "revisionist" Christology that reaffirms the "uniqueness" of Christ (attempting to satisfy critics), while still holding to a "pluralist" position—that Jesus is one savior amongst many equal saviors (chapters 4 and 5). The conclusion is put in this fashion: Jesus "does bring a universal, decisive, indispensable message"[23] (note that in one clear sense, he is an information bringer, detachable from the information/message that he brings), *and* that probably "there are *other* universal, decisive, indispensable manifestations of divine reality besides Jesus" (2:79). The basic metaphor in his argument is that fidelity to Jesus is like fidelity to one's spouse. By utterly committing ourselves to this particular person we are released to be engaged with others in all sorts of fruitful and creative ways and need not deny others their own particular and ultimate commitments. Likewise, Jesus is truly divine, but not the only divine figure; and Jesus offers salvation in a unique manner, but so do the Buddha and the Qur'an.

Knitter's Christological argument here seems to follow the Kantian pattern: all historical religions have their place in so much as they conform to the universal ethical imperative. For Kant, Jesus is the best representation of the ethical imperative. For Knitter, Jesus is the best response that he personally knows and experiences. Unlike Kant, Knitter is willing to concede that there are, no doubt, other equally good responses.[24] The Kantian notion of religion as subjective taste, an accident of particularity and culture is perpetuated in Knitter's use of the analogy about marriage as akin to religion.[25] This is the inevitable outcome of representative Christologies that are a product of modernity's erosion of the Christian narrative. What I have been arguing is that the Christian narrative has been replaced by that of modernity's. Knitter comes closest to recognizing what is at stake here when, in his later chapter on mission, he identifies a crucial issue: the difference between representative and constitutive Christologies. This is an important paragraph, so I shall quote it at length:

> Official Roman Catholic teaching has in no way opened itself to the possibility of a *representational christology* that holds up Jesus as a decisive representation or embodiment or revelation of God's saving love—a love that "predates" Jesus and is "unbounded" and universally active by the very nature of God and of creation (Ogden 1994, 9-10). Rather, the official Magisterium has adhered to a *constitutive christology*, according to which Jesus, especially in his death and resurrection, causes or constitutes the universal availability of God's salvific love. Without Jesus such love would not be active in the world; whatever experience of Divine Presence is realized in the world has to be seen as caused by Jesus and necessarily in need of ful-

> filment through membership in the church. Because Jesus *constitutes* and not just *represents* God's saving activity, Jesus has to be proclaimed as "full, definitive, unsurpassable" (2:133).[26]

Perhaps one reason why mainstream Roman Catholic theology has not opened itself to adopting a representative Christology is because it recognizes that this would be a departure from the fact that the Christian tradition takes its orientation from the trinitarian God disclosed in the narratives of the early church regarding the person of Jesus Christ and the community that he formed and which helped form him. The early church did not have a narrative into which they then inserted the story of Christ. Indeed, such a process was constantly, though not always successfully, resisted in the various forms of adoptionism and gnosticism. Christ does not "represent" God, but "is" God's very self-revelation as triune. If he is a representative, then we are able to access God without God's self being offered to us; we are, as it were, able to get behind the sign to the reality. In contrast, constitutive Christology makes the point that the signifier in this unique case, is the signified, although it is not in any sense a closed signifier or signified, because the very nature of this trinitarian sign is that it invites interrelationships with all signs within creation. I shall return to this argument later. However, to continue my point here briefly, the danger in representative Christologies is that the signified is possessed prior to Jesus, such that Jesus is seen to be an "embodiment or representation" (1:133) of what is already known prior to him. This is perhaps why volume 2, on Christology, follows volume 1, in which right values and actions have already been foundationally located. That is why one of the features of representative Christologies is the ability to abstract values and teachings from the person of Christ, so that it is his message that is all important, not his work and person, and not his resurrected body which continues in the church, the "body of Christ."[27]

At one point, in a footnote, Knitter seems to acknowledge that there is truth that could correct Christ—which is not surprising, given the logic of his project, but it is surprising as a Christian claim. He writes:

> When I called for a nonnormative christology I had in mind the traditional understanding of normativity: that Christ is a *norma nomans non normata*—a norm that norms all others but is not normed itself. I should have said more clearly than I did that I would endorse an understanding of Jesus as a *norma normans et normata*—a norm that norms others but can also be normed itself (2:169, note 9).

If there is an authority apart from Christ, then Christ is subject to something that is more normative than he, which would imply that God is subject to a more truthful and more authoritative criterion than God. (Making such a point does not commit me to any positivist or foundational account of revelation or to deny that revelation is always mediated.) Knitter's qualification regarding Jesus as norm, just cited, constitutes no real change from his early position which called for a non-normative Christology (akin to Hick's early mythologizing of the incarnation), and further justifies my claim that the Enlightenment ghost drives his Christological project.

One more feature corroborates my argument. Why does Knitter reject a constitutive Christology? The obvious answer is that he believes that the New Testament does not justify one. I have no doubt at all about Knitter's scholarly integrity here, but I want to suggest that in the plot of his book he has already decided against a constitutive Christology entirely apart from the New Testament and apart from the authority of the church. The reason is that *constitutive Christologies are not universal sites*, for they prioritize the particular and this "sectarianism" is unacceptable to Knitter. Hence, for Knitter, prioritizing the particular runs contrary to the spirit of global dialogue: "So it seems to me that traditional Christian announcements of Jesus as final, full, and unsurpassable must be, to say the least, a threat to dialogue." He continues that this runs contrary to what "is felt today to be a *moral imperative*. Anything that makes such a dialogue problematic is a problem itself" (2:62).

The logic here is that regardless of any evidence or theological reasoning, constitutive Christologies are inadmissible as they threaten the "moral imperative" (note the universal Kantian tone) that is "felt today" (by whom?). This may very likely mean that only modern liberals within the religious traditions are *allowed* to participate at Knitter's global dialogue table, for if they are not modern liberals, then they are a "threat to dialogue." I do not wish to overplay this point, but want to situate Knitter's position and its implications within the Kantian Enlightenment mastercode from whence it derives. In so much as this is the case, Knitter propounds a fundamentally non-religious form of exclusivism. In fact, as with Hick's project, it is unwittingly unhelpful in addressing the ecological, political, and interreligious tensions it tries to diffuse, for it excludes those very groups (the religions) in the process of reconciliation and peace making, by demanding that they be baptized in modernity before coming to the dialogue. In this respect, Hick and Knitter's pluralism fails not only because it cannot attain its own stated objectives (openness, tolerance, and equality of the religions); it also fails because it is a highly tradition-specific form of argument that has implicit and explicit ontological, ethical, and epistemological presuppositions that implicitly or explicitly contest alternative assumptions. It cannot but fail. Furthermore, this failure also illustrates the victory of modernity in these engagements with Christianity in generating "Christian positions" that have become detached from the trinitarian God and instead expound modernity's god.

Finally, I want to return briefly to one aspect of the issue of constitutive Christologies. For any viable theology of religions, in contrast to Knitter's project, a constituitive Christology, pneumatology, and ecclesiology, would have to be considerably developed. It may seem oblique to turn to such fundamental questions as the nature of revelation when the environment is being destroyed and suffering ravages our earth. However, it is my contention that Christian revelation is about God and created human persons, because the incarnation begins to show us what it is to be truly human, by being fully responsive to the true God, such that questions regarding socio-ecological well-being are actually properly shaped and responded to once we begin to attend to revelation, which is always a lived practice. And this, I believe, takes us to the heart of the problem: for central to the Enlightenment project is a fundamental epistemological and ontological rupture that denies the possibility of God's self-revelation in the historically particular.

If I read Knitter correctly, what he cannot accept is that God may have chosen to make himself present in Jesus Christ such that *all* history and culture are to be reconfigured through this particular narrative. Perhaps one reason for this is his supposition that this narrative is completed and hermetically sealed, for he often implies that constitutive Christologies are static, self-sufficient and fully complete packages of truth (2: 62, 72-6). I do not think one can find much evidence for such a portrayal within orthodox Roman Catholic Christologies, but in so much as this is found by Knitter, then Knitter's reaction to it is entirely understandable. However, let me briefly indicate why I think such "closure" is actually alien to Christian revelation.

To take, what I hope is a difficult example, one might cite the Roman Catholic teaching that revelation "was closed with the death of the last Apostles" (Denzinger 2020), reiterated again in Vatican II.[28] This teaching would, on the surface, seem to corroborate Knitter's point. But does it? I think not. Rather, I suggest that it indicates an important presupposition in the claim that God has revealed Himself in Jesus Christ. That is, if God has truly revealed Himself in Jesus Christ, then we can expect no new revelation as such, for the plenitude of God's being is present in Christ, although this does *not* act as a barrier to acknowledging God's presence in different modalities throughout creation. Hence the "closed" operates centrifugally to relate *all* truth as being present, hidden, disclosed, and concealed in Christ *in so much* as God is present in Christ. Such a teaching does not exclude all manner of truth and light within cultures and religions. Karl Rahner, when discussing the teaching that revelation was "closed" with the death of the last apostles, says the following:

> *Now* there is nothing more to come: no new age, no other aeon, no fresh plan of salvation, but only the unveiling of what is already "here" as God's presence at the end of a human time stretched out to breaking point.... It is because the definitive Reality which resolves history proper is already here that Revelation is "closed." *Closed, because open to the concealed presence of divine plenitude in Christ.*[29]

Rahner rightly stresses the positive nature of "closed" when he adds: "That revelation has been closed is a positive and not a negative statement, a pure Amen, a conclusion *which includes everything and excludes nothing* of the divine plenitude, conclusion as fulfilled presence of an all-embracing plenitude."[30] Rahner's quotation serves to highlight the dual logic within this teaching. First, in principle nothing can dispose of and overturn revelation—if revelation is revelation. If the economic trinity is the immanent trinity (but not vice versa, contrary to Rahner) then we cannot discover anything new about God, *in the sense* of ontologically unrelated or contradictory to Christ. I would argue that in making this claim, which is an ecclesiological and trinitarian claim, there is no need to take refuge in a positivist account of revelation which denies that revelation is mediated in human culture and through human persons, or to resort to a theory that maintains there is a final transcultural or acultural formulation of revelation. If that were so, one moment of human history would be divinized exclusively at the cost of the rest of history, whereas Christian practice is, or should be, a participation in the event of the incarnation, a furthering of this event. I return to this point in chapter four.

In conclusion, I have tried to establish three important points so far. First, that when Christian theologies of religions have assimilated themselves to modernity rather than the triune God, they end up representing modernity's gods: agnosticism (in the case of Hick) and a form of neo-pagan-unitarianism (Knitter). Second, in so much as their positions actually advance modernity's project, rather than Christianity's engagement with difference, they deny or obliterate difference and Otherness. In Hick's case, he mythologizes the differences away so that the religions can be fitted into his system. In Knitter's case, the religions are all judged by allegedly self-evident criteria that are found in the eco-system. Both Hick and Knitter know the full truth and what is ethically required of the religions independently of any of the religions. Third, and as a consequence, their pluralism turns out to be a strong form of Kantian exclusivist modernity. It cannot succeed in its claims to be more tolerant and open than forms of Christian trinitarian theology. What really is at stake is the question of whether Christianity can be genuinely open toward the Other, such as to both learn from and critically engage with difference. To this task, we return in chapter four.

However, before concluding this chapter I want to now show how Hick's pluralism is thoroughly modernist and not Christian in so much as it is transferable and can be defended by a Jew, Buddhist, Hindu or, in principle, by liberal modernists within any religious tradition. "God" is not trinitarian nor specific to any orthodox tradition, except the Encyclopedic. I have chosen a Jewish thinker, Rabbi Professor Dan Cohn-Sherbok, not because he is in any way representative of mainstream Judaism, but because in his minor differences from Hick, he seems to acknowledge his debt to the Encyclopedic tradition, and consequently invites even more objections. In thus extending the discussion, I am able to consider a Jewish pluralist and also then respond to Hick's response to the argument I have advanced in this chapter.[31]

DAN COHN-SHERBOK'S RELATIVIZING JEWISH PLURALISM

It is difficult to find Jewish pluralists and in my reading, Dan Cohn-Sherbok is almost unique within Judaism. His main work on this subject is *Judaism and Other Faiths* (1994) (page references from this book given in the text), although I shall refer to his other writings.[32] There are some Jews who are pluralists exclusively in regard to Christianity; that is, they put Christianity and Judaism on an equal par, but not in regard to other religions. Hence, in a strict sense it would be inappropriate to call them pluralists.[33] Cohn-Sherbok is a Reform rabbi, but he promotes what he elsewhere calls "Open Judaism," in contrast to a number of differing existing historical traditions within contemporary Judaism.[34]

Cohn-Sherbok fits rather well into my analysis as he explicitly adopts the threefold paradigm of pluralism, inclusivism, and exclusivism from the debate in Christianity and sees this model as apt and appropriate to analyze Jewish responses to other religions (20 ff.). Cohn-Sherbok suggests that exclusivism "is consonant with the attitude of many Jews in the past" (21). "On this view Judaism is absolutely true—its source is God" and "it excludes the possibility of God revealing himself to others" (21). He then poses the following theological problem to such a position: "If God is the providential Lord of history, it is difficult to understand why he would have hidden his presence and withheld his revelation from humanity—except for the Jews" (21).[35] He then outlines inclusivism, which he shows to be a widespread position among many contemporary Jewish writers and is also found throughout the history of the Jewish tradition:[36] "Judaism would on this view be regarded as ultimately true; its doctrines would serve as a basis for testing the validity of all alleged revelations" (22). Cohn-Sherbok's criticism of inclusivism is that it still "does not do full justice to God's nature as a loving father who truly cares for all his creation. On this model, it is the Jewish people who really matter" (23).

Finally, he proposes his version of Jewish pluralism. He proposes three arguments in support of his pluralist proposal. First, the two mentioned above against exclusivism and inclusivism can be compressed into one: a loving God could not have favorites, and so would choose all people equally. We can begin to see the specter of the Encyclopedic tradition with its assumptions that no particular can be privileged, and no revelation or tradition is to be given special status (except of course itself). Cohn-Sherbok argues that to stress Jewish particularity, in terms of the "chosen people," contradicts the universal love of God. He identifies this central tension as "internally incoherent: if God is truly concerned with the fate of all humanity, he would not have disclosed himself fully and finally to a particular people allowing the rest of humanity to wallow in darkness and ignorance" (157). The God of love revealed in Judaism requires an open tolerance and acceptance of all religions, for such a God would not have confined himself to this one religion in any definitive manner. In this respect, Cohn-Sherbok uses the same argument as Hick when Hick advanced the theistic form of his Copernican revolution.[37]

Cohn-Sherbok's second argument is theological and historical. He suggests that the "sweep of Jewish history thus points to a new goal [pluralism]—a global vision of the universe of faiths in which Judaism is perceived as one among many paths to the Divine." (6, my added bracket) The argument relies on the book's analysis of Jewish history and whether or not it really does "point" in this new direction. In terms of my argument, it would amount to asking the question whether Judaism will be entirely accommodated to liberal modernity, such that many of its central religious beliefs and practices will be radically transformed. Such transformations cannot be ruled out; neither is it possible with any ease to specify what might count as authentic Judaism or not. Certainly at present, many Orthodox Jewish intellectuals and theologians would resist such assimilation.

Finally, Cohn-Sherbok gives two related practical reasons for this shift to Jewish pluralism, the first of which amounts to an ethical requirement and the second which can only be tested retrospectively. The first is that "in contemporary society the Jewish community needs to adopt an even more open stance towards the world religions" (5). Such a need both stems from the internal theological incoherence identified by Cohn-Sherbok within the tradition and also the need to address the world's problems together as a religiously united front.[38] This latter is not unlike Knitter's plea and relates to the second practical reason. According to Cohn-Sherbok, Jews should adopt pluralism because it "paves the way for interfaith encounter on the deepest levels" (24). These levels range from common political action to interfaith prayer.

Having shown how and why Cohn-Sherbok advocates Jewish pluralism, what does this Jewish pluralism look like? The answer is that it looks entirely like Hick's Christian pluralism.[39] This is not because Cohn-Sherbok is unoriginal, but rather because both Hick and Cohn-Sherbok emerge from the same tradition, with the same epistemological, ontological, and ethical assumptions, and have the same goals: the universal acceptance of liberal modernity as the answer to the world's problems. However, there are also some interesting differences as we shall see. But first, let me look a little more closely at the similarities of Hick's and Cohn-Sherbok's pluralism. Cohn-Sherbok adopts wholesale Hick's Kantian-like distinction between the noumenal and phenomenal, so that the divine Real is seen as the ineffable noumenal and the different religions as differing phenomenal responses, none of which can be said to represent the noumenal more accurately and truthfully, let alone allow for the noumenal's self-revelation within any of the traditions. Cohn-Sherbok writes:

> Following the Kantian distinction between the world-as-it-is (the noumenal world) and the world as perceived (the phenomenal world), the Real *an sich* (in itself) should be distinguished from the Real as conceived in human thought and experience (161).

Like Hick, he suggests that this contrast, which is so crucial to the argument, is to be found in all the different religions. In Judaism, the contrast is between the "*Ayn Sof* as distinct from the *Shekinah* (God's Presence)" (161). While such distinctions are indeed to be found, it is contestable whether they equally imply such a specific form of philosophical agnosticism. However, what interests me here are the ways in which Cohn-Sherbok differs from Hick in working out the implications of this philosophical agnosticism.

The first difference lies in Cohn-Sherbok's recognition of the self-defeating relativistic implications of modernity's ethical liberalism. This is to put the matter polemically and entirely in my own terms, but this is what I believe Cohn-Sherbok's criticism of Hick amounts to. Cohn-Sherbok turns to Hick's essay on the ranking of religions, where Hick asks the question whether it is possible to rank religions as ethically better or worse, more philosophically true or false, or more historically validated or not.[40] Cohn-Sherbok agrees with Hick's argument that one cannot rank religions as a whole for they are "so internally diverse, containing so many different kinds of both good and evil."[41] However, he disagrees with Hick's argument that, even given this problem, one is nevertheless called to grade aspects of different religions. This disagreement is vital, but let me note Hick's argument so as to appreciate Cohn-Sherbok's disagreement. Hick argues that there are four objective and universally attractive and reasonable criteria. The first is one of coherence and internal consistency. The second is that of adequacy: to the particular form of experience on which that religion is based, and to the data of human experience in general. The third is that of promoting salvation and liberation. The fourth is Hick's moral criterion whereby authentic religions exhibit a turning away from the self/ego to a Reality-centeredness, seen in unselfish love and compassion.

I have elsewhere questioned the possibility of such "objective" criteria, but for very different reasons from those given by Cohn-Sherbok's response to Hick. In keeping with the position advanced in this book, I have argued elsewhere, that all criteria are tradition-specific and the more general their expression (hiding their particularity), the less helpful they are to adjudicate in conflicts; and the more specific their expression, the more clearly tradition-specific they are and therefore fail in their job of "impartial" adjudication.[42] Cohn-Sherbok, in contrast, disagrees with Hick, for he seems to recognize that once one cuts one's moorings from the noumenal, there can be no objective or universally acceptable criteria by which to grade and judge religions. In this recognition, Cohn-Sherbok seems to carry his (and Hick's) pluralism to its logical outcome. I do not want to inspect Cohn-Sherbok's detailed criticisms of Hick's criteria as they are not essential to my argument, but to note simply that they stem from a self-acknowledged relativism as the only strategy to avoid the implicit exclusivism within the strategy of "grading," for Cohn-Sherbok recognizes that grading can only implicitly advance one's own religious presuppositions. I quote Cohn-Sherbok's estimation of Hick's criteria in full:

> These proposals for evaluating religions are ultimately unsatisfactory because they fail to provide clear-cut and generally accepted bases for evaluation. Yet this should not be a surprising conclusion. In the past adherents of a particular religion judged all other religions by the criteria of their own faith; the eclipse of such an Exclusivist stance by a Pluralistic picture of the world's religions inevitably leads to a relativistic conception of the universe of faiths (167).

In so much as Cohn-Sherbok rightly recognizes Hick's exclusivism, he should in principle agree with my argument and analysis of Hick. But he cannot, for this would also call into question his own project. Hence, Cohn-Sherbok tries to steer clear of exclusivism by taking an apparently bold step in openly embracing full-blown relativism as the consequence of the inaccessible noumenal Real. However, even this step fails, for this form of relativism is as exclusivist as any other position, and is far from "open" and "tolerant"—the two virtues Cohn-Sherbok greatly prizes. This is because in Cohn-Sherbok's adopting a Kantian-like framework, following Hick, he also falls foul of the criticism I aimed at Hick's transcendental agnosticism, and indeed Cohn-Sherbok is quite explicit on this count: "in the end the Jewish Pluralist must remain agnostic about the correctness of his own religious convictions" (171).

This has the effect of putting into place some very significant ontological claims, which, despite himself, Cohn-Sherbok is committed to make in judgment *over other* religions precisely because he has adopted this Kantian framework. Most importantly, he claims that the Real cannot be known and no religions can make definitive claims to knowledge of the Real. When they make such claims, these are to be counted as false, as in principle they cannot have epistemological access to the Real, regardless of what they claim or regardless of the arguments they may present for such a claim. The irony located in Hick's position is repeated in Cohn-Sherbok's Jewish Pluralism. It is intolerant toward most forms of orthodox religious belief, be they Jewish, Buddhist, Christian or Muslim. For example, we can see this reductive hermeneutic at work when Cohn-Sherbok proceeds to "demythologize" truth claims within Judaism. Although he does not use the term, he follows Hick's demythologizing strategy very closely in this regard. This is not surprising as it is a strategy required by the epistemological and ontological assumptions within modernity as noted by Barthes, whether it be called "mythologizing" or otherwise. For example, when speaking of the Jewish understanding of the Godhead (which ironically he uses for his pluralist case viz. the distinction between *Ayn Sof* and the *Shekinah*), Cohn-Sherbok says that this Jewish understanding "cannot be viewed as definitive and final" (168). Regarding the doctrine of the "chosen people," which he acknowledges to be a "central feature of the tradition" (169), Cohn-Sherbok is now willing to dispense with it and, indeed, argues that it needs to be abandoned in so much as it suggests favoritism, parochialism, and self-justification:

> Given that the Real *an sich* transcends human understanding, the conviction that God has selected a particular people as his agent is nothing more than an expression of the Jewish people's sense of superiority and impulse to spread its religious message (169).

Revelation, providence, the doctrine of the Messiah are all accordingly abandoned, as they are within the grand narrative of modernity's recoding of history and "religion." Cohn-Sherbok is quite aware that he will be retranslating not only Judaism, but in his "tolerant" embrace will require fundamental ontological changes in self-understanding from Islam, Christianity, Hinduism, and Buddhism (162-3). For example, he says that we must question the claim that Buddhists make: "that the true understanding of the human condition is presented in the teachings of Gautama Buddha" (163). Or, to take another example, we must abandon the outmoded Christian claim that "Jesus Christ was God himself, the second person of the Trinity in human form" (163). From the pluralist perspective, "neither Jew, Muslim, Christian, Hindu, nor Buddhist has any justification for believing that his respective tradition embodies the uniquely true and superior religious path" (163).[43] Hence, Cohn-Sherbok here inevitably breaks his embargo on making judgments regarding truth in other religions, despite his criticism of Hick for making just such judgments. This should be of no surprise: this is the logical consequence and fate of pluralists, for they are finally no different from religious exclusivists, except in their differing tradition-specific starting point—modernity.

Finally, in openly embracing "a relativistic conception of the universe of faiths" such that it is just not possible to judge truth claims (167), Cohn-Sherbok invokes two further problems. First, there are no valid grounds by which his own position could commend itself. This is the age-old problem whereby relativizers relativize themselves and subsequently have no grounds upon which to commend their position to those who disagree. Hence, it is a curious argument when Cohn-Sherbok suggests that since we cannot make any judgments concerning truth, we should abandon any claims to "religious superiority" (by which he means a truth that may call into question other positions), and suggests that "instead the adherents of all faiths should regard one another with respect, acknowledging the spiritual validity of one another's traditions" (167). Since he has removed grounds for making judgments regarding the invalidity of a religion, likewise he has removed grounds for affirming their validity. At this point, Hick's thesis fares better, for at least it refuses an utter relativism, invoking instead a religious argument against all forms of naturalism.[44] Cohn-Sherbok is unable to do even this. It is a curious clarion call from someone holding a position that openly acknowledges that final and definitive claims made by traditional religions are "misapprehensions" (163), to now argue that no such negative judgments should be made in regard to the claims made by such religions. Cohn-Sherbok's attempt to avoid Hick's exclusivism has led him into this type of unintended self-contradiction.

HICK'S DEFENSE OF "PLURALISM"

I will now finally turn to John Hick's response to the argument that I have developed in this chapter. Hick makes two responses to my argument. The first is that if all I am saying is that everyone holds some form of truth criteria and that this constitutes an exclusivism of sorts, "although intelligible in a purely notional and trivial sense," such an observation "is much more misleading than helpful."[45] He argues that it is better to keep the terms exclusivism and pluralism as they are "naturally" descriptive of the positions staked out. Hence, by keeping these terms, important distinctions are kept intact, for claiming that one's own religion is the only "true" religion, for which "exclusivism" is surely the natural descriptive term and, on the other hand, the idea that there is a plurality of "true" religions, for which "pluralism" is surely the natural descriptive term requires the retention of such labels and that their logical difference be acknowledged.[46]

His second argument is to counter my claim that pluralism operates with the same logical structure as exclusivism. Hick argues that:

> religious exclusivism and religious pluralism are of different logical kinds, the one being a self-committing affirmation of faith and the other a philosophical hypothesis. The hypothesis is offered as the best available explanation . . . of the data of the history of religions. Pluralism is thus not another historical religion making an exclusive claim, but a meta-theory about the relation between the historical religions.[47]

The difficulty of Hick's reply lies in his telling resort to alleged naturally descriptive terms. We saw this same strategy in Knitter, who evokes a kind of positivist self-revealing truthfulness in relation to his own hypothesis—a point that Roland Barthes notes is a typical rhetorical form of argument employed by modernity. In Hick's response, I would contend, there is both a profound misdescription as well as a tacit claiming of high ground which obscures the debate and the real issues at stake. Let me elaborate with four interconnected points in response to Hick.

First, logically speaking, if those who claim that theirs is the only true religious tradition should be naturally described as exclusivist, it is not clear to me why "pluralists" who also believe that theirs is the only true tradition should not equally be naturally described as exclusivists. It is hardly a true description of pluralism, as found in Hick, that his explanation (or "hypothesis") is the best fit, the most "naturally" accurate interpretation of the "data of the history of religions," for as we have seen, the schema into which the religions are fitted undermines the self-understanding of most of the religions concerned. The outcome is that all religions are seen to make "mythological" (or false) claims, except for pluralists who possess a non-mythological set of ontological assumptions to sustain their own tradition (liberal modernity). As I have shown, such a position has the effect of claiming that there are no true religions, for all misunderstand themselves until they embrace the pluralist hypothesis. They must fundamentally reinterpret their self-understanding in modernity's terms. Thus it can still be argued that pluralists should be called exclusivists.

Second, Hick's distinction between a "self-committing affirmation of faith" and a "philosophical hypothesis" is highly questionable, for every hypothesis, the terms in which it is framed, and the assumptions regarding the modes of its testing and viability are tradition-specific. And, as MacIntyre and Milbank are at pains to show, in differing ways, every tradition requires an element of "self-committing faith," for there are no traditions or positions that are self-evident or neutral, and no enquiries that approach "raw data" neutrally and then explain them from some objective standpoint. Hence, in response to Hick, it might be argued that his Kantian presuppositions do not generate a neutral hypothesis, a "meta-theory about the relation between historical religions" as he claims, but are in fact "first-order" creedal statements of a philosophical faith with many epistemological, ontological, and ethical presuppositions undergirding it.[48] Hick reserves this latter category of "first-order" claims for those with religious faith. But part of my argument is to show that pluralists come from a (hidden) faith position, full of first-order truth claims which exclude truth claims other than their own.

Third, while Hick claims his position does not arise from a historical religion, I would suggest that it emerges from something very akin to this: liberal modernity, or in MacIntyre's terms, the Encyclopedic tradition. In this sense, Hick's pluralism is a historical "religion," in a formal sense, in so much as it has members who share common philosophical presuppositions (Kantian), and believe in certain forms of common practice (liberalism), and are strongly committed to a universal mission regarding their new faith. They usually belong to and support organizations that advance their common project and have rituals and ceremonies to sustain their sectarianism. That this is not so easily noticeable is simply because liberal modernity is the prevailing *mythos*, as MacIntyre and Milbank have shown.

Fourth, even if one were to reject arguments two and three above, argument one alone would make it difficult to see how Hick could commend pluralism as the "least problem-prone, explanation of the data."[49] It seems to fail to explain the data at all, as it refuses to accept the data on the terms of those that generate it. In one sense, the traditional "exclusivist" (in Hick's terms) fares better (on Hick's criteria), for he or she at least is faithful to the self-description of *one* of the religions (their own), rather than undermining all the religion's self-descriptions. On this point, dialectically, exclusivistsemerge as winners of this debate showing that pluralists fail to solve their own problem, but more so, that exclusivism solves it better.

I have tried to show that when Cohn-Sherbok's pluralism is similar to Hick's, it fails for it finally belongs to the exclusivist Encyclopedic tradition. In so much as Cohn-Sherbok differs from Hick, he simply indicates the trajectory in which the tradition finally ends up—as MacIntyre was at pains to point out. Whatever, these types of Kantian modernity seem incapable of positively engaging with difference and Otherness, be they re-presented in Christian or Jewish forms. If the effect of liberal modernity has been pervasive in western circles, and thereby deeply and corrosively affected Christian and Jewish theology, in the next two chapters we turn east, to examine the extent of modernity's influence upon a Hindu pluralist and a Buddhist pluralist. This move to the east is for four reasons. First, it is an extension of my exploration of the extent of modernity's pervasive influence: does its "god" appear in other religious traditions such as Hinduism and Buddhism? Second, it allows me to develop my argument that pluralism is deeply problematic, for it is finally no different from exclusivism. Third, it will allow me to explore non-Enlightenment forms of "pluralism" and also pursue my earlier argument that inclusivism is best seen as a form of exclusivism. Fourth, in the debate between religions where openness and tolerance are supposedly the highest goals, I suggest that Christian and other forms of "pluralism" fail to deliver on their own stated aims, and that finally, a trinitarian approach actually attains pluralist goals in taking difference and otherness utterly seriously. Trinitarian exclusivism can acknowledge God's action within other traditions, without domesticating or obliterating their alterity, such that real conversation and engagement might occur. This theological argument will be resumed in chapter four.

Notes

1. SCM, London, 1983; 2nd ed., 1994.

2. See for example, Harold Coward, *Pluralism: Challenge to World Religions*, Orbis, Maryknoll, N.Y., 1985; Paul J. Griffiths, ed., *Christianity through Non-*

Christian Eyes, Orbis, Maryknoll, N.Y., 1990; John Hick and Hasan Askari, eds., *Religious Diversity*, Gower, Aldershot, 1985.

3. See the declarations in H. Lindsell, ed., *The Church's Worldwide Mission: Proceedings of the Congress on the Church's Worldwide Mission*, World Books, Waco, Texas, 1966.

4. See the interesting comparison of these two by K. Randall Schmitt, *Death and After Life in the Theologies of Karl Barth and John Hick*, Rodopi, Amsterdam, 1986. Hick constantly uses the questionable argument against exclusivists that they automatically "consign non-believers to perdition." See for example, John Hick, "The Possibility of Religious Pluralism: A Reply to Gavin D'Costa," *Religious Studies*, 33, 1997, 161-6.

5. He began, in his own words, as a "strongly evangelical and indeed fundamentalist" Christian: see *God Has Many Names*, Macmillan, London, 1980, 2. See also my tracing of his entire pilgrimage in *John Hick's Theology of Religions*, University Press of America, London/New York, 1987, 1-16.

6. John Hick, *God and the Universe of Faiths*, Fount/Collins, London, 1977, 131.

7. Hick, *God and the Universe*, 166-7. See Gerard Loughlin's penetrating remarks in "Myths, Signs and Significations," *Theology*, 730, 1986, 268-75.

8. Hick, *God and the Universe*, 172, 177.

9. This Kantian epistemology is developed in Hick's first published book, *Faith and Knowledge*, Cornell University Press, New York, 1957. See such critics as Philip Barnes, "Continuity and Development in John Hick's Theology," *Studies in Religion*, 21, 4, 1992, 395-402; and Christopher Sinkinson, *The Nature of Christian Apologetics in Response to Religious Pluralism: An Analysis of the Contribution of John Hick*, University of Bristol, Ph.D., 1997.

10. See Roland Barthes, *Mythologies*, Paladin, London, 1983, 154. I am indebted to Gerard Loughlin for drawing my attention to the possible use of Barthes in this way. See his "Prefacing Pluralism: John Hick and the Mastery of Religion," *Modern Theology*, 7, 1990, 29-55. (Subsequent page references to *Mythologies* in the main body of the text.)

11. See also the incisive comments on this point by Joe DiNoia, "Pluralist Theology of Religions: Pluralistic or Non-Pluralistic?" in Gavin D'Costa, ed., *Christian Uniqueness Reconsidered*, Orbis, Maryknoll, N.Y., 1990, 119-34.

12. See for instance, John Milbank, "The End of Dialogue"; and Kenneth Surin, "A Certain 'Politics of Speech': Toward an Understanding of the Relationships Between the Religions in the Age of the McDonald's Hamburger," in D'Costa, ed., *Christian Uniqueness*, 174-91; and 192-212 respectively; and Loughlin, "Prefacing."

13. In this respect I agree that Cardinal Ratzinger's analysis of Knitter and Hick as Kantian relativists is correct, although he oddly attributes the turn to orthopraxis in Knitter's work as primarily influenced by Indian religions (38), rather than being the further outworking of modernity coupled with Marxism. See Cardinal Joseph Ratzinger, "Central Problem for Faith," *Briefing*, Vol 27, 1, 1997, 36-42. For a more incisive historical estimation of the genesis of liberation theology's orthopraxis, see John Milbank, *Theology and Social Theory*, Blackwell, Oxford, 1990, ch. 8. Ratzinger's estimation here is not in keeping with his analysis elsewhere when discussing liberation theology or Tissa Balasuriya's praxis solution.

14. It is instructive to see a deeply critical Muslim and Hindu response to Hans Küng's similar call for a "global" ethics. See Seyyed Hossein Nasr and Veena Das in "Special Issue: proceedings of the first meeting of the Harvard Divinity School's

Jerome Hall Dialogue Series," *The Muslim World*, LXVII, 2, 1987, 96-105, 109, 116-36.

15. Orbis, Maryknoll, N.Y., 1995; and Orbis, Maryknoll, N.Y., 1996, respectively.

16. See the co-authored volume by Knitter, John Cobb, Jr., Len Swidler, and Monika Hellwig, *Death or Dialogue*, Orbis, Maryknoll, N.Y., 1990: 20, for his critique of common essences, and 26, where he argues that this is Hick's position. See also "Dialogue and Liberation," *Drew Gateway*, 58, 1, 1987, 1-53. I do not think there is any real difference between Hick and Knitter on substantial issues, but rather a difference in emphasis. See my "Christian Theology of Religions: An Evaluation of John Hick and Paul Knitter," *Studia Missionalia*, 42, 1993, 161-78; and the excellent essays by John Milbank and Kenneth Surin in Gavin D'Costa, ed., *Christian Uniqueness Reconsidered*, Orbis, Maryknoll, N.Y., 1990, 174-91, and 192-212 respectively.

17. Knitter constantly tries to respond to postmodernist concerns regarding the danger of essentializing: "What I am saying, then, is not that there is a common essence or a common religious experience or even a precisely defined common goal within all religions" (1:56). He writes the above sentence directly under the heading: "the common human experience of suffering"—which seems to suggest that religious experience is some overlay to human experience. And then soon after, he writes, "If with David Tracy and Schubert Ogden we want to talk about a "common human experience" to which all religions can respond in order to understand themselves and others, then it is the experience of suffering and the dangers that it brings forth" (1:57). This sense of an unmediated experience, a universal foundational platform, is more explicit when he suggests of suffering, its "*universality* . . . the fact that it is found everywhere in similar forms and with similar causes—but also because of its *immediacy* to our experience" (1:89). This is a baffling claim which entirely ignores anthropological work that has deeply called such alleged similarities into question. See Robert Young, *White Mythologies: Writing History and the West*, Routledge, London, 1990, esp. 141-76. Knitter then comes clean: "I want to express this claim as cautiously as possible, but I do not want to equivocate. Suffering has a universality and immediacy that makes it the most suitable, and necessary, site for establishing common ground for interreligious dialogue" (1:89). There is an irony that when Knitter quotes Francis Schüssler Fiorenza regarding suffering: "Although it is not without interpretation and one's horizon deeply affects one's suffering, our bodily existence is affected in such a way that gives suffering a '*mediated* immediacy' " (1:89, my emphasis, quoting Schüssler Fiorenza, "Theological and Religious Studies: The Contest of the Faculties," in Barbara G. Wheeler and Edward Farley, eds., *Shifting Boundaries: Contextual Approaches to the Structure of Theological Education*, Westminster, Louisville, 1991, 135), Knitter immediately writes: "And this immediacy is available to all cultures and all religions." Schüssler Fiorenza's more cautious and correct acknowledgment of "mediated" experience has been dropped.

18. Citations referred to by Knitter: "An Earth Charter" prepared by the International Coordinating Committee on Religion and the Earth for the Earth Summit, Rio de Janeiro, June 1992; T. Berry & B. Swimme, *The Universe Story*, Harper, San Francisco, 1992.

19. John Milbank, *The Word Made Strange: Theology, Language, Culture*, Blackwell, Oxford, 1997, 258. Ratzinger makes the same point regarding the "New

Age," ibid, 39-40. For an excellent analysis of the "New Age" in sharper terms, see Paul Heelas, *The New Age Movement: The Celebration of the Self and the Sacralization of Modernity*, Blackwell, Oxford, 1996.

20. See, for example, Julius Lipner, "The Christian and Vedāntic theories of originative causality: a study in transcendence and immanence," *Philosophy East and West*, 28, 1, 1978, 53-68.

21. For two interesting alternative emphases on creation: see Cardinal Joseph Ratzinger, *"In the Beginning . . ." A Catholic Understanding of the Story of Creation and the Fall*, W. B. Eerdmans, Michigan, 1990, esp. 79-100; and Milbank, *The Word*, ch. 5.

22. See Milbank, *Theology*, ch. 8, and *The Word*, ch. 12; and Stanley Hauerwas, "Some Theological Reflections on Gutierrez's Use of 'Liberation' as a Theological Concept," *Modern Theology*, 3, 1, 1986, 67-76; and the excellent use of Hauerwas to engage critically with Moltmann's version of European liberation/political theology by Arne Rasmusson, *The Church as Polis*, Lund University Press, Sweden, 1994.

23. There is a constant ambivalence on this point in Knitter's work, see 88-93, especially highlighted when he writes that after the resurrection "The proclaimer became the proclaimed. Jesus' own Kingdom-centeredness became the early community's Christ-centeredness" (92). This view reflects accurately Pope John Paul II's view that Knitter criticizes later (127-35). However, Knitter shifts away from this position, implying that the post-resurrection preaching needs correction with pre-resurrection truth (if such a distinction is even admissible): "Being centered on Christ is the Christian way of being centered on the kingdom. As Jesus would remind us: it is more important to focus on the Kingdom than to focus on him" (92). These kinds of argument are generated from within modernity and make two strategies possible: one can identify the more primal original historical Jesus who will cut through the cultic overlay which the church imposed on him; and one can identify the values and program he taught (the social gospel) which, in principle, can be detached from him.

24. Immanuel Kant, *Religion with the Limits of Reason Alone*, Harper & Row, New York, 1960, 72-103.

25. Of course, such bridal imagery is present in the bible, but Knitter fails to explore sufficiently the accusations of infidelity made against God's own chosen people in their relations with other gods: see, for instance, Hos 1:2.

26. Citing Schubert Ogden, "Some Thoughts on a Christian Theology of Interreligious Dialogue," *Criterion*, 11, 1994, 5-10.

27. In claiming this, I do not intend to identify the kingdom and church exclusively. See Gavin D'Costa, "The Kingdom and a Trinitarian Ecclesiology: An Analysis of Soteriocentrism," in Paul Mojzes and Leonard Swidler, eds., *Christian Mission and Interreligious Dialogue*, Edwin Mellen Press, New York, 1990, 51-61.

28. See *Dei Verbum* 2, 4, and 11.

29. Karl Rahner, *Theological Investigations*, Vol. 1, Darton, Longman & Todd, London, 1965, 49, my emphasis. Rahner goes on to argue that what is contained "virtually" in Christ, both logically and "through the luminous power of the Spirit" (53), "can and must still be called 'Revelation' " (59), rather than inferred human propositions. I agree, although Rahner tends to focus too strongly on the propositional aspect of revelation in this early essay, rather than on the primary personal, historical, and relational features of revelation which would more fully support his

argument for the development of dogma. See also Edward Schillebeeckx's less propositionally oriented discussion in *Revelation and Theology*, Vol. 1, Sheed & Ward, London, 1967, 13-20. Denzinger 2020 is reiterated in *Dei Verbum* 2, 4.

30. Karl Rahner, *Theological Investigations*, Vol. 1, 49.

31. I tested a brief form of this argument in Gavin D'Costa, "The Impossibility of a Pluralist View of Religions," *Religious Studies*, 32, 1996, 223-32; and John Hick's reply: "The Possibility of Religious Pluralism: A Reply to Gavin D'Costa," *Religious Studies*, 33, 1997, 161-6.

32. I shall mainly use, *Judaism and Other Faiths*, Macmillan, London, 1994; but also refer to *Issues in Contemporary Judaism*, Macmillan, London, 1991, chs. 11 & 12 which is substantially reproduced in *Other Faiths; The Future of Judaism*, T. & T. Clark, Edinburgh, 1994, esp. ch. 7; *Modern Judaism*, Macmillan, London, 1996, esp. ch. 9. Louis Jacobs (see note 36 below) sometimes seems to veer into a pluralist position. However, see the Jewish pluralists Harold Kasimow and David M. Gordis in Byron L. Sherwin and Harold Kasimow, eds., *John Paul II and Interreligious Dialogue*, Orbis, Maryknoll, N.Y., 1999, 1-26, and 125-38, respectively. See Norman Solomon's, *Judaism and World Religion*, Macmillan, London, 1991, for an alternative "Orthodox inclusivist" overview on the matter.

33. For a classic account of exclusive Jewish-Christian pluralism, see Franz Rosenzweig, *The Star of Redemption*, trans. William B. Hallo, Routledge, Kegan & Paul, London, 1971; and Abraham Joshua Heschel, "No Religion is an Island," in Paul J. Griffiths, ed., *Christianity through Non-Christian Eyes*, Orbis, Maryknoll, N.Y., 1990, 26-40. Both Solomon, *Judaism*, and Cohn-Sherbok, *Judaism*, do not find any pluralists within their surveys of Judaism.

34. See especially, *Modern Judaism*, and his critique of contemporary Jewish traditions.

35. Strictly speaking, it is extremely difficult to find any such Jewish exclusivists, rather than Cohn-Sherbok's claimed many (21). Cohn-Sherbok's cites hardly any examples. The Noachite covenant and the notion of the "righteous gentiles" usually blocks off such a route.

36. For examples of Jewish "inclusivists," see David Hartman, *Conflicting Visions: Spiritual Possibilities of Modern Israel*, Schocken Books, New York, 1990; Norman Solomon, *Judaism*; Louis Jacobs, *A Jewish Theology*, Darton, Longman & Todd, London, 1973.

37. See Hick, *God and the Universe of Faiths*, Collins/Fount, London, 1977, 122.

38. See *Modern Judaism*, 217.

39. Cohn-Sherbok uses Hick's *God and the Universe of Faiths*, London, 1977; *God Has Many Names*, Macmillan, London, 1980; *Problems in Religious Pluralism*, Macmillan, London, 1985; and "On Grading Religions," *Religious Studies*, 17, 4, 1981, 451-67.

40. Hick, "On Grading." There is a slightly more elaborate treatment of Hick's criteria in Cohn-Sherbok, *Issues*, 139-44, but with the same conclusion—see 144.

41. Hick, "On Grading," 451.

42. Gavin D'Costa, "Whose Objectivity? Which Neutrality? The Doomed Quest for a Neutral Vantage Point from Which to Judge Religions," *Religious Studies*, 29, 1993, 79-95.

43. One might ask whether "superior" has any logical function in this sentence, as something that is "unique" exists in a class of its own and in this sense cannot be compared to other paths.

44. Hick, "Reply," 163.
45. Hick, "Reply," 162.
46. Hick, "Reply," 162-63.
47. Hick, "Reply," 163.
48. Hick, "Reply," 163.
49. Hick, "Reply," 165.

2

Advaita's Unsupported Brahman within Neo-Hindu Pluralism

WESTERN MODERNITY AND INDIA

In this chapter I will examine the thought of the distinguished Hindu philosopher, Sir Sarvapelli Radhakrishnan (1888 - 1975), regarding Hindu views of other religions. Radhakrishnan called his own position "pluralist" (or "equalist") and employed the threefold paradigm of pluralism, inclusivism and exclusivism. In so much as he does this, he provides an interesting case to see how my argument bears upon his work. If the argument so far has been convincing, then we should find in Radhakrishnan's Hindu pluralism either a form of modernist exclusivism, or some form of religious Hindu exclusivism. In a curious and interesting fashion, we will find both! This outcome is in part the result of the complex phenomenon called "Neo-Hinduism," of which Radhakrishnan is a leading example.[1] A very brief contextualization of Neo-Hinduism is in order to explain this interesting development which calls into question the notion of a "seamless narrative succession" constituting all religious traditions.

Up until the nineteenth century, traditional orthodox Hindu sources show almost no interest at all in the non-Hindu, who in Sanskrit is called *mleccha*. The only significant concern the classical texts show is in relation to how a Hindu king should deal with *mlecchas* who may be within his kingdom. Any but the most necessary dealings with such *mlecchas* incurs ritual pollution. One of the foremost historians of the relationship of Hinduism to Europe, Wilhelm Halbfass, summarizes the traditional position in the following way:

> The Indocentrism developed in "orthodox" Hindu thought transcends by far what is ordinarily called "ethnocentrism." It is not

simply an unquestioned perspective or bias, but a sophisticated theoretical structure of self-universalization and self-isolation. Seen from within this complex, highly differentiated structure, the *mlecchas* are nothing but a faint and distant phenomenon at the horizon of the indigenous tradition.[2]

The nineteenth century changed that situation dramatically. A whole generation of leading Indian Hindu intellectuals were educated within western systems of education, either in India or in England (Oxford, Cambridge, and London). This was primarily due to Britain's requirement for "properly" trained civil servants to run one of the largest outposts of its empire. This single strategy, perhaps more than any other, meant that an influential number of Hindu intelligentsia, who were also often educated within their own religious Sanskrit tradition (as was Radhakrishnan, Ram Mohan Roy and others), were highly conversant with and often deeply influenced by western intellectual currents. The Enlightenment tradition filtered in through their study of European history, philosophy, science, and theology and inevitably helped fuel the nationalist democratic movement, as it had within Europe, which was also closely allied to a revival of Hinduism. Thus neo-Hinduism designates a wide and not always entirely homogenous group of Hindu intellectuals whose re-presentation of their Hindu tradition was deeply marked by European and Christian influence. Radhakrishnan was one of the most eminent of this group's second generation figures.

For readers acquainted with Hinduism, it might be advisable to skip the next three paragraphs. I shall briefly locate Radhakrishnan's position within the complex tradition called Hinduism and define certain key recurring terms related to his position.

AN INTRODUCTION TO HINDUISM

Hindu philosophy covers a wide spectrum, and includes atheism, materialism, theism, panentheism, and monism—all under the heading of Vedānta. Vedānta means "the end of the Vedas," and the Vedas refer to the wide collection of revealed scripture (*śruti*), of which the Upanishads is often seen as of prime importance. The authority of *śruti* is assumed by all Vedāntic schools, and those schools which reject the authority of scripture are termed *nastika*, the unorthodox, such as Jains and Buddhists. The three major schools of Vedānta are Śankara's (eighth century C.E.) Advaita Vedānta, Rāmānuja's (eleventh century C.E.) Visishtadvaita, and Madhva's (thirteenth century C.E.) Dvaita.

Śankara Advaita (non-dual) is essentially monistic. Śankara, following Gaudapāda, his teacher, argues for the sole reality of Brahman (absolute reality), such that he has to "explain" creation in terms of *māyā* which can be negatively understood as "illusion" and more positively understood (as Radhakrishnan rightly argues) as beyond explanation, for it is neither real, nor unreal (as would be a barren woman's son). Śankara argued for the utter identity of the true self (*ātman*) with that of Brahman, although in a proper sense the true self is no "self" at all, for only Brahman is real. Our sense that we exist as real selves is explained in terms of a temporary association of *ātman* with the empirical self, the *jīva*, while a person is still under the spell of *māyā*. The empirical self continues to generate *karma*, which literally means "work" or "action." *Karma* is the belief that every action has a consequence, good and bad, and that all *karma* accumulates during the course of many lives, conditioning both our next birth, and determining our role within Hindu society (*jāti*, or caste). Śankara argues that *moksha*, or liberation, is attained through intellectual training, the practice of rituals, and meditation, so that eventually the *jīvanmuktī*, the man who attains liberation, "experiences" *anubhava*, which is the "experience" attested to in the Upanishads, where *ātman* is Brahman. This is an "experience" of bliss and pure consciousness, and the *jīvanmuktī* continues in his body, such that his *karma* is worked out, even though now he accrues no *karma*, for he is beyond good and evil. The reason why "experience" is marked in quotation marks is because properly speaking there is no experience, for all experience is marked by duality, subject and object, name and form (*nāma rūpa*), whereas there is no subject and object, name and form, in Brahman, for Brahman is one without a second. Śankara developed a two-level theory of reality whereby the lower level (*apara vidyā*), in which most of us live, is characterized by name and form, subject and object, and tends to be seen as real—which is simply the condition of *māyā*. However, in truth, on the higher level (*para vidyā*) of reality, only Brahman is real. Radhakrishnan is a neo-Advaitin. He follows Śankara's Advaita, but is keen to engage with the various criticisms of Advaita, both from western scholars and Christians on the one hand, and also alternative forms of Hindu philosophy on the other. In undertaking this task, he also employs western philosophy, theology, social sciences, natural sciences, and comparative religious literature.

Rāmanuja's Visishtadvaita (qualified, or limited non-dualism) evolved out of a critique of Śankara, and, as with all Vedāntins, a commentary on scripture. It is basically panentheist, in so much as it supports devotional theism and holds to a personal God as an ultimate reality, as well as arguing that the world is analogically to be understood as God's body. This latter was required to maintain that the world is not to be understood as utterly other to God, for where could such other derive? Even Thomas Aquinas realized that *ex nihilo* was not a satisfactory philosophical answer on its own. For Rāmanuja, the soul, *ātman*, or self, has an eternal reality, although distinct from God and, in principle, distinct from other souls. Madhva's *dvaita*, which means "dualism," runs the difference between God, self, and matter to the extent that he posits three eternally distinct entities. Only grace can save, and good *karma* is only possible through grace. Madhva has often been seen as being influenced by Christianity, which is not impossible given the existence of the Syrian Church since at least the fourth century in South India.

Neo-Hinduism can be seen to have affected all these three schools within Vedānta, and many other forms of Hinduism. For the west, the main figures were often related to Advaita (Radhakrishnan, Rāmakrishna, Vivekananda, and Christopher Isherwood), although Gandhi is closer to Madhva and Vaishnavite (Gujarati) *bhakti* traditions. Admittedly, there was also a response to Christianity from other groups, often very hostile and critical (centered around the Ārya Samaj) and perhaps the most articulate being the traditionally trained Sanskrit pandits. Paul Griffiths writes of these debates, that "because they were conducted entirely in the learned language of Sanskrit—a necessary condition for participation in them by the pandits—they have had little effect upon Hindu-Christian dialogue in the present century."[3] Given the increasing westernization and modernization of India, most non-Sanskrit-trained lay Hindu intelligentsia are more familiar with the key figures of neo-Hinduism than the early pandits. In this respect, John Milbank's stipulation that Christians should not engage with modern Hinduism's most eloquent spokesmen, but instead learn about Hinduism from an "attentive readings of 'dead' texts pre-dating western intrusion and practices relatively uncontaminated by Western influence" is simply unconvincing.[4] Hinduism is going through all sorts of changes and developments, such that the notion of an uncontaminated original is a somewhat ahistorical and idealized notion. The same process is evident as we have seen in Christianity and Judaism, and will see in Buddhism.[5] Admittedly, Radhakrishnan's departure from the orthodox Advaitin view of the authority of *śruti* (primary scripture) weakens his argument considerably, as we shall see, but for logical, not historical, reasons. With this brief and sketchy contextualization of neo-Hinduism, let me now turn to the work of Radhakrishnan.

RADHAKRISHNAN'S NEO-HINDU PLURALISM

Radhakrishnan was an immensely influential spokesman for "neo-Hinduism," which was at its peak during the early twentieth century. He was a prolific writer and provided one of the most articulate accounts of a Hindu pluralist position available in English. The works that I cite were written during the period 1920-1956.[6] He is also particularly apt for my study as he develops his own position in terms of the threefold paradigm of pluralism, inclusivism, and exclusivism, some sixty years before Alan Race.[7] This may well be due to his reading of John Farquhar, upon whom Race is also dependent, but Radhakrishnan does not explicitly acknowledge Farquhar in this particular respect.

We can situate his own self-positioning in relation to this typology. Interestingly, he used Christian theologians' attitudes to other religions to define the field. This is significant, as with many neo-Hindus Radhakrishnan was keen to establish the superiority of Hinduism over Christianity. Radhakrishnan was perhaps understandably antagonistic to Christian missionaries. He wrote of his formative years: "my pride as a Hindu roused by the enterprise and eloquence of Swami Vivekananda was deeply hurt by the treatment accorded to Hinduism in missionary institutions."[8] By this he meant a derisory and negative treatment. Consequently, one must contextualize some of his polemical passages, which also bear the passion of the political independence movement, which many neo-Hindus saw as intrinsically connected with Hindu religious self-respect.

Radhakrishnan defines "exclusivism" in terms of Karl Barth's position, which he sees as establishing total discontinuity between Christian truth and all other forms of religious "truth." Radhakrishnan accurately summarizes the early Barth: "Barth is definite that the glimpses and intuitions of God found in other religions are not a preparation for the full revelation in Christ but are misdirections."[9]

The "second view," inclusivism, or "fulfillment" as Radhakrishnan properly calls it, is an advance on the first as it acknowledges that other religions are not simply characterized by error but are positive preparations for the full revelation in Christ and/or Christianity—by which they are fulfilled. Radhakrishnan cites John Farquhar as an example.[10] While Radhakrishnan appreciates Farquhar's positive affirmation of Hinduism, he finally thinks there is little difference between exclusivism and inclusivism (somewhat substantiating my own thesis). He says of exclusivism and inclusivism:

> These two attitudes are common to all missionary religions. Each claims with absolute sincerity that it alone is the true light while others are will-o'-the-wisps that blind us to the truth and lure us away from it. When it attempts to be a little more understanding, it affirms that the light of its religion is to that of others as the sun is to the stars, and the minor lights may be tolerated so long as they accept their position of subordination.[11]

In contrast, he writes of the pluralist attitude: "An increasing number of Christians adopt a third attitude, the Hindu one"—which he terms "equalist."[12] He finds this advocated by a small group of writers such as William Hocking, Ernst Troeltsch, and Bernard Lucas.[13] He sees these writers as accepting all religious traditions as equal in terms of truthfulness and in their capacity to disclose God. They recognize strengths and weaknesses in all religions. Equalism is "definitely against proselytism," and instead advocates that the "relation of religions must take increasingly hereafter the form of a common search for truth."[14] The "religions reform themselves by interpretation and adjustment to one another."[15] Radhakrishnan argued that it is this position of equalism or pluralism that is, and always has been, advocated by Hinduism.[16]

The model of the relation between religions that he advances is that of a form of democratic liberalism:

> The cosmopolitanism of the eighteenth century and the nationalism of the nineteenth are combined in our ideal of a world-commonwealth, which allows every branch of the human family to find freedom, security and self-realization in the larger life of mankind.[17]

Citing such sources of authority, Radhakrishnan would appear to be more of an Encyclopedic traditionalist than a Hindu, but one must also recognize that such a use of authority in his form of argument (the preferences within modern political life), derive from his connection of Hinduism with nationalism, and his resistance to British imperialism. In an often employed image, first used in a lecture to an English audience in Oxford (1926) and often repeated in his writings, Radhakrishnan suggests the forum of a "civilized" "parliament of religions":

> The different religions are slowly learning to hold out hands of friendship to each other in every part of the world. The parliaments of religions and conferences and congresses of liberal thinkers of all creeds promote mutual understanding and harmony.[18]

Radhakrishnan contrasts this Hindu "tolerant" approach with that of Christianity's basically "intolerant" approach.

At this point, I should note a typically pluralist ambivalence within his position. On the one hand, in some writings, he argues that his is a Hindu approach to the question—as we have just seen. In this context, Hindu tolerance is exalted above Christianity's intolerance. For instance, when advocating pluralism he writes: "Hinduism is wholly free from the strange obsession of some faiths that the acceptance of a particular religious metaphysics is necessary for salvation."[19] On the other hand, in different places and texts, he argues that his position is positionless, that it can be argued from any and every religious tradition:

> In my writing my main contention has been to make out that there is a perennial and universal philosophy which is found in all lands and cultures, in the seers of the Upanishads and the Buddha, Plato and Plotinus, in Hillel and Philo, Jesus and Paul, and the medieval mystics of Islam. It is this spirit that binds continents and unites the ages that can save us from the meaninglessness of the present situation, and not any local variant of it which we find in the Indian tradition. It is absurd to speak of any Indian monopolies of philosophic wisdom.[20]

This ambivalence within his position is in part due to the tensions that are inherent within pluralism as a species within historical modernity, which I have already charted. That is, he is wanting to advance a non-partisan argument, when in fact all arguments are partisan and tradition-specific. However, Radhakrishnan's ambivalence also stems from the fact, as I shall be arguing below, that finally he opts for Hindu Advaitin epistemology and metaphysics, and not for modernity's agnosticism or unitarianism. This choice will be seen in his analysis and criticism of Kant, in contrast to Hick, Knitter, and Cohn-Sherbok's assimilation of Kant.

While there are a number of arguments put forward by Radhakrishnan for his Hindu pluralist outlook, I shall only focus on what I take to be the two most important.[21] I have therefore made judgments that I cannot justify here, concerning the importance of his various arguments. Some, for example, I think are weak and ontologically inappropriate to his own position. For example, in speaking of Hinduism in contrast to Christianity, he says that Hinduism's

> scheme of salvation is not limited to those who hold a particular view of God's nature and worship. Such an exclusive absolutism is inconsistent with an all-loving universal God. It is not fair to God or man to assume that one people are the chosen of God, that their religion occupies a central place in the religious development of mankind.[22]

Radhakrishnan is in part reacting to the claim of superiority made by Christians which seems to privilege a particular scripture and a particular people. He advances precisely the same argument as do Hick and Cohn-Sherbok on this count, even though he is not finally a theist, nor obviously a Christian. For Radhakrishnan, as with theistic pluralists, an all-loving God is incompatible with the particularity of revelation. This tenet seems to be universal among pluralists—even when they do not believe a theistic "God" has any ontological status, as is the case with Hick, Cohn-Sherbok, and Radhakrishnan.[23]

The first of his two major arguments establishes his (Hindu) pluralist position on what he takes to be a universally accessible basis: *mystical experience*. For Radhakrishnan, religion is primarily a matter of inner "personal realization." He notes that for Hinduism:

> Intellect is subordinated to intuition, dogma to experience, outer expression to inward realization. Religion is not the acceptance of academic abstractions or the celebration of ceremonies, but a kind of life or experience. It is the insight into the nature of reality (*darśana*) or experience of reality (*anubhava*).[24]

His use of the term *anubhava* is significant as he associates this with Śankara's non-dual Advaita Vedānta and Śankara is clearly the most influential Hindu philosophical influence upon Radhakrishnan.[25] We will return to this shortly. Radhakrishnan cites Evelyn Underhill, and a host of contemporary authors on mysticism, to the effect that one "cannot honestly say, that there is any wide difference between the Brahman, the Sufi, or the Christian mystics at their best."[26] They all testify to the common divine reality at the heart of mystical experience.

Mystics, according to Radhakrishnan, testify to three things. First, that there is a common core to mysticism. This is materially the most crucial element of the argument. Second, mystical experience transcends all expressions such that no expression is adequate or appropriate. In mystical rapture, "the soul is lifted above itself and above all words and signs."[27] Third, and relatedly, there is an important distinction between the experience and its subsequent interpretations.[28] It would be futile to criticize Radhakrishnan's arguments purely on the basis of the vast subsequent literature on comparative mysticism. Much of this literature strongly calls into question both the claim to a common core in all mystical experiences, and the thesis that mystics relativize their own claims so thoroughly, such that interpretation and experience can formally be prized apart. Stephen Katz is perhaps one of the most significant critics of the type of approach utilized by Radhakrishnan.[29] If we contextualize Radhakrishnan in terms of the literature on mysticism that was then available, it must be acknowledged that some, if not most, of it broadly supported his position. Radhakrishnan was deeply influenced by writers like Evelyn Underhill, Dean Inge, and William James. One critic, Paul Hacker, actually argues that Radhakrishnan was more influenced by William James than he was by Śankara's Advaita Vedānta.[30] While I shall be contesting this claim, it certainly indicates the unique cocktail that constituted neo-Hinduism, and specifically the work of Radhakrishnan.

However, for my purpose, it is immaterial whether these three claims regarding mystical experience can be historically or epistemologically defended. What is germane to my argument is the question: what precisely did Radhakrishnan believe to be the core mystical experience, open to all, and testified to within all traditions? Answering this will allow me to identify Radhakrishnan's basic ontological convictions. Hence, even if his arguments from experience are problematic, which I believe they are, pursuing the matter in this way will at least allow us to see the logic of his underlying exclusivist presuppositions—which is the purpose of my investigation.

In a key number of texts, Radhakrishnan does specify the "contents" of this perennial mystical experience which is so seminal to his position. Admittedly, "contents" is an inappropriate word, for in this "experience" (which is an equally inappropriate word), there is no "subject" or "object," no duality, but pure undifferentiated identity between the self, *ātman* (who at a lower level of insight is conceived as a distinct person) and the divine, *Brahman*. The common core experience is always therefore suggested indirectly by language, symbols and thought, for in it there is no distinction between the knower and the known, between the real self (*ātman*) and the ultimate divine reality *(Brahman)*. In most of his writings this position clearly resembles Advaita Vedānta's classical non-dualist realization, which constitutes final liberation from the cycle of birth and death, the attainment of *moksha*.[31] Radhakrishnan writes, "in the experience itself the self is wholly integrated and is therefore both the knower and the known" and thus, all "dualities disappear."[32] This non-dual state of undifferentiated pure consciousness, characterizes *anubhava* and Radhakrishnan explicitly relates it to Śankara's Advaita: "Saṃkara admits the reality of an intuitional consciousness, *anubhava*, where the distinction of subject and object are superseded and the truth of the supreme self is realized."[33]

Hence, Radhakrishnan can write, in full accordance with Advaita Vedānta, the "true and ultimate condition of the human being is the divine status."[34] That is, the non-empirical self (*ātman*) is *identical* with the divine *(Brahman)*. He loosely employs a Christological term to express this identity, whereby there is ultimately no difference between the true self and the divine: "The consubstantiality of the spirit in man and God is the conviction fundamental to all spiritual wisdom."[35] However, it should be registered that this is certainly not what orthodox Christianity, let alone Judaism and Islam, hold to be true. For Radhakrishnan's ontological assumptions in this claim are that finally, all created persons are not in any sense real, for in the ultimate liberative state there is no such thing as relations, nor persons, but only pure consciousness of pure being, intelligence and joy—*satcitānanda*—all analogically understood. To put it crudely there is no distinction between God and creation, for in a final ontological sense, there is no creation.

One significant difference between Śankara and Radhakrishnan at this point of the argument is that for Śankara the authority of *anubhava*, non-dual realization, is finally scriptural. This is very important for Śankara as a good religious Advaitin, for truth is always exegeted from scripture upon which the certainty of truth is established. Certainly, to experience the authority of the truth of scripture requires personal realization; but even without such experience, the authority of scripture certifies the veracity of such an interpretation. Radhakrishnan inverts this order. He prioritizes the experience and argues that it suggests its own self-interpretation, that is then found to conform to that in the Upanishads, but not only the Upanishads. One reason for this inversion of the tradition is because Radhakrishnan is trying to advance a pluralist position, and to prioritize any scripture or revelation would be counter to his proposals. This central claim is based on

> verifiable truth and not on the correct solution to creedal puzzles. It is not opposed to science and reason. It is not contingent on any events past or future. No scientific criticism or historical discovery

> can refute it, as it is not dependent on any impossible miracles or unique historical revelations. Its only apologetic is the testimony of spiritual experience.[36]

Note, in this quotation, Radhakrishnan's invocation of the "gods" of modernity: a critique of the authority of tradition; the exaltation of science and reason as the universally accessible means to truth; the deprivileging of historical revelation; and the importance of experience in so much as it is thought to be unmediated. The interesting blend between Advaita and modernity comes from prioritizing Advaitin metaphysics and supporting its findings and conclusions with the authority of modernity. I am going to suggest later that Radhakrishnan's particular concoction simply does not work, for Advaitin metaphysics cannot be detached from the tradition-specific context which gives authority to its interpretation of the nature of reality. Modernity (with its notion of reason and experience alone) is incapable of substantiating Radhakrishnan's conclusions. But I shall return to this critique shortly after further developing the exposition of Radhakrishnan's position.

To summarize, the first argument presented by Radhakrishnan for (Hindu) pluralism is that mystical experience testifies to the universality of non-dual identity mysticism; the self is recognized as divine, and there is thus no "self," but only *Brahman*. Even if this were not a universal testimony among mystics, which it is not, I have been able to identify Radhakrishnan's fundamental ontological presuppositions which drive the motor of his pluralist project—which is my first task. Whether this accords with his claim regarding the equality of the religions seems doubtful, but let me now turn to his second argument.

In this argument, Radhakrishnan develops the traditional Advaitin distinction between "God" (who is an analogue to the notion of the *jiva*, the empirical self—and both are provisional constructs) and the "Absolute" (which corresponds to pure non-dual consciousness). While he sometimes uses these terms loosely and even interchangeably, in other works he makes important, perhaps even crucial, distinctions between them. It is here that we see Radhakrishnan's difference from Hick and Cohn-Sherbok, defined precisely through his criticism of Kant. Remember, Hick makes the distinction between the noumenon (the divine reality which we cannot know) and the phenomena (the many images of the divine, both personal and non-personal, theistic and non-theistic). Cohn-Sherbok follows him in this. However, Radhakrishnan makes a distinction between the "Absolute" —"the changeless noumenal reality," "God as he is" in himself[37] —and the phenomenal: "These different representations do not tell us about what God is in himself but only what he is to us."[38] However, the crucial difference is that for Radhakrishnan, unlike Hick, we *do* have direct access to the Absolute via non-dual-identity mystical experience. It is in this context that he both praises and criticizes Kant.

He praises Kant for showing the "logical indemonstrability of God" and for Kant's recognition that our "capacities of knowledge are limited to the phenomenal world, and if we extend the principles of space and time experience to regions beyond it" we are led to false understanding.[39] Reason, knowledge, and the mind are always limited within the empirical world, and this is in keeping with the Advaitin understanding of the *apara vidyā* level of understanding—truth on the level of duality, empirical truth. This is in contrast to *para vidyā*, absolute truth. Of *para vidyā* Radhakrishnan says, significantly, "Its contents is the oneness of Ātman and the sole reality thereof."[40] However, he strongly criticizes Kant, as did other contemporary Indian philosophers on this point,[41] for failing to consider intuition (as understood by Advaita) as a proper mode of knowledge:

> God is not an object of perception or of inference, and if he exists, his being must be apprehended in some way other than that which holds for the finite world. But unfortunately Kant did not discuss the question of the possibility of a different mode of apprehension. . . . Kant thinks that intuitive understanding is a prerogative of God and not a possession of the human spirit. Such a misconception is traceable to the arbitrary limits he imposed on human knowledge.[42]

For Radhakrishnan, intuitive apprehension, exemplified in *anubhava*, bridges the gulf between the noumenal and phenomenal.[43] Kant limited this type of intuition to God and denied it to man. However, because for Radhakrishnan there is ultimately no difference between the true self (*ātman*) and the divine (*Brahman*), he sees Kant's limits as arbitrary—which of course they are not. Kant assumed a real ontological difference between the immortal soul and God, whereas Radhakrishnan does not because of his Advaitin presuppositions. Hence, Radhakrishnan often and rightly says, "it is a sound religious agnosticism which bids us hold our peace regarding the nature of the supreme spirit."[44] In this regard some critics have incorrectly, though not implausibly, read Radhakrishnan and Hick as holding the same position.[45] However, to leave the matter there would be inaccurate, for Radhakrishnan is also of the conviction that in the core of mystical experience one has (and here we are bedeviled by dualistic language, for strictly speaking there is no "one" to have the experience) "direct communion" with the Absolute. Here "we" experience the Supreme Spirit, discovering "our" identity with it and can proclaim the "consubstantiality of the spirit in man and God."[46] In this respect Radhakrishnan is committed to affirming the definitive ontological status of *nirguna Brahman* (*para vidyā* level of knowledge), that is, God who is beyond all name and form, beyond all attributes, over that of *saguna Brahman* (*apara vidyā*), that is, the Absolute—who only when characterized by name and form gives us philosophical theism which is a provisional truth only appropriate to the level of duality. Hence, Radhakrishnan's agnosticism is of a very particular tradition-specific type, which is also concerned to maintain other very particular ontological claims about the divine reality and the world.

My reading of Radhakrishnan will, I think, be further substantiated in what follows. I want to analyze critically his equality/pluralism claim. By now, the shape of my analysis will be predictable. I will show that despite his claims of tolerant equality, Radhakrishnan's position exemplifies the characteristics of a rigorous exclusivism. We should not be surprised at this, but we will discover that in contrast to Hick, Knitter, and Cohn-Sherbok, Radhakrishnan's rigorous exclusivism is based on Advaita Hinduism, whereas in principle, it would be impossible to distinguish between Hick and Cohn-Sherbok regarding actual metaphysical claims made: i.e., they are both fundamentally agnostics, and belong to the Encyclopedic tradition. The same can ultimately be said of Knitter's eco-Encyclopedianism.

Given that the core mystical experience is one of Advaitin non-dual identity, one can see how Radhakrishnan is forced in practice to grade the different religions and their experiences in so much as they conform and differ with regard to this ultimate and definitive standard. Like all pluralists, he cannot succeed in escaping history and particularity, for even though he formally rejects the authority of scripture and revelation, he fundamentally prioritizes some, rather than other, experiences. In so doing, he prioritizes and gives particular status to certain forms of Hinduism (and alleged corresponding forms of such claims in other traditions). In a very telling passage he reveals the basic implicit hierarchy that operates within his approach:

> Hinduism insists on our working steadily upwards and improving our knowledge of God. "The worshippers of the Absolute are the highest in rank; second to them are the worshippers of the personal God; then come the worshippers of the incarnations like Rāma, Krishna, Buddha; below them are those who worship ancestors, deities and sages, and lowest of all are the worshippers of the petty forces and spirits."[47]

Such a grading exercise finally displays Radhakrishnan's Advaitin metaphysics clearly. Advaita comes first. "Theism" ranks second, especially demythologized forms which are not related to any historical and particular revelation. The latter, incarnational-based forms of theism, represent the third nearest to the truth. This hierarchy of truths is inevitable and a corollary of holding various truth claims, but it certainly runs against Radhakrishnan's avowed "equalism." At times, it would seem that his rhetorical edge blunts his own self-consciousness when, for instance, only a few lines above the quotation just cited and within the same paragraph, he writes: "Hinduism does not distinguish ideas of God as true and false, adopting one particular idea as the standard for the whole human race."[48]

This is manifestly not true, for he does apply a single exclusivist standard to the entire religious life of humankind, so that they are fitted into higher and lower levels of development and progression.

One might want to say that this amounts to inclusivism, or in Radhakrishnan's terms, fulfillment, but this would be inaccurate on three counts. First, Radhakrishnan has himself called into question whether exclusivism and inclusivism can be formally distinguished in so much as the standard of truth by which all others are judged is tradition specific, and therefore others are tolerated "so long as they accept their subordination."[49] In his own terms he would refuse the label of inclusivism, and I am inclined to think he is right in so doing. Second, Radhakrishnan's Hindu tolerance is not based on an indifference to questions of truth, but rather on a different conception of time and freedom from many of the Christians of whom he is critical. The doctrine of *karma* and rebirth allows an entirely relaxed attitude toward religious pluralism, for it is Radhakrishnan's belief that over time, and preserving human freedom, men and women will eventually come to the full realization (*anubhava*) of their divine nature.[50] Radhakrishnan specifically argues against predestination in terms of damnation, and then criticizes the very notion of damnation and hell.[51] This is quite in keeping with most of Hinduism, with the interesting exception of Madhva who is unique in proposing a doctrine of predestination and damnation.[52] However, the effect of holding this Advaitin position means that rebirth facilitates the eventual opportunity to come to the right (Advaitin) view and with it, concomitantly, the final liberative "experience" of *moksha*.[53] In this sense, Radhakrishnan is a universalist and claims that

> Cosmic history is working towards its highest moment when the universal tendency towards spiritual life becomes realized in one and all. . . . As matter was delivered of life and life of mind, so is man to be delivered of the spirit. That is his destiny.[54]

Thus, "fulfillment" would be passing through the various hierarchic stages, through the different levels of development from animism, incarnational theism, philosophical theism, and finally into Advaita Vedānta which would bring about final release. This is typically the case with inclusivists, who only accept others in a provisional and restricted sense, and only until others come to recognize fully the (inclusivist's) truth. This is a further reason why, strictly speaking, Radhakrishnan is not inclusivist, if indeed such a type exists. In this respect, it is difficult to find an inclusivist who isn't, in the final ontological analysis, an exclusivist.

The third reason for suggesting that his position be read as exclusivist is that strictly speaking Radhakrishnan's viewpoint requires fundamental changes within the religions of the world if they are to be acceptable, otherwise, in a strict ontological sense he would have to regard them as erroneous. The changes that he requires would mean conforming Christianity, for example, to Advaita Vedānta. Consider an argument advanced by Radhakrishnan that helps illustrate my point:

> Suppose a Christian approaches a Hindu teacher for spiritual guidance, he would not ask his Christian pupil to discard his allegiance to Christ but would tell him that his idea of Christ was not adequate, and would lead him to a knowledge of the real Christ, the incorporate Supreme. Every God accepted by Hinduism is elevated and ultimately identified with the central Reality which is one with the deeper self of man.[55]

Two points regarding this quotation. First, the Advaitin teacher (quite rightly) would "lead" his pupil to the "real" Christ, contrary to Radhakrishnan's rhetoric elsewhere about the "common search for truth," pitted against Christianity's alleged dogmatic claims to truth.[56] Second, this "real" view of Christ would certainly run counter to mainstream orthodox Christianity and in historical terms, at least, raise the question as to whether this would be Christianity's fulfillment or destruction. Christianity, for Radhakrishnan, got it right about Jesus Christ, but got it wrong in limiting the claim of divine consubstantiality to Jesus alone. I would question whether Radhakrishnan employs "consubstantiality" in the way in which it was used by the orthodox councils of the church. Whether Jesus' real humanity is preserved within Radhakrishnan's scheme of things is open to doubt.[57]

If any reader thinks that I am engaged in a polemic against Hinduism on behalf of Christianity, I should make it clear that this kind of criticism cuts both ways. Of course, both "sides" in this debate could point to "converts" whereby some Christians who have become Hindus would agree with Radhakrishnan and vice versa. This reversibility relates to dialectical argumentation. However, this fact does not materially affect the logical point that I am making about the historical traditions that do exist: that fulfillment of one (X) by another (Y) means the death of that other (X), as it actually exists. Hence, within (Y) there are therefore profoundly discontinuous elements with (X), within which there may exist some continuities with (X) even if those within (X) would not see them to be continuous in so much as they have become transformed within the intrasystematic logic of (Y). I do not want to question the logic and viability of Radhakrishnan's position as such, but simply want to show how a clear form of exclusivist neo-Advaitin Hinduism is operative within what Radhakrishnan presents as his Hindu "tolerant" and "equalist" approach to interreligious relations. In effect, we should not accept his own self-description as a pluralist, but recognize that he is an Advaitin exclusivist. If my argument has been in the least convincing, then it will indicate that such labels like "equalist" or "pluralist" are deceptive and therefore entirely unhelpful. They conceal different forms of exclusivism—in this instance, a neo-Advaitin form of exclusivism rather than modernity's Encyclopedic exclusivism.

Although at this point I could finish the chapter, I want to go one step further and ask whether Radhakrishnan's Hindu pluralist proposals are actually sustainable, even if they are exclusivist rather than pluralist. Despite his final adherence to a form of Advaita Vedānta, he departs from the entire Vedāntic tradition, as we saw, in refusing authority to the Vedic scripture. This actually has very serious consequences for his entire argument, because it becomes questionable, apart from a leap of faith, as to how Radhakrishnan can assert that the height of mystical experience is non-dual identity with the divine. Logically, there is no one to know this when it takes place, because there is no distinction between subject and object, knower and known; and since all interpretations operate at the level of duality, the bridge between this intuitive realization and its expression is impossible to build.[58] Here, Thomas Urumpackal rightly concludes his analysis of Radhakrishnan with this same puzzlement:

> According to him [Radhakrishnan], whatever the nature of direct experience, the moment it is conceptually expressed, there is a duality which means that there is an element of error in it. Therefore the expressed form of spiritual experience is not absolutely valid. We do not understand how he can maintain then the absolute validity of the reports of the Hindu mystics about the realization of identity with the Absolute, how he can dogmatize the doctrine of the oneness of man and God.[59]

Śankara, or any orthodox Vedāntin would have recourse to scriptural exegesis to support the interpretation of such experience, but Radhakrishnan has denied this possibility to himself as it would appear sectarian. This failure in "sectarianism" is precisely why Ignatius Gnanapragasam concludes that Radhakrishnan's failure is attributable to his defending by reason and experience alone that which his "Hindu ancestors defended theologically, that is, on the authority of the supposed revealed word of God."[60] Hence, my point is that Radhakrishnan actually weakens the credibility of his arguments by resisting tradition-specific authority, even though, as we have seen, he inevitably ends up within a tradition-specific position. His particular position, based as it is on non-dual mystical realization, is actually extremely weak when it relies on experience and reason alone, for neither on their own nor together can they properly support his conclusion. Radhakrishnan needs to be more Hindu, so to speak, for this part of his thesis to work; even if in so doing, it would then actually weaken his thesis by displaying a partisan starting point and privileging certain scriptures.

Let me conclude this chapter by summarizing my findings. First, Radhakrishnan's pluralism has been shown to be exclusivism and therefore fails to attain the goals it claims to achieve. Second, Radhakrishnan's exclusivism is seen to be a form of neo-Advaita Vedānta, which is a fusion of Advaita with various elements from the Encyclopedic tradition. Third, this particular form of neo-Advaita actually fails, for traditional Advaita bases its claims regarding *anubhava* on the authority of scripture that is supported by experience. Logically speaking, if the argument is advanced on rational experiential grounds alone, as it does within Radhakrishnan's neo-Advaita, it is unsustainable. Had he advanced these arguments from a more traditional basis, relying on the authority of scripture, he would have succeeded in terms of coherence, but failed by his own criterion in privileging one historical revelation (even if eternal), the Upanishads, over that of other forms of revelation. Hence, Radhakrishnan's pluralism fails, as all pluralisms have so far failed, even though it is of a different species from Enlightenment exclusivism. Fourth, my study of Radhakrishnan provides one case study to suggest that inclusivism is logically better characterized as exclusivism. Fifth, we are therefore still searching for a genuinely religious tradition-specific form of pluralism that is viable. We shall find this in the next chapter, when we turn to the Dalai Lama, but we shall also find that such a discovery entails a very orthodox exclusivist Tibetan Buddhism. We will also find that Tibetan Buddhism has, in the Dalai Lama's terms, nothing at all to learn from difference. This is not a problem for the Dalai Lama, nor should it be, but it puts an end to the notion of a tolerant and open east in comparison to a dogmatic and closed west. I shall also be arguing that while the Dalai Lama's orthodox form of Tibetan Buddhism fares best of all our exclusivist/pluralists, he fails actually to teach a position on other religions that follows logically from his basic position. We shall see a form of internal contradiction of an entirely new type.

Notes

1. For an excellent historical contextualization of Neo-Hinduism, see Percival Spear, *A History of India*, Vol. 2, Penguin, London, 1965, 194-271; and Arvind Sharma, ed., *Neo-Hindu Views of Christianity*, E. J. Brill, Leiden, 1988. For a more deconstructive critical account, see Paul Hacker, "Aspects of Neo-Hinduism as Contrasted with Surviving Traditional Hinduism," translated by Dermot Killingley, from Lambert Schmithausen, ed., *Kleine Schriften*, Harrassowitz, Wiesbaden, 1978, 580-608. See also J. L. Brockington, *The Sacred Thread*, University Press of Edinburgh, Edinburgh, 1981, ch. 9. In ch. 10, like Hacker (to whom he does not refer), Brockington suggests the historical "triumph" of traditional Hinduism. On Hindu reception in the west, see Wilhelm Halbfass, *India and Europe: An Essay in Understanding*, State University of New York, Albany, 1988.

2. Wilhelm Halbfass, *India and Europe*, 187.

3. Paul J. Griffiths, ed., *Christianity through Non-Christian Eyes*, Orbis, Maryknoll, N.Y., 1990, 192-3.

4. John Milbank, "The End of Dialogue," in Gavin D'Costa, ed., *Christian Uniqueness Reconsidered*, Orbis, Maryknoll, N.Y., 1990, 174-91, 178.

5. It is clearly evident in Islam as well. See for example, Paul J. Griffiths, ed., *Christianity through Non-Christian Eyes*, 135-90; and J. O. Voll, *Islam: Continuity and Change in the Modern World*, Longman, London, 1982.

6. This is the main period (1926-45) of his engagement with religious pluralism. See Ishwar C. Harris, *An Exposition of the Concept of Universalism in S. Radhakrishnan's Thought*, Ph.D., Claremont Graduate School, California, 1974, 17ff. In this period Radhakrishnan alternates between Hindu apologetics in response to western criticisms (see *The Hindu View of Life* [1926], Unwin, London, 1980) and a more "neutral" philosophical approach dictated by his concern not to privilege any particular religion (*An Idealist View of Life* [1929], Unwin, London, 1980).

7. See Alan Race, *Christians and Religious Pluralism*, SCM, London, 1983. Radhakrishnan uses this typology rather loosely in *Hindu View* ch. 2, and most fully in *Eastern Religions and Western Thought*, Oxford University Press, Oxford, 1939, 343ff.

8. Radhakrishnan, "My Search for Truth" in V. Ferm, ed., *Religion in Transition*, George, Allen & Unwin, London, 1937, 14. P. Fallon, in "Rāmakrishna, Vivekananda, and Radhakrishnan," in Richard De Smet and Josef Neuner, eds., *Religious Hinduism*, St. Paul's Press, Allahbad, 1964, 288-91, suggests that Radhakrishnan outlines a caricature view of Christianity, often relying on "anti-Christians" such as Gibbon and Loisy (290). Stephen Neill goes so far as to say that Radhakrishnan's writings display a "passionate hatred of Christianity." See Neill, *Christian Faiths and Other Faiths*, Oxford University Press, London, 1961, 82.

9. Radhakrishnan, *Eastern Religions*, 343.

10. *Eastern Religions*, 344.

11. *Eastern Religions*, 344-5.

12. *Eastern Religions*, 345. I shall subsequently use equalist and pluralist interchangeably.

13. *Eastern Religions*, 297, 327, 345, 347.

14. *Eastern Religions*, 345, 346.

15. *Eastern Religions*, 335.

16. I am not concerned here with his historically inaccurate depiction of Hinduism. See for example, Chuni Mukerji, *A Modern Hindu View of Life*, SPCK, London & Calcutta, 1930, which, while lapsing into polemics, nevertheless greatly qualifies Radhakrishnan's claims. A. R. Wadia's "The Social Philosophy of Radhakrishnan" in Paul Arthur Schilpp, ed., *The Philosophy of Sarvapelli Radhakrishnan*, Tudor Publishing Co., New York, 1952, 755-87, is a balanced criticism of Radhakrishnan regarding his glossing over questions of caste and social structure. Often, Radhakrishnan makes sweeping claims for "Hinduism," while he is well aware of its complexity and varieties as is evinced in one of his best works, the 2 volumes of *Indian Philosophy* (1923), George, Allen & Unwin, London, 1977.

17. Radhakrishnan, *Hindu View*, 42.

18. *Hindu View*, 43.

19. *Hindu View*, 28.

20. Radhakrishnan, "Answer to the Critics," in Schilpp, ed., *The Philosophy of Radhakrishnan*, 820.

21. See Thomas Urumpackal, *Organized Religion According to Radhakrishnan*, Universita Gregoriana Editrice, Rome, 1972, pt. II, for an extremely detailed outline of Radhakrishnan's various arguments.

22. *Hindu View*, 37. See also *Recovery of Faith*, George Allen & Unwin, London, 1956, 21.

23. Radhakrishnan's "theism," as will be shown below is not an ontological theism, but a pragmatic and provisional one that gives way to his ontologically monistic outlook. Radhakrishnan also foreshadows Hick's universalism when he writes, "if every soul is precious to God, universal salvation is a certainty. If some souls are lost, God's omnipotence becomes problematical." Radhakrishnan, *Idealist*, 227.

24. *Hindu View*, 13; *Eastern Religions*, 73.

25. See especially his telling defense and total lack of criticism of Śankara in *Indian Philosophy*, Vol. 2, 656-8. Nevertheless, there are problems reading Radhakrishnan as a straight-forward Advaitin, both in his failure to recognize the eternal authority of the Vedas and other traditional departures from Advaita, and in his philosophical idealism. See Hacker, "Aspects"; and A. C. Mukerji, "Reality and Ideality in the Western and the Indian Idealistic Thought," in W. R. Inge, et al., eds., *Radhakrishnan: Comparative Studies in Philosophy in Honour of his Sixtieth Birthday*, George Allen & Unwin, London, 1951, 216-31. Nevertheless, D. R. Tuck, *Māyā: Interpretative Principle for an Understanding of the Religious Thought of Śankara and Radhakrishnan*, Ph.D., School of Religion, Iowa University, 1970, and P. T. Raju, "Radhakrishnan's Influence on Indian Thought," in Schilpp, ed., *Radhakrishnan*, 513-41 (519) both identify Radhakrishnan as primarily a creative follower of Śankara.

26. *Hindu View*, 26, citing E. Underhill, *Essentials of Mysticism*, London, 1920, 4.

27. *Hindu View*, 27, citing Augustine's *Confessions* from Hermann, *The Communion of the Christian with God*. No further bibliographical information given.

28. Radhakrishnan, *Hindu View*, ch. 3 for these three claims.

29. Katz addresses the typologies that existed during Radhakrishnan's main period of writing (James, Underhill, Inge) and those that immediately followed (Stace, Zaehner, et al.)—which are well summarized and criticized by Stephen Katz in his important "Mysticism and Philosophical Analysis" in S. Katz, ed., *Mysticism and Philosophical Analysis*, Sheldon, London, 1978, ch. 9; and see the subsequent debate generated by Robert K. C. Forman's edited book, *The Problems of Pure Consciousness: Mysticism and Philosophy*, Oxford University Press, New York, 1990. Forman counters Katz and recasts a position not unlike that of Radhakrishnan. See also Katz's subsequent response in Stephen Katz, ed., *Mysticism and Language*, Oxford University Press, New York, 1992.

30. Hacker goes so far to claim that Radhakrishnan was more influenced by William James than any other person: see Hacker, "Aspects," 601.

31. In some parts of his work, there seems to be a concerted effort to give history a more dynamic ontological status, which is in direct reaction to the critiques of western missionaries regarding Hindu ethics and the status of history. *Idealist*, 208-47, 263-73, is the most mature example of this struggle. However, in my reading, *Idealist*, 271-3, is a final resolution toward Śankara.

32. *Idealist*, 76, 79.

33. *Indian Philosophy*, Vol. 2, 510-11.

34. *Idealist*, 80.

35. *Idealist*, 81; see also 215 to support this reading.

36. *Eastern Religions*, 294-5.

37. *Idealist*, 84.

38. *Hindu View*, 23.

39. *Idealist*, 127.
40. *Indian Philosophy*, Vol. 2, 518.
41. J. G. Arapura, *Radhakrishnan and Integral Experience*, Asia Publishing House, London, 1966, 44, cites K. C. Bhattacharya, G. R. Malkani, and A. C. Mukerji's criticisms of Kant as indicative of this trend.
42. *Idealist*, 130-34.
43. *Hindu View*, 33.
44. *Hindu View*, 20.
45. See Duncan Forrester, "Professor Hick and the Universe of Faiths," *Scottish Journal of Theology*, 29, 1, 1976, 65-72, where Forrester argues that Hick is indistinguishable from an Advaitin (69).
46. *Idealist*, 81. This use of the word "God" in the final sentence just cited should be "Absolute" in Radhakrishnan's own terms. His sometimes loose use of language could be attributable to the fact that the books originated as lectures.
47. *Hindu View*, 24. Presumably Jesus would rank equal along with Rāma, Krishna, and Buddha. It is not clear why Radhakrishnan puts the main section in inverted commas and he does not give any citation. However, this happens in a number of places within the book, and this hierarchy is repeated in other texts of Radhakrishnan's.
48. *Hindu View*, 24.
49. *Eastern Religions*, 344-5.
50. *Idealist*, 218-23; 227-39.
51. *Idealist*, 222-7.
52. On Madhva see Radhakrishnan, *Indian Philosophy*, Vol. 2, 738, who suggests that such a dualist tradition may have had a precedence in the earlier tradition of Vedānta. See also Eric Lott, *Vedāntic Approaches to God*, Macmillan, London, 1980, 163-8.
53. *Idealist*, 241-7.
54. *Idealist*, 242. Such evolutionary optimism is present in his earliest writings, and are then fueled by such emphasis in western writers such as Henri Bergson. For example, see *Idealist*, 107-8.
55. *Hindu View*, 34.
56. *Idealist*, 345f.
57. See his discussion on Jesus in *Idealist*, 53-9, 75-93, 164-5, 267. M. M. Thomas contextualizes this Christological view which was quite common among neo-Hindus. See M. M. Thomas, *The Acknowledged Christ of the Indian Renaissance*, SCM, London, 1969, esp. ch. 7.
58. This question has been incisively probed with regard to Radhakrishnan's theory of intuition. See for example, in order of importance, R. Browning, "Reasons and Intuition in Radhakrishnan's Philosophy" in Schilpp, ed., *Radhakrishnan*, 173-279; J. G. Arapura, *Radhakrishnan*, ch. 2, section I.1; Urumpackal, *Organized Religion*, ch. 3; V. T. Lee, *The Concept of History in S. Radhakrishnan*, Ph.D., Northwestern University, 1977, 175-94; and P. T. Raju, "The Idealism of Sir S. Radhakrishnan," *Calcutta Review*, August 1940, 168-84.
59. Urumpackal, *Organized Religion*, 228.
60. Ignatius Gnanapragasam, *Dr. Radhakrishnan and Jnana: An Essay on the Metaphysical Aspects of a Spiritual Wisdom*, Ph.D., Gregorian University, Rome, 1956, 33.

3

The Near Triumph of Tibetan Buddhist Pluralist-Exclusivism

Buddhism, since its beginnings in India six centuries before the time of Christ, has always had to deal with religious plurality. On the one hand it offered a penetrating critique of Hinduism, abandoning caste, the authority of the Vedas, and questioning the entire Brahminical priestly system; and on the other hand it had to deal with Jain asceticism and doctrine. It offered itself as the middle way. Buddhism soon developed in very different but related forms throughout Asia. It is an enormously complicated phenomenon and in these brief introductory paragraphs I want to try to locate the Dalai Lama's Buddhism and also introduce beginners to some key terms. Those knowledgeable about Buddhism should skip the next four paragraphs. As with my brief introduction to Hinduism, I am unable really to discuss the contentious portrait I offer here, and specialists would rightly question much that I say. My main request to specialists would be to exercise their talents on what follows after these introductory paragraphs.

AN INTRODUCTION TO BUDDHISM

Buddhism developed in Tibet when Padma-Sambhava was invited to teach there in the mid-eighth century and introduced a form of Tantric Buddhism, often associated with spells, magic, and mandalas. For various reasons it began to disappear from Tibet after its initial success, and was fanned into life again by Atisha (Dipankara Srijnana) who, in the early eleventh century, began missionary work there. Atisha probably represented North-Indian Buddhism, which was extinguished by the advance of Islam, and possibly represented a mixture of Tantric and Mahāyāna Buddhism. The major development of the Mahāyāna form of Buddhism practiced by the Dalai Lama comes through the work of the sixteenth-century philosopher Tsong kha pa, who follows the tradition of Nāgārjuna within Mahāyāna Buddhism.

The roots of Mahāyāna might go back to the Council of Vesāli, with the Mahāsanghikas (the great Sangha party) who were more liberal about the rules of the sangha, paid greater attention to the role of the laity, and emphasized both meditation and devotion to Buddhas. It forms the basis of Buddhism in Nepal, China, Korea, Japan, and of course, Tibet. This is in contrast to the Theravāda school (meaning "the teaching of the elders"), which was more conservative, very focused on monastic life, and is prevalent in Sri Lanka, Malaysia, Thailand, and Cambodia. The Theravāda is just one of the eighteen sects of Hinayāna ("lesser vehicle," a name given by Mahāyānists), although the most historically widespread. Within Mahāyāna, there developed many differing schools, possibly the two most important being the Madhyamaka (founded by Nāgārjuna in the second century C.E.) and the Yogācāra, or Cittamātra tradition as it is also called (probably founded by Maiteryaratha in the third century C.E.). Madhyamaka, meaning "middle position," is philosophically important for Tibetan Buddhists. It is also called Śūnyavāda (the emptiness school). Its middle path was negotiated between the Sarvāstivādins (also called Vaibhāṣika), who were dharmic realists, and the Cittamātra, who were absolute idealists. Nāgārjuna's great achievement was in defending the doctrine of emptiness (*śūnya*), as the middle way between these two schools, that is, that nothing has inherent existence or independent real existence. In chapter 15 of his Madhyamakākarikā, verses 1-2, Nāgārjuna argues that independent existence is incoherent on the basis that everything we know is affected by cause and effect:

> The origination of inherent existence from causes and conditions is illogical, since inherent existence originated from causes and conditions would thereby become contingent. How could there be contingent inherent existence, for inherent existence is not contingent, nor is it dependent on another being.

Nāgārjuna develops this analysis to apply to absolutely everything, such that the mind trained to see this will be able to realize emptiness in meditation. Hence there is both a highly analytical aspect and practical counterpart to Madhyamaka. Within Tibet, the development of the Madhyamaka school is charted in a particular way, which has no parallel in China or India, but is important in locating the Dalai Lama. First, it branched into two traditions, the Prāsaṅgika tradition (founded by Buddhapālita c. 470-540, with its greatest exponent Candrakīrti c. 600-650), and the Svātantrika tradition (founded by Bhāvaviveka c. 500-570). The latter then branched into the Yogācāra-Svāntantrika. The Dalai Lama is located within the Prāsaṅgika school. The main differences between the two schools,

Prāsaṅgika and Svāntantrika, are methodological (viz. the manner in which one must dispute with opponents to lead them into truth) and substantive. The Svātantrika accept inherent existence conventionally, while denying its ultimate existence, whereas the Prāsaṅgika insist that inherent existence is a fiction on any level.

One major feature of Mahāyāna is the notion of the *bodhisattva* (*bodhi* means enlightenment, and *sattva* means being), to which we will return in more detail later. Attaining enlightenment entails a proper conceptual grasp of emptiness, which generates the attainment of *śūnya* in meditation, coupled with the practice of compassion. Those who set themselves upon this path seriously strive to be *bodhisattva*. Basically, the *bodhisattva*, who must traverse five paths and ten stages, is one who on the sixth (or seventh) stage may pass into *nibbāna*, but relinquishes it to be able to help all suffering sentient beings. The Dalai Lama (meaning "ocean"—in Mongolian, and "superior" respectively) is thought to be the reincarnation of the great *bodhisattva* Avalokitésvara who is full of compassion. The fourteenth Dalai Lama fled to India after the brutal invasion of Tibet by China. He has had help from Christian quarters and writes out of the context as an exile, greatly desiring western support for the cause of his Tibetan homeland. In contrast, other Buddhist interaction with Christianity begins in the nineteenth century and is closely connected with colonialism and mission in South and South East Asia. Hence, many of the writings from these traditions are much more rigorously critical (and sometimes polemical) regarding Christianity. Now, let us turn to the writings of the Dalai Lama.

THE "SKILLFUL" PLURALISM OF THE DALAI LAMA

The sources for outlining the Dalai Lama's views on religious pluralism come from various talks and interviews given during the period 1963-1981.[1] A methodological note of caution should be added regarding the source material. There are three literary genres within the source materials: talks given in English; talks given in Tibetan delivered to an entirely Buddhist audience; and talks given in Tibetan (and simultaneously translated) to either Buddhists in the west or a mixed audience of Buddhists and others (usually in the west). The first genre is often loose and sometimes *ad hoc*, so that we should be careful not to press this material extensively. The second genre is often the most rigorous and technical and also sometimes represents the least guarded of the Dalai Lama's comments. The third genre, while often rigorous and technical is also sometimes more self-conscious regarding the western context in which they were delivered. These generic types do not represent a conflict of teaching *per se*, but rather show the Dalai Lama's use of "skillful means" (*upāyakauśhalya*) in communicating with different audiences who have differing needs, capacities, and expectations. Furthermore, recognizing these varying modes of communication will help us analyze more carefully the coherence, or otherwise, of his position, which I will now describe.

The Dalai Lama does not refer to the threefold paradigm of exclusivism, inclusivism, and pluralism, but he is usually thought to represent a tolerant, pluralist view of the relationship between religions. Congressman Charles G. Rose is typical, when in his introduction to the Dalai Lama's celebrated talk in Constitution Hall, Washington, D.C., Rose said: "The visionary humanism of His Holiness may even help us find a more authentic expression of the religions with which we are familiar. All the world's religions lead along the same path."[2] Such a pluralist impression may be formed from sections of the Dalai Lama's teachings. Here is an example:

> Among all those who accept religion, each follower has his own sort of system, his own method in order to achieve that goal. I want to stress that it is not necessary for everyone to follow one path, nor is there only one way. . . . You cannot say that there is only one religion and that one religion is the best, or that a particular religion is the best. Now for example I am a Buddhist but I cannot say Buddhism is best, although for me Buddhism is best. . . . For certain people Christianity is much more influential than Buddhism, so for them Christianity is the best.[3]

Is the Dalai Lama really a pluralist as this quotation would indicate? To answer this question let me turn to two seminal arguments advanced in his writings which help to explain the path by which he comes to the conclusions expressed in the quotation above.

First, he consistently prioritizes practice over doctrines, or rather he suggests that one should assess doctrines in regard to the practices they produce. According to him this is more fruitful than focusing on their conflicting metaphysical implications. It is important to note that the Dalai Lama is clear that there are in fact conflicting metaphysical claims and in no way does he try to deny this. For example, he says: "Among spiritual faiths, there are many different philosophies, some just opposite to each other on certain points. Buddhists do not accept a creator; Christians base their philosophy on that theory."[4]

There are three reasons why he thinks that it would not be productive critically to engage with these metaphysical differences between traditions. First, one may not succeed in convincing the other person, leading to "endless argument" with the result that "we irritate each other," "accomplishing nothing."[5] Second, after such a discussion or dispute with a person from another religion, "you may have weakened the trust they have in their own religion, so that they may come to doubt their own faith."[6] Consequently, they will not be able to reap the good benefits obtainable from their own tradition. The third reason takes us to the heart of the matter. Doctrines, he argues, should be assessed in terms of their possible good fruits and this commonality, an emphasis on what "is shared," should be the focus for the meeting of religions—not that which divides them.[7]

The Dalai Lama is convinced that all the major religion's doctrines are at least employed toward one goal:

> The development of love and compassion is basic, and I usually say that this is a main message of religion. . . . The important thing is that in your daily life you practice the essential things, and on that level there is hardly any difference between Buddhism, Christianity, or any other religion. All religions emphasize betterment, improving human beings, a sense of brotherhood and sisterhood, love—these things are common. Thus, if you consider the essence of religion, there is not much difference.[8]

(This could almost be a quotation out of Hick, Cohn-Sherbok, or Radhakrishnan.) The Dalai Lama gives a very concrete example of how this process can be seen in instances of differing doctrines. He recognizes the difference between Buddhism and Christianity on the question of God, as noted above. Hence, for the Dalai Lama, compassion and love are the heart of Buddhism, predicated upon the doctrine of emptiness (*śūnyata*). He then explains how Christian (or theistic) doctrine works to the same end as Buddhist doctrine:

> Those faiths which emphasize Almighty God and faith and love of God have as their purpose the fulfilment of God's intentions. Seeing us all as creations of and followers of one God, they teach that we should cherish and help each other. The very purpose of faithful belief in God is to accomplish His wishes, the essence of which is to cherish, respect, love, and give service to our fellow humans.[9]

Unlike Hick, Knitter, Cohn-Sherbok, or Radhakrishnan, the Dalai Lama is relentlessly clear that his proposal comes out of his Buddhist tradition-specific context. For example, he cites the founder of the dGe lugs school (pronounced: Geluk), the fourteenth-century philosopher, Tsong kha pa, as substantiating the approach of focusing on practice rather than doctrinal disagreement:

> By concentrating on the actual practice of each individual devotee, we shall discover with absolute certainty that we share the same sublime aim. To cite the great mentor, the saint-scholar Tsong Khapa:
>
> > All precepts when realized are found free of contradiction.
> > Every teaching is a precept for actual practice.
> > This is the easy way to penetrate to our Teacher's meaning,
> > And to avoid the great ill of abandoning the path.[10]

Tsong kha pa was not of course applying this to interreligious dialogue, but to differences within Buddhism. The Dalai Lama extends this same intra-Buddhist principle to other religions in a way in which Buddhism has done so from its beginnings. Paul Griffiths writes that in contrast to Hinduism, there is considerable evidence that Buddhists have

> been accustomed to thinking about religious pluralism since the very beginning. The Buddha himself was active in India about five hundred years before the beginning of the Christian era, during a period when a number of new religious movements were being founded and when the orthodox Brahminism of the time was being challenged. Buddhists therefore quickly developed some conceptual tools to deal with the questions raised by the existence of manifold and apparently incompatible religious claims and communities.[11]

Griffiths identifies the two arguments that I am focusing on in this chapter as the two main ways in which Buddhists have engaged with religious difference.[12]

The second important argument used by the Dalai Lama to sustain his position is that one should recognize that different people are formed by various factors and are therefore to be addressed differently. What might be helpful for one person's religious development might be harmful for another. Hence, each person should be encouraged within the religion to which they belong. For example, he writes: "Religion can and should be used by any people or person who finds it beneficial. What is important for each seeker is to choose the religion which is most suitable to himself."[13] In another place, he compares religious choice in an analogy of choice between spicy, bland, or sweet foods and the dependence of choice upon differing tastes. We should not force someone to eat spicy foods when they prefer bland food. Similarly, for

> certain people the idea of God as creator and of everything depending on his will is beneficial and soothing and so for that person such a doctrine is worthwhile. For someone else, the idea that there is no creator . . . is more appropriate. For certain people, it may be a more effective method of spiritual growth, it may be more beneficial.[14]

This argument, in turn, helps us more fully understand the Dalai Lama's reticence to engage in rational debate and critical assessment of doctrinal claims made within other religions, as noted above. It also helps us understand why he is explicitly against mission, for the most important thing is the encouragement of compassion in each person's context, and not *per se*, the following of Buddhism. In response to a question regarding the importance of Buddhist mission toward non-Buddhists, the Dalai Lama answers: "I am not interested in converting other people to Buddhism but in how we

Buddhists can contribute to human society, according to our own ideas."[15] Neither is he interested in forming a single world religion, but instead rejoices in plurality: "It is a wonderful thing to have variety."[16]

Addressing people according to their context amounts to the Dalai Lama's traditional use of the doctrine of skillful means. This is a key doctrine within the Mahāyāna tradition.[17] It was employed to explain why it was that the Buddha's teachings within the scriptures appear to be inconsistent when in fact they are not. The Buddha employed different teachings according to the appropriate context of his audience. The ability to thereby adapt Buddhism through the use of arguments and devices appropriate to one's audience was one of the major factors of the success of Mahāyāna Buddhism in East Asia. This success is sometimes contrasted with Theravāda or Hinayāna Buddhists, who were in this respect, according to Edward Conze, "inflexible literalists."[18] They were unable to adapt themselves as skillfully as the Mahāyāna tradition. Together, these two arguments, the pragmatic interpretation of doctrines and the use of skillful means, form the conceptual basis for the Dalai Lama's attitude to religious pluralism.[19]

In regard to my overall argument, I shall propose that first, the Dalai Lama's "pluralism" is in fact a strict form of exclusivist Tibetan Buddhism of the dGe lugs variety.[20] His "tolerance" and "acceptance" of plurality is entirely in keeping with this exclusivist form of Buddhism and indeed predicated upon it. In this respect, and in this respect only, some of his comments made to western audiences regarding the "legitimacy" of religions need to be carefully contextualized. However, nowhere can we find that the Dalai Lama is in any sense intentionally misleading or self-deceptive and I would not wish to suggest this. Second, underpinning his exclusivism is a profoundly religious exclusivism, not one shaped by modernity and the Encyclopedia tradition. Third, his apparent pragmatic viewpoint regarding doctrine is entirely consistent with the dGe lugs doctrinal position which underpins and justifies such pragmatism. However, I shall engage with a particular defense made of the Dalai Lama's position regarding this specific point which does raise some critical difficulties for the Dalai Lama. Fourth, the Dalai Lama's approach also shows that inclusivism always finally collapses into exclusivism—and must so do to retain internal coherence. Fifth, I shall show that other religions in principle have nothing at all to teach the Dalai Lama, which is not a criticism of the Dalai Lama or Tibetan Buddhism as such, but a point that helps dissolve the Romantic European view of the "tolerant" and "open" "East" and also problematizes some of the empirical and philosophical claims made by the Dalai Lama.

First, then, let me locate the Dalai Lama's exclusivist dGe lugs position from within which his whole approach is generated.[21] Whenever appropriate, the Dalai Lama makes clear his adherence to the dGe lugs form of Tibetan Buddhism. Within Buddhism itself there is, for the Dalai Lama, a hierarchy of truths. The different Buddhist systems are "ranked according to the subtlety with which they identify and rectify the various forms of ignorance considered to prevent liberation and omniscience."[22] This follows Candrakirti texts, where each school is outlined and then shown to be wanting according to the canons of rationality acceptable to these schools. These texts are still the major texts that form the curriculum in Tibetan monastic universities, and the type of argumentation bears close parallels to the form of dialectics located by MacIntyre in twelfth-century Paris. Hence, each system is learned and then criticized so as to move beyond it, working through Vaibhāṣika and Sautrāntika schools associated with Hinayāna, followed by the Cittamātra/Yogācāra school of Mahāyāna, ending finally with Madhyamaka. Then, within Madhyamaka, arguments are addressed against the Svātantrika in favor of the Prāsaṅgika school to show that it is both the most rational form of Buddhism and the only effective way to attain Buddhahood via the paths of the *bodhisattva*. The Dalai Lama therefore makes a quite traditional claim, which would surprise the likes of Congressman Rose, that "there is within Tibetan Buddhism the complete practice of all Buddhism," and it is therefore the highest and complete form of Buddhism.[23] According to the Dalai Lama this is because Tibetan Buddhism externally maintains the Hinayāna system of ethics, internally maintains the Mahāyāna Sūtra generation of altruism, love, and compassion, and secretly maintains the practice of Tantra.[24] In this respect he claims that "Buddhism in Tibet includes a complete form of practice of all systems within Buddhism—Low Vehicle, Sutra Great Vehicle, and Mantra Great Vehicle."[25]

This latter claim, according to the dGe lugs, can be argued for and arrived at by rational analysis. The truth and uniqueness of the dGe lugs position is not based on sectarian or fideist claims, and can be defended rationally. In this respect, the dGe lugs tradition has been said to represent the high point of the intellectual "Scholastic" achievement within Buddhism.[26] Hence the Dalai Lama views Hinayāna Buddhists, those Buddhists who lack the highest aspirations of a *bodhisattva*, as being able to attain only the two lower forms of enlightenment: as *arhats* (who obtain liberation for their own sake); and as *pratyekabuddhas* (who obtain liberation for their own sake, and in their last life are not dependent on a teacher). In contrast, the highest liberation is that attained by a *bodhisattva*: "While the first two ranks (*arhat*, *pratyekabuddha*) may be obtained by following the Hinayāna path, the rank of Buddhahood is only reached by engaging in the Mahāyāna."[27] The path of the *bodhisattva* is itself a highly complex model, with substantial regional variations. I shall attempt a brief summary of the Tibetan dGe lugs view.

The *bodhisattva*, on his journey to perfect Buddhahood, practices six (or ten) perfections and traverses the five paths (*mārga*) and ten stages (*bhūmi*). With the attainment of an Awakened Mind, the beginning of *bodhicitta* (the mind of enlightenment), there is an increasing realization of emptiness. When direct non-conceptual awareness of *śūnya* is attained, the second path has begun where the person is no longer ordinary, but a fully-fledged *bodhisattva*. Paul Williams writes of this stage:

> This stage is associated with the particular (although by no means exclusive) cultivation of the perfection of giving. It follows that actually to attain the perfections of giving and so on it is necessary to have had direct nonconceptual awareness of emptiness. They are not truly *perfections* unless they are underpinned with a direct realization that, e.g., the giver, recipient and gift all lack inherent existence.[28]

At the fourth or fifth path, the process of the ten stages begins; which includes all sorts of powers such as living for aeons, manifesting and withdrawing one's body. The second stage, the Stainless, *vimalā* is the achievement of perfect morality. (That there seem to be repeats of attainments at certain points is often attributed to the fusing of earlier traditions into a more complex later one.) At the sixth or seventh stage, depending on which sources are followed, there is the perfection of skill in means and the complete eradication of the obscuration of moral taints such that the *bodhisattva* is totally free from rebirth and could enter *nibbāna*. However, given that the *bodhisattva* is full of compassion, he chooses to renounce this option and instead returns to teach and lead all suffering sentient beings out of ignorance, toward Buddhahood. Eventually, beyond the tenth stage lies omniscience, and this is a path to nowhere, for now the *bodhisattva* is a Buddha, and the Buddha is everywhere.

It is therefore clear that the Dalai Lama has a strict hierarchy of lower levels of "truth," which are finally coordinated and practiced purely and correctly only within the dGe lugs tradition. While the Dalai Lama has not done so, one can envisage that implicitly there must be a hierarchy whereby the other religions would slot in below the differing forms of Buddhism, with non-dual Advaita probably at the top, given its close philosophical proximity to Buddhism. The reader may recall that Śankara had been accused of being a crypto-Buddhist, and his teacher Gaudapāda has very strong affinities with the Yogācāra idealist school. Returning to the Dalai Lama, Paul Williams makes the point I am suggesting most clearly:

> In terms of reasoning to find the ultimate truth, if carried out correctly and without bias the Dalai Lama holds as himself a Buddhist, in common with all dGe lugs practitioners, that only Buddhism will be found to make final sense. Even within Buddhism, however, there are different teachings, and only certain teachings will be found to articulate in the last analysis that ultimate truth. It is a widespread Mahāyāna view upheld by the dGe lugs that the Buddha taught all these other teachings as stages on the path, suitable for people at particular levels. For those at certain stages in their spiritual progress

these other teachings make more sense, and will be more appropriate. The Dalai Lama has applied these same intra-Buddhist points to the issue of inter-religious contact.[29]

The doctrine of emptiness (*śūnyata*), that nothing has inherent existence (*svābhāva*), is central to Madhyamaka Buddhism and Tsong kha pa's dGe lugs view. I shall briefly attend to this doctrine as it is central to the Dalai Lama's beliefs and will allow me later to address some questions to his position.[30] The ultimate truth is emptiness, that is, absence of inherent existence. This can be analytically shown following Nāgārjuna's analysis. All things depend one way or another on causal processes. For example, nothing resists analysis into its parts, and therefore all things are composite and dependent on their parts. In contrast, anything that has inherent existence would resist analysis, for it could not have parts as this would mean that it was dependent on an aggregating process for its existence. But nothing resists analysis, therefore there is no inherent existence: everything, absolutely everything, is emptiness.

> All, absolutely all, is dependent, relative. Emptiness is the ultimate truth—that is, the ultimate truth is told when we say that all things, no matter how exalted, be they Buddha, nirvana or worms, are empty of ultimate, i.e. independent, existence. The range of this even includes emptiness itself.[31]

Rational analysis is essential to attain this insight for it is through rational analysis that we see that nothing has inherent existence. But this same conceptuality also allows the mind to realize emptiness: both conceptually, and through non-dual, non-conceptual, direct experience. This is quite unique to the dGe lugs who hold that: "Conceptuality—from rigorous scholastic debate to the cultivation of subtle mental images—is seen not as an impediment but as a *necessary* auxiliary to non-dualistic experience."[32] Through properly listening, thinking, and meditating, rational analysis can bring about a conceptual experience of emptiness, which then provides the means for direct non-conceptual, non-dual experience.

This analysis also establishes a doctrine of two levels of truth. The first level, related to our normal everyday, subject-object dualistic experience, is where we tend falsely to identify objects, including ourselves, as having inherent existence. This the Dalai Lama calls the "conventional" level of truth (*kun rdzob bden pa*), as opposed to the second level, the level of "ultimate truth" (*don dam bden pa*).[33] This latter is the truth of emptiness, that there is no inherent existence, in which there is no subject-object distinction, and the metaphor of pure water being poured into pure water is used to describe the direct experience of this truth by a *bodhisattva*. Of course, it is *only* first by means of conceptual analysis that this truth is arrived at, which then allows for, indeed facilitates, the direct-experience of emptiness following its conceptual identification and analysis.

It is arguable that compassion can both help to arrive at the insight of emptiness as well as follow from it, although Tsong kha pa recognizes that there is no logically necessary connection between emptiness and compassion as it is quite possible for an *arhat* to attain direct insight into emptiness without practicing compassion. Some, such as Śāntideva seem to argue that there is a logical connection between compassion and emptiness, but it must be acknowledged that the logical relation between emptiness and compassion was and is much disputed.[34] I do not wish to enter this debate except to suggest that, in so much as the Dalai Lama sides with one particular view on it, various problematic consequences follow for his position, with regard to my concerns.

The role of compassion in generating *bodhicitta* within the dGe lugs tradition is vital in terms of generating compassion, and therefore *bodhicitta*, for it explains the Dalai Lama's affirmation of other religions. There are two types of meditation techniques employed by the Dalai Lama for generating *bodhicitta*. The two types of meditation, the "switching of self and other" and, secondly, the "sevenfold quintessential instructions of cause and effect" are the "two main techniques for developing . . . an altruistic attitude" and increasing compassion.[35] It is for this reason that the Dalai Lama is keen to promote the practice of compassion within all religions. Compassion will help adherents develop right motivation which will, in turn, lead toward *bodhicitta*, which will in turn lead to liberation. In effect, his encouragement of compassion is to be understood within a tradition-specific ontological context: the realization of emptiness and the practice of compassion both lead to buddhahood, which is the basic goal. Hence, what appears to be an endorsement of compassion within all religions *per se*, is in fact harnessed toward a further aim: the attainment of *bodhicitta* as a step toward the attainment of buddhahood. Hence, the Dalai Lama understandably construes the "essence" of religions as a hierarchy of attainments pointing toward the fullest attainment via the path of the *bodhisattva* and the realization of emptiness. The pragmatic approach to doctrine serves a higher purpose: skillfully moving people toward the right goal and the right view.

Furthermore, given the doctrine of rebirth and the usual need for many reincarnations before attaining Enlightenment, there is no need to hurry people toward following the *dharma*. Each person must come to fuller knowledge in accordance with their *karma*. This helps contextualize the Dalai Lama's attitude to mission. He writes:

> We Buddhists ourselves will not be liberated at once. In our own case it will take time. Gradually we will be able to reach *moksha* or *nirvana*, but the majority of Buddhists will not achieve this within their own lifetimes. So there's no hurry. If Buddhists themselves have to wait, perhaps many lifetimes, for their goal, why should we expect that it would be different for non-Buddhists?[36]

Hence, it should be clear by now that Enlightenment and even the first really significant stage of the *bodhisattva* path is predicated upon the realization of the truth of emptiness that is attained through conceptual analysis and discrimination. Without it, there can be no release from the cycles of birth and death, and subsequently no liberation. The Dalai Lama is clear about this point, as one would expect him to be, but interestingly, this particular quotation is found within the first generic type in our source material (talks given in English). In answer to a questioner who presses him three times (in traditional Buddhist fashion!) on the questioner's own stated presupposition "that teachers of other religions, no matter how great, cannot attain liberation without turning to the Buddhist path," the Dalai Lama finally answers: "Liberation in which 'a mind that understands the sphere of reality annihilates all defilements in the sphere of reality' is a state that only Buddhists can accomplish."[37] This is an absolutely vital admission and entirely consistent with his basic position. The point, then, is that regardless of the practice of compassion, on its own, it *only* has the role of building up good motivation for a mind that can therefore eventually more clearly attain *bodhicitta*. Therefore, and this is all important, it is only the practice of compassion *in unity* with the realization of emptiness that brings about real progress, and only then, true entry upon the *bodhisattva* path leading to buddhahood.

We are now in a position to see the inner coherence of the Dalai Lama's position and understand how his exclusivism is able to generate an apparent pluralist tolerance, thereby exemplifying my first contention: that all pluralists are exclusivists. However, the Dalai Lama is in a strong position in contrast to Hick, Knitter, and Radhakrishnan, who do not acknowledge this logic. When Cohn-Sherbok seems to acknowledge this logic, he explicitly tries to avoid it by unwittingly adopting a self-refuting form of relativism which also suffers from breaking a further stipulation of his own in so much as he requires that all religions adopt it.

Regarding my second contention, the Dalai Lama is a religious Tibetan Buddhist rather than an Encyclopedic exclusivist. Regarding my third contention, his position shows that despite his emphasis on the pragmatic significance of doctrine, such an approach is only facilitated by his commitment to the ontological truth of the doctrine of emptiness. Doctrine, practice, and ethics are inseparable. While this supports my own argument, it may well be problematic to the attractiveness and coherence of the Dalai Lama's position. I will return to this shortly. Fourth, his position also indicates that there is no such thing as inclusivism for finally the Dalai Lama's truth claims are exclusivist—that is, all religions and all forms of Buddhism will eventually come to the insight of truth held by and practiced by the dGe lugs. Consequently all religions, including rival forms of Buddhism, are ontologically false and erroneous. Fifth, the Dalai Lama has rightly nothing to learn from other religions and from difference and Otherness. This claim regards the ontological issues, whereas it is clear that the Dalai Lama gives many instances of practical learning, such as the way in which Christianity teaches social action and social compassion. His doctrine of *śūnya* is perfectly complete. Learning may operate on a pragmatic level only. This, I should reiterate, is not a criticism of the Dalai Lama. It is entirely consistent with his position and would require an intra-Tibetan response to suggest otherwise. However, it does call into question the perception that Tibetan Buddhism promotes a better dialogue between religions or is more open or tolerant than other approaches or, indeed, is pluralist in any sense at all. However, as I shall argue below, it does suggest that some of the Dalai Lama's statements need careful contextualization and some require constructive critique regarding their intrasystematic coherence.

In one sense, the argument of this part of the book has come full circle.[38] However, before concluding, and proceeding within my own trinitarian reflections, I would like to respectfully probe what I take to be some unresolved tensions within the exclusivist logic of the Dalai Lama's position. This will amount to two main questions, with the first containing two subquestions.

One criticism of the Dalai Lama is that while claiming to treat all religions equally (pragmatically), he in fact does not. He holds to the ultimate doctrinal truth of emptiness while he nevertheless relativizes *all other* doctrinal truths and views them pragmatically. On this very count he has been defended by Jane Compson who draws upon what seems to be a traditional Buddhist answer. We should recall that emptiness applies to everything, the Buddha, *nirvāna*, even the teaching of emptiness itself. The doctrine of emptiness is itself a pragmatic tool to attain the realization of emptiness. Whilst the teaching of emptiness linguistically points to the ultimate truth, it, too, is empty, and should not become the object of attachment. The famous Buddhist parable of the raft is pertinent here. In the Middle Length Sayings (1:173) the Buddha tells an important story:

> Monks, as a man going along a highway might see a great stretch of water, the hither bank dangerous and frightening, the further bank secure, not frightening, but if there were not a boat for crossing by a bridge across for going from the non-beyond to the beyond, this might occur to him: "This is a great stretch of water . . . suppose that I, having collected grass, sticks, branches, and foliage, and having tied a raft, depending on that raft, and striving with hands and feet, should cross over safely to the beyond?" To him, crossed over, gone beyond, this might occur: "Now, this raft has been very useful to me. I, depending on this raft, and striving with my hands and feet, crossed safely over to the beyond. Suppose now that I, having put this raft on my head, or having lifted it on to my shoulder, should proceed as I desire?" What do you think about this, monks? If that man does this, is he doing what should be done with that raft?

There is no point carrying the raft that we use to cross a river once we have crossed. After crossing, it can be discarded. Compson cites José Ignacio Cabezón regarding the relativity of all doctrinal expression in relation to the raft parable: "This too is the nature of the linguistic aspect of doctrine; it is a pragmatic and provisional entity that has no ultimate value in and of itself."[39] Compson therefore concludes:

> The fact that, ultimately, the linguistic aspect of the doctrine of emptiness is a pragmatic tool, devoid of inherent value, enables the Dalai Lama to advocate the ultimacy of this view without contradicting his pragmatic and non-dogmatic treatment of religious theories in general.[40]

However, for two related reasons, I am not sure that Compson's defense is entirely convincing. First, as we have seen, it is a unique feature of the dGe lugs that rational analysis, language, and concepts are seen as actually bridging the gulf between ignorance and enlightenment. They are not an obstruction, but vital for the crossing. While the raft may be eventually disposable, there is only one raft and it is actually not disposable until attainment of buddhahood, so that the dGe lugs refuse to concede that there is some inexpressible, ineffable reality (emptiness) which cannot be expressed by language. Compson's use of Cabezón should be contextualized within Cabezón's text, as his argument is that this linguistic provisionality is asserted *within* the context of two excesses: on the one hand, meditative traditions (e.g., certain schools of Ch'an Zen) which repudiate the need for scriptural study and argument; and on the other hand, the scholastic traditions which forget that intellectual pursuits are only useful for "transformative experience."[41] For Cabezón the raft parable is a reminder to both to follow the middle way, not a discarding of language. Furthermore, later on, Cabezón approvingly points out that rJe btsun pa, the Tibetan exegete, criticizes the Vaibhāṣika view that language and words are completely transcended in realization. For rJe btsun pa, without words, nothing would be left from which meaning could be derived for meditation, even that of emptiness.[42]

Second, and relatedly, it would therefore seem that while the linguistic conceptual expression of emptiness is dispensable and devoid of inherent value, what is really at stake is the claim being made by such an expression: the truth regarding the way things really are (*yatabhutadarsana*); that is, emptiness (*śūnyata*). This is a truth claim that cannot finally be relativized, even though its expression can be, and even though we can see that it is expressed not only because it is true but also because it pragmatically leads one to realize this truth in unitive non-dual meditation. The point is analogous to the debate that took place in Tibet over whether Nāgārjuna's negations finally meant that he had no thesis himself. Such a reading was denied by Tsong kha pa, who

> maintained that Nāgārjuna's denial of a thesis is only a denial of an inherently existing thesis. For Tsong kha pa, Nāgārjuna clearly has a position, and obviously makes assertions. Any alternative involves paradoxes.[43]

Hence, what is at stake is not the question of "attachment" to true doctrines, as Compson puts it, but rather the fact that argumentatively and experientially the truths held were in fact defensible and true in an ultimate sense. Tibetan Buddhism cannot be coherently reduced to a form of pragmatism without any ontological claims, and in this sense the Dalai Lama's claim to treat all religion equally pragmatically does not work. He holds to the ultimate doctrinal truth of emptiness while nevertheless relativizing all other doctrinal truths and views them pragmatically.

It is for this reason that Paul Williams writes, in a quotation already cited above, that by the impartial use of reason, the Dalai Lama would hold that the truth of Tibetan Buddhism would be "found to make final sense," in contrast to all rival claims and other religions.[44] Hence, within this view a rigorous rational argument will succeed in showing that alternative views ultimately fall short of "final sense" in comparison to the dGe lugs view. To put it in another way, Compson's argument really amounts to saying that there is no contradiction in the Dalai Lama's position, but only in so much as one already agrees with the theory of two levels of truth and already acknowledges a hierarchy of religious doctrines with varying degrees of pragmatic efficacy. However, with these two qualifications in place, the nature of the defense is altered significantly. Basically, the Dalai Lama's form of pragmatism is predicated upon the tradition-specific truth of emptiness, rather than being a general "pragmatic and non-dogmatic" reading of all doctrines as Compson suggests. It is a dogmatic interpretation of all doctrines as pragmatic, because of the dogmatic truth of a single doctrine: that of emptiness.

I do not think that the Dalai Lama is guilty of advancing Compson's argument, but, in so much as her argument is problematic, it then indicates that while he has every right to treat all religious doctrines as pragmatic, he does so because of the dGe lugs *religiously true doctrine* of emptiness that he understandably prioritizes and which subsequently allows him to see all doctrines, including his own, as pragmatic. But this is only possible because his own doctrine is true. One would not expect anything else from a good dGe lugs pa, but whether this amounts to treating all religious doctrines on an equal footing, as Compson suggests, is therefore called into question. Hence, we are led to two further sub-questions regarding the nature of the Dalai Lama's "tolerance."

First, this form of "tolerance" does mean that finally all religious doctrines are *not* treated on their own terms, except the dGe lugs' doctrines. This is not to suggest that the claims of different religions should be accepted as true. That would be absurd. However, it seems to me that within the Dalai Lama's outlook, the claims of other religions are neutralized from the start if they are not even considered as challenges, problems, or puzzles, but instead translated into pragmatic injunctions. For example, the Dalai Lama's pragmatic interpretation of theism implies that theism leads not to adoration of God for God's own sake, as Augustine and Aquinas held, but rather to compassionate action toward all sentient beings (which in one limited sense Augustine and Aquinas do hold). Is it tolerant to affirm other religions entirely on grounds which negate or fail to engage with the fundamental claims to truth within them? Christianity, for instance, is valued purely in terms of its fruits/actions, not because of its truthfulness regarding the triune God as such. Like any good Buddhist, the Dalai Lama is suspicious of the doctrine of God, and in a talk to an exclusively Tibetan Buddhist audience (hence causing no offense to his listeners), he advances five arguments against the existence of God, and the "problematic side-effects" of holding such a belief.[45] (Congressman Rose should study this text carefully.)

I reiterate, this is not a criticism of the Dalai Lama's Tibetan Buddhism *per se*; rather, I question whether this kind of "tolerance" and "openness" is actually open to learning anything at all, or tolerant in any than the weakest sense. It is perhaps ironic that Paul Williams, after presenting a brilliant critique of Raimando Panikkar's Christian proposals for religious harmony and tolerance, commends the Dalai Lama's tolerance in the following terms. The Dalai Lama "represents a rare tolerance and humanity—all the real tolerance that is required of a religious practitioner. It is a tolerance based on Buddhist premises, but perhaps with a universal appeal."[46] I say this is ironic because Williams shows that Panikkar's proposals are hardly conducive to tolerance when they amount to denying the epistemological and soteriological teachings of the dGe lugs by claiming that the Real is ineffable and transcends expression. But the Dalai Lama's claims have the same logical consequence: they deny the epistemological and soteriological claims of Christianity (to take just one example). If Williams denies Panikkar's helpfulness regarding tolerance on the grounds that he gives, I cannot see why the same objections could not be leveled at the Dalai Lama. And I certainly cannot see why there should be a "universal" appeal if the premises are Buddhist, except in so much that in principle, from the dGe lugs standpoint, one could arrive at them through rigorous rational argument. However, by now we should realize that such terms as tolerance only have tradition-specific meanings and cannot therefore be too easily compared and assimilated. I would agree with Williams that: "There is a danger of the word tolerance becoming a slogan."[47] Hence, let me move to the second sub-question.

The dGe lugs tradition is committed to the view that one can arrive at the conceptual truth of emptiness by the correct use of analytical reasoning. Hence, while it is clear that in some interreligious situations the suggestion that all doctrines be treated pragmatically is appropriate to that particular situation, in principle this need not be the case. It is this last point that is important. The Dalai Lama's position is advanced without the sense that any such rational analytical exchange could ever be appropriate in the interreligious context, and this seems to run against the flexible use of skillful means. Are there no situations at all, such that arguing against theism might help those interested in that type of argument who are attached to the untruth of theism? Would the dGe lugs engagement in such argument not be a form of compassionate service to humankind? It also seems to run against the grain of the dGe lugs epistemological tradition which places such a supreme emphasis on the role of rationality. Such a moratorium on rational and analytical debate in interreligious matters will surely, in the long run, stifle rather than help understanding and encountering each other. That this plea be made to the dGe lugs is an irony, given their pre-eminent status in the Buddhist scholastic tradition and their engagement in rigorous and complex debate. However, one must consider the Dalai Lama's particular political context such that to engage in critical debate of this sort may not further a higher aim regarding Tibet and China. Or it may be that one so adept at skillful means knows that the time is not right, for all sorts of reasons, to engage in traditional scholastic debate with other religions. Nevertheless, those sympathetic to his position, such as Williams, have helpfully brought the dGe lugs critical rigor to analyze and question the pluralist theses advanced by Christians.[48] This kind of rigor is to be welcomed and forms a serious part of taking other religions seriously—at least from my particular perspective.

My last question raises a serious problem regarding the Dalai Lama's pragmatic claim that the religions are equal in promoting compassion and human well-being. Williams says, rightly:

> For the Dalai Lama the sphere of Truth is not of primary importance either between religions or in society generally. Primary concern is that of human relationships, loving kindness. . . . Our concern should be with goodness, and between religions the issue of Truth is relatively not so important.[49]

I want to raise the question as to whether the divorce between the good life and the question of truth is internally coherent within the dGe lugs tradition—or within any tradition for that matter. MacIntyre assumes that there cannot be a divorce within the western ambit of the debate and I suggest that it applies here with equal force. My contention amounts to the question, which we have already touched on, as to the relationship of compassion to emptiness—which, admittedly, is a much debated and unresolved question within Tibetan Buddhism itself.

To put it starkly, this is what I see as incoherent. On the one hand, the Dalai Lama holds that love and compassion are the goal and essence of all religions, which makes them equal. On the other hand, compassion is never finally practiced perfectly without wisdom: the attainment of buddhahood. Without the realization of emptiness, compassion and morality will always be tinged (in various degrees) with imperfection. Hence, on the question of the apparently perfect morality of the *bodhisattva* on the sixth or seventh stage we find that:

> Nevertheless, in spite of this morality, as Tsong kha pa points out, following Candrakīrti, "if they do not abandon the view that phenomena inherently exist, then their ethics will not be pure but will be faulty though apparently proper." That is, the morality of one who does not understand emptiness cannot be pure, even if it appears to be so, for it is not the perfection of morality.[50]

This means that the empirical claim the Dalai Lama makes regarding the essence and goal and therefore equality of all religions, including Buddhism, cannot *in principle* or *in practice* be the case. It cannot be the case in principle because it is held that *only* those with right view and realization of emptiness can attain to perfect compassion, and these are by definition Tibetan Buddhists of the dGe lugs tradition who are on the higher stages of the *bodhisattva* path. If this view is held, which it is, then it cannot be the case, in principle *and* in practice, that such perfect untainted compassion could be practiced in another religious tradition. That this is the nature of the dGe lugs outlook is neither arrogant nor incoherent, but it certainly means that even the claim for a pragmatic equality of religions is in principle ruled out. How then can such a claim be made by the Dalai Lama?[51]

Williams writes of the Dalai Lama's equality claim regarding universal compassion:

> It must be admitted, incidentally, that the idea that all religions are aiming at the welfare and benefit of sentient beings, that this is in some sense their common core or essence, strikes one as a noble but highly contentious and perhaps naive claim concerning a very complex situation and issue.[52]

Hence, while Williams is correct in his gentle qualification of the Dalai Lama's claim in empirical terms, it is not clear whether his qualification is in terms of the principle I have sought to isolate: that regardless of the material evidence, and leaving aside the difficulty of making such judgments, it would be impossible, in principle, to claim the pragmatic equality of all religions regarding the attainment of compassionate practice. The question then arises as to the logical basis from which the Dalai Lama makes such a claim. His good intentions in doing so and his sincere commitment to interreligious relations are not at all in question. What is at stake is the logical coherence of such a claim from within the intrasystematic coherence of Tibetan dGe lugs Buddhism.

In conclusion, I have tried to show the following regarding the Dalai Lama's position on interreligious harmony. First, the Dalai Lama is a rigorous exclusivist. Second, even the proposals that he makes regarding the pragmatic (rather than doctrinal) equality of religions cannot be sustained on his own internal presuppositions. It is impossible to attain pure moral action or intention outside the highly tradition-specific path of the *bodhisattva*, and then only at a particular stage within this journey. Both practically and in principle this argument fails in terms of internal coherence. Third, the defense that he does not privilege his own doctrines when comparing religions is found to be unsustainable. This is not perhaps a problem for the Dalai Lama, but for some of those who would defend his position from criticisms of exclusivism. Fourth, the Dalai Lama cannot be seen as defending some sort of inclusivism, for he clearly holds that *bodhicitta* is a precondition to attaining *śūnyata*, and that both can only be attained within dGe lugs Buddhism. The value of other traditions is that they lead one nearer to this goal, but can never attain it in their own right. Fifth and finally, he is perhaps the most successful of the four theologians/philosophers that I have examined in so much as he alone seems to realize that pluralism is always exclusivism.

The Dalai Lama is fully aware that the tradition-specific way in which the problem is perceived and resolved is something one cannot escape, and that desiring to escape this is impossible. However, his position still reflects some seriously unresolved problems that I have noted, and calls into question some of the claims he makes that have made his position so attractive to many Buddhists and non-Buddhists alike. In terms of dialectics, I have tried to show that intrasystematically the Dalai Lama's position cannot deliver what it promises. Rhetorically, I want to commend an alternative position on the relationship between religions. While my alternative may be dialectically more defensible, it is an open question as to whether it will be rhetorically more persuasive.

Finally, before moving to Part II of the book, I would like to draw together some further conclusions in the light of the entire argument and findings of Part I. First, my explorations have been limited, both in terms of authors and religious traditions examined. There are other pluralists within the religions I have examined, and I have not examined Islam at all. However, this limitation does not necessarily invalidate the tentative conclusion that I have argued for: that pluralism simply does not exist. It is always some or other form of either explicit or implicit exclusivist tradition-specific narrative. This has been shown to be the case in all four thinkers, and given the logical feature of making any claims, it is, I suggest, the features we would find in anyone making a pluralist claim. So, the first conclusion is that pluralism does not constitute a particular position on the threefold typology of pluralism, inclusivism, and exclusivism.

The second conclusion is that Enlightenment exclusivism fares worst of all the cases examined, because despite its claims about granting equality to the religions, it grants no such thing and in fact can be seen to do the opposite. It privileges liberal modernity as the mastercode within which all the religions are positioned, and neutered. At least Radhakrishnan and the Dalai Lama hold one religion to be true, even if Radhakrishnan, in so doing, contradicts the claims that he makes about pluralism and equality; as does the Dalai Lama albeit in a very different way. I do not want to suggest that my trinitarian position views other religions as true, but I do want to argue that it will lead to an outcome where other religions cannot be deemed true or false, or both, outside of specific historical instances and engagements. In this respect, there is a genuine openness toward other religions, rather than an *a priori* mythification (Hick and Cohn-Sherbok), or an *a priori* universal subjugation to an ethical universal (Knitter), or this *a priori* being rendered in pragmatic terms (the Dalai Lama), or religions *a priori* being fitted into a hierarchic chain (Radhakrishnan). Of course, the judgment that this is a better "openness" than the alternatives I've examined is more of a rhetorical issue, but surely not unimportant when this value is so highly prized by so many involved in this debate.

Third, I have in the course of Part I tried to show that when pluralists are unmasked as exclusivists, it is better to locate them in these terms, rather than as inclusivists. Radhakrishnan saw what was at stake on this point, better than any of the other four thinkers and rightly classifies inclusivism as a weak form of exclusivism. This does not help him when his own position is subject to critique. Nevertheless, in showing that no position is able to affirm another on that other's own terms, inclusivism fares no differently from exclusivism. This critique would also be applicable to that most famous of Christian inclusivists, Karl Rahner, who in two very important respects was clearly and explicitly an exclusivist. First, in his insistence that the beatific vision constituted salvation; and second, in his insistence that "lawful" religions only had any existence up until their historical and existential confrontation with Christianity.

Fourth, I have tried to conduct the entire exploration of Part I as an exercise in dialectics, following MacIntyre's project, such that I have tried to show why these four positions all fail to attain their own stated goals, and fail to do so because of the internal contradictions generated within their own positions. In contrast, I shall be wanting to commend a rhetorical alternative. In Part II rhetoric takes over, as I turn to develop and defend a trinitarian orientation on the question of other religions.

However, there is one final and fifth observation that is worth making—and it relates further to the question of rhetoric. Terms such as "tolerance," "openness" and "equality" are only to be understood as tradition-specific terms, such that I cannot entirely develop and defend my position as being *more* open and tolerant than the rival traditions that I have examined. What I can show, which is what I have tried to do, is that these alternative positions fail to deliver on what they themselves call tolerance, openness, and equality. What is then left to me is to show whether the position I advance actually meets some of the claims made by these other traditions, even if it meets them by changing the ground rules.

In the second part of the book I shall be jettisoning the threefold typology. Since I think that every position is exclusivist, and that the terms pluralism and inclusivism mask this, it will be better for the debate that they be seen as a raft that got us here, and now it is time to jettison the raft. I also wonder whether that particular raft might have taken us over the wrong river, for it failed to focus in on the particular historical engagements, which provide the only material we have for thinking through the questions viz. Christians and other religions. In conducting this argument against the typology I have also sought to call into question meta-theories which place Christianity (or any other religious tradition) within a grander meta-narrative which then narrates the religions. What I will seek to show is that a trinitarian meta-narrative does a very good job in narrating an unfinished story regarding other religions, while also allowing other religions their own voice. While not entirely jettisoning the claims regarding tolerance, openness, and equality, we will do well to remember (MacIntyre's paraphrased) question: whose god, which tolerance, what openness? The most important question of these three is the first, and then, I believe, the rest will follow.

Notes

1. I shall be using: the Dalai Lama (Tenzin Gyatso), *Kindness, Clarity and Insight*, Snow Lion, New York, 1984 (a collection from his visit to the United States and Canada during 1979-1981); *Universal Responsibility and the Good Heart*, Library of Tibetan Works and Archives, Dharamsala, 1980 (visits abroad as well as teachings in India during 1963-80); John F. Avedon, ed.,*An Interview with the Dalai Lama*, Littlebird Publications, New York, 1980 (interviews during his visit to the United States in 1979, plus the final interview in India); José Ignacio Cabezón, ed., *The Bodhgaya Interviews*, Snow Lion, New York, 1988 (interviews given between 1981-1984). His more recent writings, such as *The Good Heart: A Buddhist Perspective on the Teachings of Jesus*, Wisdom, New York, 1996, do not signify any change of position from the material analyzed and I shall not use it in what follows.
2. *Kindness*, 10.
3. *Heart*, 36.
4. *Kindness*, 45.
5. *Kindness*, 47.
6. *Bodhgaya*, 22-3.
7. *Kindness*, 47.
8. *Kindness*, 13, and see 46; see *Heart*, 40, 73.
9. *Kindness*, 46; see also *Heart*, 35-6.
10. *Heart*, 73, source of quotation not given. Regarding the spelling of transliterated Tibetan Buddhist terms, I have sought to remain consistent in the style of spelling words as there is immense variety in the literature—and I have no

preferences myself. For the main part, I have followed Paul Williams's style of spelling—see note 17 below.

11. Paul J. Griffiths, ed., *Christianity through Non-Christian Eyes*, Orbis, Maryknoll, N.Y., 1990, 136. See also one of the best introductions to the topic of Buddhist and Christian encounter: Joseph J. Spae, *Buddhist-Christian Empathy*, The Chicago Institute of Theology and Culture, Chicago, 1980.

12. Griffiths, *Christianity*, 136-8.

13. *Heart*, 26.

14. *Bodhgaya*, 13; see also *Kindness*, 74.

15. *Kindness*, 48; see also *Heart*, 82-8; *Bodhgaya*, 12.

16. *Bodhgaya*, 13.

17. Paul Williams, *Mahāyāna Buddhism: The Doctrinal Foundations*, Routledge, London, 1989, 143. For an extensive examination of primary materials on skillful means, especially from the Lotus Sutra, see Michael Pye, *Skilful Means: A Concept in Mahāyāna Buddhism*, Duckworth, London, 1978, chs. 2 and 3.

18. Edward Conze, "Buddhism: The Mahāyāna" in R. C. Zaehner, ed., *The Concise Encyclopedia of Living Faiths*, Hutchinson, London, 1971 (2nd ed), 309.

19. Paul J. Griffiths, as noted in the main text, suggests that the first argument undergirds most Buddhist assessments of other religions within the modern period, although countries directly affected by western colonialism have increased antagonism toward Christianity. See Griffiths, ed., *Christianity*, 136-7. This might well explain the very positive approaches advanced by Japanese Buddhists such as Masao Abe, Daisaku Ikeda, and D. T. Suzuki. See Masao Abe, (Steven Heine, ed.), *Buddhism and Interfaith Dialogue*, University of Hawaii Press, Honololu, 1995; and D. T. Suzuki, *On Indian Mahāyāna Buddhism*, Harper Torchbooks, New York, 1968, ch. 9.

20. Richard Haynes argues that the Buddha's own teachings could never be presented as "pluralist," and are strictly exclusivist. With him, I too have been arguing that "pluralism" is a "distinctly modern ideology." See Richard Haynes, "Gotama Buddha and Religious Pluralism," *Journal of Religious Pluralism*, 1, 1991, 65-95.

21. In what follows I shall focus exclusively on this tradition, for the various Buddhist alternatives would facilitate very different responses and tactics.

22. Anne Klein, *Knowledge and Liberation: Tibetan Buddhist Epistemology in Support of Transformative Religious Experience*, Snow Lion, New York, 1986, 19, see also ch. 1.

23. *Kindness*, 51.

24. *Kindness*, 51-4.

25. *Kindness*, 52.

26. Such is the argument of José Ignacio Cabezón's, *Buddhism and Language: A Study of Indo-Tibetan Scholasticism*, State University of New York, Albany, 1994; and Klein, *Knowledge and Liberation*, 23, 206-16.

27. See *Interviews*, 74, and 82, note 40, although the citation is from a note representing the Dalai Lama's view, not his own words. Avedon conflates the stages of the *bodhisattva* with that of buddhahood. The relation between the two is complex and quite different in various Buddhist schools. See also Williams, *Mahāyāna*, ch. 9; and in Japanese Mahāyāna, Susumu Yamaguchi, *Mahāyāna Way to Buddhahood*, Buddhist Books International, Tokyo, 1982, esp. ch. 14; Beatrice

Lane Suzuki, *Mahāyāna Buddhism*, George Allen & Unwin, London, 1981 (4th ed.), 61-9; Conze, "Buddhism," 297-305. In this brief outline I am simplifying considerably!

28. Paul Williams, *Mahāyāna Buddhism in India: A Doctrinal Overview*, University of Bristol, ms., 1999, 70: forthcoming in *Buddhist Thought: An Introduction to the Indian Tradition*, Routledge, London, 2000.

29. Paul Williams, "The Recent Work of Raimundo Panikkar," *Religious Studies*, 27, 1989, 519-20.

30. In what follows I rely mainly on Williams, *Mahāyāna*; and Williams, "Panikkar," 511-21; Klein, *Knowledge and Liberation*; Cabezón, *Buddhism and Language*.

31. Williams, "Panikkar," 516.

32. Klein, *Knowledge and Liberation*, 216, my emphasis. Cabezón, *Buddhism and Language*, 50, qualifies this as a sufficient, not necessary, cause of enlightenment.

33. *Kindness*, 193, and see 192-99 for his full exposition of this. See also Williams, *Mahāyāna*, 69-72; Klein, *Knowledge and Liberation*, ch. 2. One can see the close similarity with Radhakrishnan's employment of the two levels of truth, following Śankara. It is not by chance that Śankara, like his teacher Gaudapada, was accused of being a crypto-Buddhist!

34. See Paul Williams, in *Altruism and Reality: Studies in the Philosophy of the Bodhicaryāvatāra*, Curzon, London, 1998, section 5 where he discusses Śāntideva's contention. Williams concludes that Śāntideva's argument destroys the *bodhisattva* path! This focuses on Śāntideva's "faulty" (according to Williams) suggestion that one can refer to pains without the specific subjects who are in pain; see 164-76.

35. See *Kindness*, 11-2; 32-44; Williams, *Mahāyāna*, 200 ff..

36. *Bodhgaya*, 22.

37. *Bodhgaya*, 22. The sentences that follow are important, but do not, I think, contradict the reading offered here, for Tushita is a provisional heaven not required or linked to *bodhisattvas*, who, once they are advanced will not be reborn in such abodes, but will in fact master them.

38. To start the circle in motion again, one could now return to question Hick's pluralism in regard to both his explicit denial of the possibility of non-dual meditative realization (*An Interpretation of Religion*, Macmillan, London, 1989, 292-8); and his extremely questionable use of skillful means (Hick, *Interpretation*, 343-59). See Cabezón in contrast, *Buddhism and Language*, 171-87.

39. Cabezón, *Buddhism and Language*, 47. See Jane Compson, "The Dalai Lama and the World Religions," *Religious Studies*, 32, 1996, 271-9, 276.

40. Compson, "Dalai Lama," 276.

41. Cabezón, *Buddhism and Language*, 47-8; and see Klein, *Knowledge and Liberation*; her subtitle, *Tibetan Buddhist Epistemology in Support of Transformative Religious Experience*, makes the same point.

42. Cabezón, *Buddhism and Language*, 46 ff.; see also ch. 9. ("*bstun*" should be "*btsun*." There is a misprint in Cabezón.)

43. Williams, *Mahāyāna*, 64; and see also Paul Williams, "rMa bya pa Byang chub brtson 'grus on Madhyamaka Method," *Journal of Indian Philosophy*, 13, 1985, 205-25.

44. Williams, "Panikkar," 519. I am clearly unsympathetic with this claim

and have argued against it on internal grounds within Radhakrishnan's position. I will not pursue this argument here, as would a number of other Buddhist schools, as it is not relevant to my present purpose.

45. *Heart*, 10-1.

46. Williams, "Panikkar," 521.

47. Williams, "Panikkar," 521. In contrast, Williams's own taking the religiously other with full seriousness, admittedly in an aside, should be noted; see *Altruism*, 175.

48. See Paul Williams, "Panikkar," and also, "Some Buddhist Reflections on Hans Küng's Treatment of Mahāyāna Buddhism in *Christianity and the World Religions*," *World Faiths Insight*, n.s. 22, 1989, 13-26.

49. Williams, "Panikkar," 520-1. In a footnote following this sentence Williams refers to *Bodhgaya*, 11-4, and 21-3 to substantiate this reading.

50. Williams, *Mahāyāna*, 209. The internal quotation is from J. Hopkins, *Compassion in Tibetan Buddhism*, Rider, London, 1980, 195, who is citing Candrakīrti's *Madhyamakāvatāra* 2:3ab.

51. Admittedly, some of his expressions indicate a reservation: see the citation viz. note 8 where he uses phrases "hardly any difference" and "not much difference" between religions. I have also noted that one should not press statements made in the first generic type of literature and it is in this class that all such claims are made.

52. Williams, "Panikkar," 521, note 23.

PART II

Trinitarian Theology and the Religions

4

Trinitarian Theology: An Invitation to Engagement

In this chapter I want to establish a Roman Catholic trinitarian orientation in relation to other religions. I want to make three points regarding the relation of this part of the book to that of Part I. First, given the tradition-specific nature of all thought and practice, this part of the book is unashamedly Roman Catholic in method, orientation, and accountability. It is written with the desire to develop an intrasystematic dialectical argument to convince other Roman Catholics, and other Christians, that this type of approach is both defensible, faithful to major currents within the tradition, and also creatively innovative and responsive to the reality of other religions. Second, this trinitarian orientation more rigorously meets the demands for openness, tolerance, and equality that pluralists have stipulated for interreligious meetings, but in a manner in which all three terms are transformed. In this sense, what follows contains both rhetorical and intrasystematic dialectical arguments. Third, in the same manner in which I have examined other religions regarding their view of religious pluralism, I would be honored for those who are not Christians to engage in criticism of my position.

The chapter will be divided into three parts, each of which forms a cumulative argument in trying to establish the approach I am advancing. In the first part, I turn to Vatican II and post-Conciliar documents to assess the Fathers of the church and the Pope's attitude to a single question. Since it is uncontroversial within Catholicism that non-Christians may be saved, one particularly controversial question is: are non-Christian religions, *per se*, vehicles of salvation? This question is important for my overall argument for two reasons. First, if the answer is that there is no evidence to suggest that the Catholic tradition up until now sees other religions, *per se*, as salvific structures, then we have some evidence to counter pluralist and inclusivist theologies—which both argue for such a conclusion. We already have logical reasons to call these two positions into question in the light of Part I, but now I want to show that the material evidence also confirms my arguments. I should acknowledge that even if the church documents support my point, there is no definitive reason why further documents might move in a different direction, although I do not think this likely. Second, in suggesting that this is indeed the answer we find within the documents, I want to show that this apparently negative answer still allows for a radical openness to other religions, still affirms the saving work of God within other religions, and still means that other religions are infinitely interesting and complex. This point will be developed in theological terms in the second part of the chapter.

Before proceeding, a word to readers who are not Roman Catholic. The reason for taking the Council and post-Conciliar documents so seriously is precisely because I take tradition seriously, for after all, it is only through the tradition that we have the Bible, and only through the authority of church that we have the Bible and tradition. Hence, there is an intrinsic and dynamic interrelationship between Bible, tradition, and magisterial authority. If the documents that I discuss have no authority to some readers, I invite them to listen in on a discussion between Christians who take their tradition very seriously indeed, while recognizing that it must be recast, rethought, and even "developed" in the slow and ambiguous process of history. Furthermore, while the documents may have no authority for some readers, there is still a form of argument going on that can be assessed for its persuasiveness and for its fidelity to the biblical tradition that is shared by all Christians (even if differently).

The second part of the chapter will then turn to the question of what precisely these same documents say about the trinity and other religions. I focus more precisely on one issue: the meaning of the affirmation that the Holy Spirit may be actively present in other religions. The "may be" is respectful toward the historical task of affirming such a reality, rather than a cautious or mean-spirited qualification. First, I will argue, that this theological affirmation requires *both* a serious engagement with the other religion on its own terms, which is an on-going process, and also allows for what I will call legitimate hetero-interpretation, that is, a theological evaluation of the meaning of that religion, or various parts of it, that may not necessarily be in keeping with the sense of those within that tradition—what I call auto-interpretation. While auto and hetero-interpretations may coincide, the latter is always reliant on auto-interpretation. Second, I want to explore the way in which the affirmation of the Holy Spirit in other religions has serious ecclesiological implications for the church, for the Spirit is always both a trinitarian and an ecclesiological doctrine. To elaborate this second point, I turn to a close exegesis of John's gospel, before then constructively outlining the trinitarian orientation so far established.

The third part of this chapter will then turn to the rhetorical out-narration of the four thinkers in Part I. I will show how openness, tolerance, and equality are all granted to other religions in a more rigorous and non-contradictory fashion than achieved by pluralists. In this process, it will be clear that the three terms are transformed within my tradition-specific narration such that "openness" becomes "taking history seriously," "tolerance" becomes the "qualified establishment of civic religious freedom for all on the basis of revelation and natural law." This transformation will also indicate a major development (or corruption, as some theologians see it) within the Roman Catholic church, and indicates the uneasy inculturation of the best of the Enlightenment within the Roman Catholic tradition. "Equality" will become the "equal and inviolable dignity of all persons," such that there is no *a priorism* on questions of truth *per se* within the religions when renarrating these three terms. On the basis of the establishment of this trinitarian orientation, I will then address a single question in the final chapter: that of prayer, and interreligious prayer.

THE STATUS OF OTHER RELIGIONS AS SALVIFIC STRUCTURES

The *Declaration on the Relationship of the Church to Non-Christian Religions* (*Nostra Aetate* in Latin) promulgated on October 28, in 1965, marked a decisive step in Roman Catholic theology of religions. In 1962 Pope John XXIII had personally requested Cardinal Bea to oversee the drafting of a statement on the Jews. This was to be have been chapter 4 of the schema of the *Decree on Ecumenism* (*Unitatis Redintegratio* in Latin), but eventually mutated into a separate Declaration on the world religions, not just Judaism.[1] In the process the Secretariat for Non-Christian Religions was created in 1964 under Cardinal Marella. The Secretariat is now called the Pontifical Commission for Interreligious Dialogue.

The resulting document on *Nostra Aetate* was both a miraculous triumph as well as a painful failure. The triumph was at least twofold. First, as Cardinal Bea noted in introducing the final document, it was the first time that the Church has made an official pronouncement regarding the non-Christian religions. The tone was entirely positive and the concern was to focus on what was held in common so as to build together from shared strengths. This was a gigantic step for the Roman Catholic church. This is not the place to trace the pre-Vatican II history on the question of other religions except to say that the traditional teaching *extra ecclesiam nulla salus* (no salvation outside the church) was never formulated or applied to non-Christian religions in the technical sense in which they are understood in the 1965 document, *Nostra Aetate*. Furthermore, and ironically, Leonard Feeney, S.J., was excommunicated in 1949 for refusing to retract his literal application of the *extra ecclesiam nulla salus* to those from other religions and also non-Roman Catholic Christians. I refer readers to the footnote for further reading on the pre-Vatican II history.[2]

Second, the Jewish question had allowed the African and Asian bishops to express concern about the invisibility of religions that partly formed their own cultures: Islam, African religions, Hinduism, and Buddhism. Many of the bishops in Arab and Muslim countries also feared Muslim reaction to a document exclusively on the Jews, in the light of the Middle East crisis. In consequence, the document addressed itself to the much wider question of relations with religions. However, the tragic counterpoint to this is the way in which the original schema on the Jewish people was revised, finally failing to acknowledge Christian culpability in the long history of anti-Jewishness and the church's need for forgiveness. Even though the Vatican has taken some serious steps forward since then, Rabbi David Polish said of the document at the time that it was "a unilateral pronouncement by one party which presumes to redress on its own terms a wrong which it does not admit."[3]

In what follows I want to pursue a single question and one of the most important questions raised in the light of *Nostra Aetate*: are non-Christian religions, *per se*, vehicles of salvation? Can it be said that according to Vatican II non-Christian religions are mediators of supernatural revelation to their followers? This question absolutely takes for granted, following both pre-Conciliar and post-Conciliar teachings, that there is no doubt that the non-Christian may be saved. To answer my question, are non-Christian religions, *per se*, ever viewed as vehicles of salvation, I shall briefly inspect the Conciliar documents to see what kind of answer they give. I shall be arguing that they are silent, and this silence has in fact been read in two quite differing ways by post-Conciliar theologians. The types of readings, furthermore, are deeply affected by the presuppositions concerning nature and grace. Hence, there are theologians who argue that the documents affirm the possibility that non-Christian religions are means of supernatural revelation. These theologians tend to envisage a very close relationship between nature and grace. On the other hand there are those who disagree and tend to envisage a sharper distinction between nature and grace. I will briefly show that the present Pope, John Paul II, is in the latter group of readers. He does not understand the documents to teach that non-Christian religions, *per se*, can be viewed as supernatural means to salvation.

What does *Nostra Aetate* teach about other religions in terms of their being possible mediators of supernatural revelation and therefore salvation to their adherents? At least three things must be said in contextualizing the silence that is found on this explicit question. First, the religions are seen to be differently related to the Church in theological and historical terms: Judaism first, then Islam, and finally Hinduism, Buddhism, and "other religions to be found everywhere" (NA 2). This latter phrase is taken to refer to "primal" religions in Africa, although some argue that it should be extended to Shinto, Confucianism, and other Asian religions. In the official commentary, it is clear that these traditions cannot be regarded as monolithic entities, but such a brief pastoral document cannot enter into detailed historical descriptions. Judaism is seen as the root from which the church springs, out of "Abraham's stock." In this section we find the single exclusive use of the term *Revelationem* (revelation) in regard to other religions, although the sentence in which the term is used refers to the "Old Testament" so that it is difficult to speak here of another religion bearing revelation *per se*. Rather it denotes what Christians view as revealed and sacred scripture—the Old Testament—as do Jews. The sentence reads: "The Church, therefore, cannot forget that she received the *revelation* of the Old Testament through the people with whom God in his inexpressible mercy deigned to establish the Ancient Covenant" (NA 4, my emphasis). It is worth noting that the term was not part of the original text, but was introduced in the second drafting, in September 1964 when the document was widened to refer to non-Christians. This is highly significant, for the term "revelation" is not used in any of the sections dealing with other religions. This also highlights the *sui generis* relationship with Judaism, and implies that the non-use of the term "revelation" regarding other religions can be seen as significant. Supernatural revelation is clearly related to Christian scripture. This is confirmed in the *Dogmatic Constitution on Divine Revelation* 14-16 (*Dei Verbum* in Latin).

Second, *Nostra Aetate* is silent on the question of the salvation of the non-Christian. For this we must turn to *The Dogmatic Constitution on the Church* 16 (*Lumen Gentium* in Latin), and again we find a silence on the matter of the non-Christian religions *per se*, but not about the non-Christian's possible salvation. *Lumen Gentium* is unequivocal about the latter. The unique place of the Jews is acknowledged: "the people to whom the covenants and promises were given." Note that the document stops short of affirming the validity of Judaism *per se*. Islam, as in *Nostra Aetate*, is commended for its theism and belief in a creator God. However, it should be recalled that Vatican I already held that it was possible for women and men to come to knowledge of a creator God through the use of reason and in this respect, one does not have to impute supernatural salvific status to Islam as a religion, *per se*, by virtue of this belief.[4] This interpretation is supported by the fact that in the same section of *Lumen Gentium* the Council Fathers indicate that non-religious theists may "sincerely seek God, and moved by His grace, strive by their deeds to do His will as it is known to them" (LG 16). Logically, this places them in a similar category to Muslims regarding their theism, and this theism requires no religious structure to mediate such belief.

Then, and this is most important, the Council Fathers make it clear that salvation can be attained by *anyone*, be they religious or not, whether they have explicit belief in God or not, under three conditions. First, that they "through no fault of their own do not know the gospel of Christ or His Church." Second, that the non-culpably ignorant "who have not yet arrived at an explicit knowledge of God, but who strive to live a good life, thanks to

His grace" are not lost. When we ask how a person lives the good life, various Conciliar documents give a uniform answer: through conscience and the natural law that is written within the hearts of all and is part of the created order (see *Pastoral Constitution on the Church in the Modern World* 16, 29, *Gaudium et Spes* in Latin; *Declaration on Religious Freedom* 2, 3, *Dignitatis Humanae* in Latin; *Decree on the Church's Missionary Activity* 9, *Ad Gentes* in Latin). This is not supernatural revelation in the technical sense, although it is assisted by grace and leads to salvation. Third, these positive realities are but a preparation *(preparatio evangelica)* for the full and undiminished truth of the gospel. This is explicitly stated in *Lumen Gentium* 16, with a note referring to Eusebius of Caesarae's *preparatio evangelica*. This is a restatement of the Thomistic principle: *gratia non tollit naturam, sed perficit* (grace does not destroy nature but perfects it).

All this indicates precisely what is said in *Nostra Aetate* regarding truth outside the Church: that these are a "ray of that Truth which enlightens all men" (NA 2). In the previous sentence when speaking of the truth and holiness found in non-Christian religions "*vera*" is used, whereas *Veritatis* with a capital letter is used in the phrase just cited and translated with a capital "T." Hence, truths found in non-Christian religions, it is implied, are never more nor can they be, than the Truth found in Christ: "that Truth which enlightens all men." Therefore, it is no accident that the next sentence in *Nostra Aetate* says of the Church: "Indeed, she proclaims and must ever proclaim Christ, 'the way, the truth, and the life' (John 14:6), in whom men find the fullness of religious life, and in whom God has reconciled all things to Himself" (NA 2; cf. 2 Cor 5:18-19).

Third, and last, the final context of the silence on this question is to be found in the way that negative qualifications are entered in documents apart from *Nostra Aetate* in regard to the reality of goodness and truth found outside the Church and their relation to the Church. This is connected to the previous point regarding fulfillment or *preparatio evangelica*. "[T]ruth" (*veritas*) is only used twice in all the Conciliar documents to refer to truth outside revealed Christian Truth: once, in *Nostra Aetate* 2, as just noted; and the second occurrence is in *Ad Gentes* 9. Recall that *Nostra Aetate* explicitly focuses on the positive aspects of other religions. Here, in *Ad Gentes* we find a much more nuanced appreciation of the context of truth and goodness:

> But whatever truth and grace are to be found among the nations, as a sort of secret presence of God, this [missionary] activity frees from all taint of evil and restores to Christ its maker, who overthrows the devil's domain and wards off the manifold malice of vice. And so, whatever good is found to be sown in the hearts and minds of men, or in the rites and cultures peculiar to various peoples, is not lost. More than that, it is healed, ennobled, and perfected for the glory of God, the shame of the demon, and the bliss of men (AG 9).

This contextual qualification shows fulfillment proceeding via both continuity ("perfected," "ennobled") and discontinuity ("secret," "free from all taint of evil," "healed"). The same mix is also to be found in *Lumen Gentium* 17.[5] This is also in keeping with my own argument in Part I. This therefore indicates that other religions are a complex mixture of both truth and error, and rarely are they likely to be simply one or the other.

In the light of the above comments, I hope to have shown that it is difficult to read the Conciliar documents as giving a positive answer to the question: can other religions, *per se*, in their structures be mediators of supernatural revelation and salvific grace? While it is true that there is no explicit negative answer, there is certainly no positive answer. In the light of the last part of the analysis above it may well be the case that the documents' silences are intentional and could be read, as I would suggest, as prohibiting any unqualified positive affirmation of other religions as salvific structures, or as containing divine revelation.[6] This is all held, while holding at the same time, without contradiction, that supernatural saving grace is operative in other religions and that in those other religions there is much that is true, good, and holy, and much to be admired and learned by the church.

Before moving to look at two recent papal documents that throw further light on our question one may ask why it is that the reading I have suggested has been somewhat marginalized. In fact Paul Knitter observes that: "The majority of Catholic thinkers interpret the Conciliar statements to affirm, *implicitly but clearly*, that the religions *are ways of salvation*."[7] If Knitter is empirically correct in this judgment, then are most Catholic thinkers wrong in coming to such conclusions, if I am right in my findings? The issues here are many and complex but I want to make two brief points before proceeding. First, while many Catholic theologians have indeed put forward this view, it is interesting to note that Karl Rahner, most often associated with the defense of non-Christian religions as possible means to salvation, agrees that the Council texts are silent on this very point. He acknowledges that this "essential problem" has "been left open" and that "*Nostra aetate* gives us no information about the questions."[8] I have been arguing that in the silence of the text, the position has not been left open in the manner Rahner suggests, but rather that it was an intentional silence given the truth of the gospel. Second, the polarized readings of the document are perhaps explicable in terms of the perceived relationship between nature and grace held by the interpreter. For those wanting more sharply to distinguish supernatural grace in terms of the explicit Christian revelation, the silence is seen as an intended restraint. For those wanting to relate nature and grace more closely, such as Rahner in his intrinsicism, the silence is seen as an open question to be answered—affirmatively.[9]

I want to now further probe my question in the light of two papal documents: *On the Permanent Validity of the Church's Missionary Mandate* (*Redemptoris Missio*, after its opening Latin words, 1991), and *Crossing the*

Threshold of Hope (subsequently referred to as CTH), 1994.[10] There are many other documents that one could draw on, and the authoritative status of these two documents requires further clarification, but in what follows I simply want to present a number of features in Pope John Paul II's thinking that helps sharpen our reading of the Conciliar texts. *Crossing the Threshold of Hope* represents a running commentary on *Nostra Aetate*. With regard to the recognition in *Nostra Aetate* 2, that the church rejects "nothing that is true and holy in these religions," the Pope recalls the tradition of *semina Verbi* (seeds of the Word) to explain this statement, thereby locating his reading within the *preparatio evangelica* tradition. However, in so doing, he fully acknowledges that explicit elements within a religion (not the whole structure) may be used by the Holy Spirit in mediating grace to those who seek God sincerely:

> In another passage the Council says that the Holy Spirit works effectively even outside the visible structure of the Church (cf. *Dogmatic Constitution on the Church* 13), making use of these very *semina Verbi*, that constitute a kind of *common soteriological root present in all religions* (CTH 81).

This last statement should not be read as endorsing other religions as structures *per se* for the following reasons. It is in keeping with the affirming of a supernatural desire, moved by grace, implanted by God within all creation. In *Sources of Renewal, The Implementation of the Second Vatican Council*, the then Cardinal Wojtyla commented on the Council's depiction of Hinduism and Buddhism by saying that "the main emphasis is laid on the search for God which for man is the core of religion, and which seems to constitute the basis of ordination between the People of God."[11] This "ordination" indicates the common *telos* shared by all women and men. Furthermore, when the phrase is used in *Ad Gentes* 9, it is seen in terms of "a sort of secret presence of God" which indicates both that this may refer to the inner workings of God through conscience and the natural law (i.e., not necessarily in explicit religious structures) or to those grace-filled explicit elements that may or may not be recognized and affirmed as such by a non-Christian. Clearly, each historical case must be decided *a posteriori*. Furthermore, the Pope gives precise illustrations to indicate what in a religion may act positively and what in a religion may not. It is immaterial whether he is right or wrong in these judgments, but the fact that he makes them in such a manner is significant. There is never the question of any wholehearted "yes" or "no," but rather always both a "yes" and "no," and the balance of each is in accordance with the subject matter to hand.

Hence, to take an example, with "primitive" and "animistic" religions which stress ancestor worship, the Pope sees a "kind of preparation for the Christian faith" with a direct parallel drawn between faith in ancestors and faith in the communion of saints. As the latter leads ultimately to faith in

Christ, the Pope sees in this the explanation for why animists become Christians more readily than followers of the "great" religions of the Far East (CTH 82). This is why he cites Hebrews 11:6, noting the possibility of "implicit faith" in these animist traditions. Alternatively, regarding Buddhism he challenges (rightly or wrongly) its central doctrine of salvation which he claims is "an almost exclusively *negative soteriology*" (CTH 85). And with Islam, he says of the Qur'an in regard to the Old and New Testaments that one

> clearly sees the *process by which it completely reduces Divine Revelation*. It is impossible not to note the movement away from what God said about Himself, first in the Old Testament through the Prophets, and then finally in the New Testament through his Son (CTH 92).

Regardless of these deeply critical judgments the Pope has no difficulty in affirming Muslim's "religiosity" in, for example, their fidelity to prayer (CTH 93). This indicates that the Pope is doing no more than recognizing those rays of Truth that enlighten men and women, in mixture with error. He is not endorsing or criticizing religions in general, or any one in particular, and is clearly dialectical (in the yes/no sense) in his judgments in recognizing various commonalities and differences.

Finally, and perhaps somewhat definitively, *Redemptoris Missio* 29 is clear that the Pope sees the natural questing of men and women as also related to the action of the Holy Spirit within their lives. There is no clear and unambiguous nature apart from grace. In section 28 he writes: "The Spirit, therefore, is at the very source of man's existential and religious questioning, a question which is occasioned not only by contingent situations but by the very structure of his being." Hence, this line of thinking is in explicit continuity with the Conciliar documents for it acknowledges that grace is mediated both by the inner teleological search and also through the contingencies faced in history. This stress on history is most important, and breaks out of the theoretical structures of the threefold typology. History really counts and cannot be predicted prior to its becoming. Nevertheless, this grace is not the fullness of sanctifying and redeeming grace found in Christ's eschatological Church. Hence, all these actions of the Spirit cannot facilitate a theology of religions which affirms the various religious quests as authentic in themselves, apart from Christ, the trinity, and the Church. Here the Pope is keen to counter those views which seem to legitimate a reading of other religions as independent means to supernatural grace. It is worth quoting a sizable portion of section 29, for it is most important in terms of supporting my conclusions and illuminating our problem:

> Thus the Spirit, who "blows where he will" (cf. Jn 3:8), who "was already at work in the world before Christ was glorified," and who

> "has filled the world, . . . holds all things together (and) knows what is said" (Wis 1:7), leads us to broaden our vision in order to ponder his activity in every time and place. I have repeatedly called this fact to mind, and it has guided me in my meetings with a wide variety of peoples. The Church's relationship with other religions is dictated by a twofold respect: "Respect for man in his quest for answers to the deepest question of his life, and respect for the action of the Spirit in man." Excluding any mistaken interpretation, the interreligious meeting held in Assisi was meant to confirm my conviction that "every authentic prayer is promoted by the Holy Spirit, who is mysteriously present in every human heart."
>
> This is the same Spirit who was at work in the Incarnation and in the life, death and Resurrection of Jesus, and who is at work in the Church. *He is therefore not an alternative to Christ, nor does he fill a sort of void which is sometimes suggested as existing between Christ and the Logos*. Whatever the Spirit brings about in human hearts and in the history of peoples, in cultures and religions *serves as a preparation for the Gospel and can only be understood in reference to Christ*, the Word who took flesh by the power of the Spirit "so that as perfectly human he would save all human beings and sum up all things."
>
> Moreover, the universal activity of the Spirit is not to be separated from his particular activity within the Body of Christ, which is the Church (RM 29, my emphases).

I shall return to this. However, regarding my question here, and going back to *Crossing the Threshold of Hope*, even with regard to Judaism, the Pope clearly maintains a fulfillment theory, and as with *Nostra Aetate*, refrains from suggesting any form of mission, although never explicitly repudiating the universal need for evangelism as *Redemptoris Missio* makes clear. In an important passage, the notion of fulfillment is clear even in the context of the *sui generis* relation with Judaism:

> The New Covenant has its roots in the Old. The time when the people of the Old Covenant will be able to see themselves *as part of the New* is, naturally, a question to be left to the Holy Spirit. We, as human beings, try only not to put obstacles in the way" (CTH, 99-100, my emphasis).

In conclusion, it is to be noted that while the Pope acknowledges, as with the Council, much that is good, true and holy in non-Christian religions, he is clear in keeping the Council's silence intact regarding non-Christian religions as salvific structures *per se*. If anything, in *Crossing the Threshold of Hope* we see him pose major and radical questions to the heart of both Buddhism and Islam. It is also clear that the grace encountered in non-Christian religions is viewed as a *preparatio evangelica*, though *not* in terms of a division between the grace of creation and the grace of salvation, or natural and supernatural grace, but only because within the historical church is this grace finally properly ordered toward its eschatological fulfillment. Therefore, this grace is "not an alternative to Christ" (RM 29).

In terms of my overall argument and in relation to Part I, I hope to have shown three things. First, the silence, indeed refusal, to acknowledge other religions, *per se*, as possibly being salvific structures, indicates that pluralism and inclusivism are not sanctioned by the Conciliar and post-Conciliar documents. Second, despite this, there is no hesitation within the newly developing tradition on this question that other religions contain much that is good, true, and holy, and Christians have much to learn from them. Furthermore, there is no ambiguity that non-Christians may be saved (given various qualifications). Hence, there is room, beyond pluralism and inclusivism to develop a theology of religions which acknowledges that the history of religions is an important site where God may be acting. But what does this mean, both with regard to our use of the word "God," and its implications for the church?

I shall also be asking, whether the above findings necessarily negate the importance of the self-understanding of the Other, or leads to a domestication of difference. It is already clear that the latter question is answered "no" from what we have seen above, and our further readings will not suggest otherwise.

THE HOLY SPIRIT'S INVITATION TO RELATIONAL ENGAGEMENT: THE CONCILIAR AND POST-CONCILIAR DOCUMENTS

To find a mention of the Spirit and other religions in the Conciliar documents, and more broadly, the Spirit within human cultures, we have to turn to *Gaudium et Spes*. Here we find an explicit reference to the presence of the Holy Spirit within cultures outside the explicit and visible church. The key section reads:

> Pressing upon the Christian, to be sure, are the need and the duty to battle against evil through manifold tribulations and even to suffer death. But, linked with the paschal mystery and patterned on the dying Christ, he will hasten forward to resurrection in the strength which comes from hope.
>
> All this holds true not only for Christians, but for all men of good will in whose hearts grace works in an unseen way. For, since Christ died for all men, and since the ultimate vocation of man is in fact one, and divine, we ought to believe that the Holy Spirit in a manner known only to God offers to every man the possibility of being associated with this paschal mystery (GS 22).

Here then is an explicit statement regarding the possible active presence of the Holy Spirit in the non-Christian such that they are associated with Christ's redemptive death, even if it is left unclear how the Spirit is present. This is extremely important. However, it is also important to note that this affirmation is framed within a parameter, which at first sight seems to contradict the affirmation. That is, the Council explicitly taught that the church is necessary for salvation. *Lumen Gentium* clearly states that the church "is necessary for salvation" (LG 14). The Council documents do not try to reconcile these tensions, but there has been much speculation since the Council on this point. The main route for reconciling these tensions lies within the Conciliar teaching that whenever God is present, this is the presence of the triune God; and it is this triune God who is the foundation of the church. Hence, one very important point follows from these Conciliar statements: the Holy Spirit's presence within other religions is both intrinsically trinitarian and ecclesiological. It is trinitarian in referring the Holy Spirit's activity to the paschal mystery of Christ, and ecclesial in referring the paschal event to the constitutive community-creating force it has, under the guidance of the Spirit. This much is clear, even though much more elaboration is required as to the significance of these connections. This and the next chapter are a small contribution to elaborating these connections.

In the debates that have followed, some theologians have gone beyond the parameters set out here regarding the necessary and intrinsic, though not fully specified, relations between the persons of the trinity, the church, and the presence of the triune God in the world.[12] Some, like Paul Knitter, have tried to argue that the Spirit's presence within other religions might actually free Christianity of its Christological fixation in its engagement with other religions so as to facilitate a better dialogue that overcomes the alleged impasse raised by orthodox Christological claims.[13] However, it is clear that the Spirit cannot be disassociated from Christ. Others like Raimundo Pannikar have sought to rehabilitate a Logos Christology. However, Panikkar makes the Logos a universal revelation, of which Jesus Christ is one instantiation, and then reads other revelations in like manner. The prioritizing of the economy of salvation in the particularity of Adam and Eve and Jesus and Mary's history is bypassed, and the series of relations specified in the Conciliar documents is made subordinate to a higher controlling idea of "Logos."[14] Others, like the Belgian Jesuit Jacques Dupuis, have suggested that it is necessary and right to relate Christ to the Spirit's presence, but it is not credible intrinsically to relate this to the church and kingdom. While Dupuis's position is extremely nuanced, it still falls short of retaining this delicate Conciliar balance by removing some of the terms of the relations (church), rather than by fruitfully engaging with them as necessary parameters.[15] Yet others, like Karl Rahner, have argued that these Conciliar claims are best explained by the concepts of the "anonymous Christian" and "anonymous Christianity." Although I have reservations regarding Rahner, at least it can be said of him that he explains the intrinsic relations between the affirmation of God in the religions and the relations between the trinity, the kingdom, and the church, without conflating or excluding any of the terms.[16] I have developed my criticisms of Rahner elsewhere.[17] The point I am making here is that in affirming the Spirit's presence in the world, there is a tacit acknowledgment that in a mysterious and hidden manner, there too is the ambiguous presence of the triune God, the church, and the kingdom. It is these claims that require further explication.

Let me return to my documentary search regarding the Holy Spirit's presence within other religions so as to develop such an explication via perhaps the most important post-Conciliar statement explicitly referring to this matter: *Redemptoris Missio*. Sections 28 and 29 are the most important, and I have already quoted a large part of section 29 above. They continue the Conciliar tradition in holding that the Holy Spirit is present in relating Christ's paschal mystery to all women and men. *Gaudium et Spes* 22, is explicitly cited. It also continues the Conciliar tradition in maintaining, in a somewhat undialectical and uneschatological fashion, that the presence of the Spirit in other religions constitutes a "preparation for the Gospel" (GS 29).[18] Let me attend to this point as it is of considerable importance to my concerns. I do not question the actual theology behind the notion of *preparatio*, which simply expresses the radical novelty and difference that the triune God constitutes, while nevertheless affirming possible elements of continuity between Christianity and other religions. However, I would want to ask why "fulfillment" is conceived in such a unilateral manner.

Contrast the straightforward notion of fulfillment stated above, with the very important insight and "concession" made in relation to western secular culture (in GS 44), but nowhere made so clearly in Conciliar documents in relation to other religions. In *Gaudium et Spes* 44, it is acknowledged that elements of goodness and truth within western modernity may be a preparation for the gospel. However, it *also* goes on explicitly and boldly to acknowledge that such cultures may therefore have elements which will *challenge and even change elements within the church*, in its structure, formulations, and practice. None of this is to be regarded as detracting from the claim that God's fullness is known in Jesus Christ through his Spirit within the church, but is rather understood as the church deepening its own understanding and practice of the gospel, and even coming to see the ways in which it has obscured the gospel. I shall cite the complete relevant section:

> With the help of the Holy Spirit, it is the task of the entire People of God, especially pastors and theologians, to hear, distinguish, and interpret the many voices of our age, and to judge them in the light of the divine Word. In this way, revealed truth can always be more *deeply penetrated, better understood, and set forth to greater advantage*.

> Since the Church has a visible and social structure as a sign of her unity in Christ, she can and ought to be enriched by the development of human social life. The reason is not that the constitution given her by Christ is defective, but so that she may *understand it more penetratingly, express it better, and adjust it more successfully to our times*.
>
> She gratefully understands that in her community life no less than in her individual sons, she receives a variety of helps from men of every rank and condition. . . . Indeed, the Church admits that she has greatly profited and still profits from the antagonism of those who oppose or persecute her (GS 44, my emphases).

This is quite a remarkable section in acknowledging that both the practice and self-understanding of the church may be transformed in the encounter with the Other, even if in this instance, and perhaps especially because in this instance, the Other is modernity. Yves Congar does not overstate the case when in his commentary on this section he writes:

> The Church has . . . never before acknowledged so plainly that it too receives from the world. . . . we must go briefly into the question of what the possibility of receiving from the world in this way means for the Church. In the first place it means that its dialogue with the world cannot simply consist of the conversation between doctor and patient, of which the encyclical *Ecclesiam Suam* speaks (AAS 56 [1964], 638f.). It is a question of dialogue, and this involves reciprocity; the world has something to contribute.[19]

This concession to modernity in *Gaudium et Spes* has been criticized in some quarters, but even with my own serious reservations regarding modernity's grand-narrative, I do not think that section 44 can be interpreted as sanctifying modernity. Its entire Conciliar context mitigates against such a reading, even if section 44 became the favorite quotation of those who sought to accommodate the church to modernity. Rather, *Gaudium et Spes* represents an honest acknowledgment of positive aspects of the church's learning from modernity in recent western history.

Gaudium et Spes also clearly acknowledges that the church, here on earth, is not identical with the eschatological church, and in this sense, is not yet the church triumphant. It is perhaps a matter of time before similar acknowledgments regarding other religions enter into post-Conciliar documentation, but will do so only, and should do so only, on the basis of the historical experience of the local churches. Various regional synods have already begun to find and reflect upon such historical realities, not least the Asian bishops.[20]

Having reflected on the undialectical and therefore impoverished manner in which fulfillment is sometimes understood and the way in which *preparatio* is in danger of domesticating the Other, let me turn to another aspect of *Redemptoris Missio* which illuminates the implications of acknowledging the Holy Spirit in other religions. In *Redemptoris Missio* there is an unambiguous acknowledgment that the Spirit's activity in other religions has important structural and cultural dimensions, and does not take place solely in the secret of the heart, or in some asocio-acultural location. Recall *Gaudium et Spes* 22's reticence about the manner of the Spirit's presence. Here, John Paul II is clearly developing *Gaudium et Spes*, highlighted by his close use of the documents, but prefacing his usage with an interestingly developed interpretation.

> The Spirit's presence and activity affect not only individuals but also society and history, peoples, cultures, and religions. Indeed, the Spirit is at the origin of the noble ideals and undertakings which benefit humanity on its journey through history: "The Spirit of God, with marvelous foresight directs the course of the ages and renews the face of the earth" [*Gaudium et Spes* 26]. The Risen Christ "is now at work in human hearts through the strength of his Spirit, not only instilling a desire for the world to come but also thereby animating, purifying and reinforcing the noble aspirations which drive the human family to make its life one that is more human and to direct the whole earth to this end" [*Gaudium et Spes* 38, and see 93] (RM 28).

The two citations do not refer to cultures and religions, and the Pope clearly wants to push beyond any individualist reading of *Gaudium et Spes*'s far-reaching affirmations. Hence *Redemptoris Missio* 28 marks an important development in affirming the implications of the Spirit's activity in structural and social terms, rather than as a matter purely relating to the heart and the individual's inner-self.

However, *Redemptoris Missio* then makes it absolutely clear that this recognition of the Spirit's transforming activity within other religions does not confer independent legitimacy upon other religions (in terms of their own self-understanding), because this very positive judgment is itself a Christian theological recognition (hetero-interpretation) *and* therefore relates to the reality of the trinity within the church. This is a very important move in the argument and must be clearly distanced from any pluralist or inclusivist reading, for the reasons outlined in Part I. In *Redemptoris Missio* there is a critique of the *types* of theology that have come to be advanced by Knitter, Panikkar, and Dupuis whereby, respectively, the Spirit is shorn of its relationship to Christ or the church, or when Jesus is seen as one of many instantiations of the eternal Logos, or when the trinity is potentially envisaged within the economy of history as apart from, or out of relation to, the historical church and the kingdom. To counter such positions that stray from the parameters within which discussion should take place, the encyclical first states that the presence of the Spirit is

> not an alternative to Christ, nor does he fill a sort of void which is sometimes suggested as existing between Christ and the Logos. Whatever the Spirit brings about in human hearts and in the history of peoples, in cultures and religions, serves as a preparation for the Gospel and can only be understood in reference to Christ (RM 29).

If we follow *Redemptoris Missio*, we see that after these important qualifications, the document turns to the ecclesiological implications of acknowledging the Holy Spirit in other religions. Hence, after this trinitarian section, *Redemptoris Missio* then relates these trinitarian themes to the church, reiterating its treatment of the "inchoate reality" of the "kingdom of God" present outside the church within other religions, but a reality that must nevertheless be related to the historical church:

> It is true that the inchoate reality of the Kingdom can also be found beyond the confines of the Church among peoples everywhere, to the extent that they live "Gospel values" and are open to the working of the Spirit who breathes when and where he wills (cf. Jn 3:8). But it must immediately be added that this temporal dimension of the Kingdom remains incomplete unless it is related to the Kingdom of Christ in the Church and straining toward eschatological fullness[21] (RM 20).

Hence, it is clear and unambiguous that through the Spirit, God's trinitarian presence within other religions and cultures is a possibility, and one that is discerned by signs of the kingdom inchoately present within that culture. The insight of *Gaudium et Spes* 44, should also remind the church that in propounding the notion of other cultures as "preparation for the Gospel," it is in danger of domesticating the activity of the Spirit in that religion, for the Spirit within that culture may call for an even deeper penetration, understanding and application of the truth of God's triune self-revelation entrusted to the church. That is, if the church is not attentive to the possibility of the Spirit within other religions, it will fail to be attentive to the Word of God that has been entrusted to it. In this sense, if one were to retain and utilize the category of fulfillment in a very careful sense, then it is not only the other religions that are fulfilled in (and in one sense, radically transformed) their *preparatio* being completed through Christianity, but also Christianity itself that is fulfilled in receiving the gift of God that the Other might bear, self-consciously or not. *Redemptoris Missio* certainly moves in this direction, even if it does not make "fulfillment" a more dialogical and carefully qualified term. To support this reading, let me look more closely at the way in which the Spirit, both inside and outside the church, is related to the single issue of making the church more Christ-shaped, and therefore reiterating the fact that pneumatology is always ecclesiologically oriented:

> Moreover, the universal activity of the Spirit is *not to be separated* from his particular activity within the Body of Christ, which is the Church. Indeed, it is always the Spirit who is at work, both when he gives life to the Church and impels her to proclaim Christ, and when he implants and develops his gifts in all individuals and peoples, guiding the Church to discover these gifts, to foster them and receive them through dialogue (RM 29, my emphasis).

Three important points follow from this section. First, if the Spirit within the church has the role of helping the church to follow Christ more truthfully, and coming to indwell the trinity more completely, then this same Spirit, when outside the church must also have an analogous role within the other cultures, to help make women and men more Christ-like, individually and in community, however frustrated and thwarted. This surely is the significance of acknowledging the inchoate presence of the kingdom in other religions. Second, there is a real trinitarian basis to Christianity's openness in meeting other religions, knowing that in "dialogue" the Church must be attentive to the possibility of God's gift of himself through the prayers, practices, insights, and traditions found within other religions. Such an acknowledgment facilitates a critical and reverential openness toward other religions. Clearly, the positive appreciation and challenge to the church need not necessarily reflect how these other religions see themselves, but they may well do so, although it is clear that hetero-interpretation is utterly dependent on auto-interpretation first. This is not unlike MacIntyre's learning a second language first, prior to any serious critical and constructive engagement with that tradition. Thus, and thirdly, the discernment of the activity of the Holy Spirit within other religions must also bring the church more truthfully into the presence of the triune God. *Redemptoris Missio* makes this important connection quite clear and brings out the ecclesiological character of any talk about the Holy Spirit. There is to be no separation of the Spirit's "universal" activity and "his particular activity within the Body of Christ." This accounts for the final sentence just quoted in section 29 above: if the Spirit is at work in the religions, then the gifts of the Spirit need to be discovered, fostered, and received into the church. If the church fails to be receptive, it may be unwittingly practicing cultural and religious idolatry.

One important implication of this possible inner transformation of the church is related to the possible reconfiguring of Christian practice and understanding (inculturation—or fresh Christian auto-interpretation), and it is a point clearly recognized within the encyclical, because immediately after its acknowledgment that the "gifts" from outside the church need to be received "through dialogue," the question of the discernment *and* incorporation of such gifts is seen as an ecclesial task, not that of particular theologians or talented individuals alone. Immediately after the sentences just cited from section 29, the document continues:

> Every form of the Spirit's presence is to be welcomed with respect and gratitude, but the discernment of this presence is the responsibility of the Church, to which Christ gave his Spirit in order to guide her into all the truth (see Jn 16:13).

We have here one decisive clue as to how to think through the now clearly established Conciliar and post-Conciliar teaching that the Holy Spirit is present within cultures and religions (in ways that need to be *a posteriori* specified).[22] If the Spirit is present, Her activity bears an analogical relationship to the guiding task of the Spirit within the church, that is, She leads the church more deeply into a life with Christ. The Johannine quotation in *Redemptoris Missio* 29 is very important and one to which I will return shortly.

This claim has two fields within which elaboration is required. First, there is the question as to what the claim that the Spirit is present in other religions or cultures might mean for the church and its task of trinitarian theologizing and practice. Second, there is the question as to what the claim that the Spirit is present in other religions might mean for that religion. This latter can only follow within the process of historical engagement and only retrospectively, and thus I cannot pursue this question further here. The important thing is not to allow these two questions to be conflated. However, the first question requires painstaking attention to the inner logic and intrasystematic richness within another religion (i.e., auto-interpretation) prior to being able to affirm, critique, and engage with that tradition. Hence, I am arguing that while both these operations: (a) learning about the Other, and viewing the Other as genuinely Other so that they do not become domesticated or negated; and (b) critical and constructive engagement with the Other—are distinct and logically different, they are mutually interdependent. One possible way of pursuing this, for example, would be to attend to accounts of those who have been Muslims or Hindus and have subsequently become Christians. Both these distinct operations are important for such converts.[23] However, I will now pursue my question within this first field of enquiry by means of turning to an exegesis of the Johannine passage cited at the conclusion of *Redemptoris Missio* 29 regarding the Spirit as guide into the truth of Christ.

Before turning to this task, however, let me offer a summary of my findings so far. First, in examining the Conciliar and post-Conciliar documents we find a positive affirmation of the activity of the Holy Spirit within the religions and cultures of non-Christians. This is not simply some sort of preserving grace, by virtue of creation being God's creation, but the sanctifying grace of the triune God such that the Spirit's activity is related to the paschal mystery of Christ and thus "inchoately" forming children of God celebrating God's kingdom. Second, this affirmation neither leads to pluralism which grants equal status to the religions, nor to inclusivism, in affirming structures *per se*, even if in a provisional sense. Third, this affirmation operates within a form of *trinitarian ecclesiology* such that it requires: (a) the church to listen to other religions, as they understand themselves; (b) to engage critically with the religions (mission in dialectical and rhetorical fashion); (c) to be open to the reality of the church being challenged, developed, and deepened in its commitment to the triune God in so much as God may speak through the other religions, either despite them (despite their auto-interpretation) or through them (in their auto-interpretation). In the latter case it is clear that auto- and hetero-interpretation cannot fully coincide, for Christ and the trinity are never the object of proclamation and worship. The point about this trinitarian ecclesiology is that it has already been set in motion regarding modernity's engagement with the church (*Gaudium et Spes* 44), even if that particular engagement is always in danger of turning into an ill-conceived marriage, as is the case in the theologies of Hick and Knitter. Such dangers cannot mean retreat, but only a careful attention to the difficulties and problems that lie ahead in the meeting with religions. Furthermore, such a trinitarian ecclesiology helps to make us aware that talk of Jesus Christ, the Spirit, and the Father is always ecclesiological grammar even when used of revelation outside the church. Hence, there is a real cost to the church in making any affirmation of the Spirit's activity outside the church, for this might always call the church into question in a way that cannot be predicted *a priori*.

Having established this much from the documents that I have inspected, I now want to turn to John's gospel as an avenue to further explore the feasibility and coherence of what has been said. Am I conceding too much to other religions in according them such an important ecclesiological role? (Needless to say, this role does not exhaust their meaning and significance.) To answer this, let us turn to the high Christology and trinitarian ecclesiology of John's gospel.

THE SPIRIT AS ADVOCATE AND GUIDE: A SELECTED HISTORICAL WITNESS

Three qualifications should be made before proceeding. First, I do not want to suggest that the section of the gospel that I shall inspect is in the least concerned with my particular question viz. the Holy Spirit and other religions. On the contrary, John's circumstances were such that this is probably the last question on his mind. If anything, John understands the non-Christian, the Other, as a persecutor and destroyer of the church and not a person in whom the Holy Spirit is found. Second, John's concerns are relentlessly ecclesiological, but also relentlessly trinitarian. John realizes that the shape of the church is utterly dependent on the narrated shape of God's self-revelation. Hence, I will focus exclusively on the question of the role of the Spirit in ecclesiological formation and how John's notion of the Spirit keeps in balance a very high Christology which is also fundamentally an understanding that the church *continues* to be Christ to the world, or it is an utterly worthless "body of Christ." Third, I will look at John on his own terms, while also recalling that John is today to be read in the light of the church's teaching that the Holy Spirit is to be found within other religions. I shall make these latter connections after I have conducted a brief exegesis.

When we turn to John to pursue our question, we are immediately confronted with a complex nexus of further issues. In John, to look at the Spirit, we must also look at the resurrection, and with it, pentecost and the ascension. It would be no exaggeration to say that for John, the resurrection is pentecost. John, as Raymond Brown puts it well, should have logically "joined the author of the Epistle to the Hebrews in having Jesus go directly to the Father from the cross, for the resurrection does not fit easily into John's theology of the crucifixion."[24] This ill fit has more to do with John's profundity than with any ideological impatience or demythologization of the problematic details of the tomb, or the nature of Jesus' risen body—as Bultmann prefers to read it.[25] For John, the crucifixion, resurrection, ascension, and pentecost are all part of the same event: Jesus' presence to his disciples in the Spirit. In the chronological sequence of time, John can only deal with the eternity of God's self-revelation by narrative, that is, by structuring the story in a particular way, even if each and every part of the story (as we shall see) relates to all other stories, and requires the retelling of all stories for its own meanings to deepen and unfold.

Luke also sees this, although in a quite different manner. Jesus, after the resurrection and prior to the ascension, tells his disciples to "stay in the city, until you are clothed with power from on high" (Lk 24:49). Acts 1:8 makes it clear that this "power" is that of the Holy Spirit and it empowers the followers of Christ to begin to interpret their own story and Jesus' in the way that the risen Christ did for them on the way to Emmaus (Lk 24:13-35). John's grasp of the resurrection as the inauguration of a new community and a new creation is yoked to his theology of the Holy Spirit. For John, the resurrection is pentecost (whereas Luke separates these events). For John the resurrection/pentecost is also the beginning of the world—a new creation; just as for Luke, this new beginning is the reversal of Babel. John's gospel ends where it began: the creation of the world.

When the risen Jesus appears to his disciples behind locked doors, after his greeting of peace and commission, the account continues: "he breathed (*emphysaō*) on them, and said to them, "Receive the Holy Spirit" (Jn 20:22). John's gospel began with the theme of creation (Jn 1:1f), and now at this decisive point of the narrative, where all life is changed, *emphysaō* echoes the Septuagint version of Genesis 2:7, where the same Greek verb is used when God gives life to his creation through his "breath" of life. If that "breath" animated all creation which then became disfigured through sin, this "breath" restores creation, but with such abundance so as to inaugurate a new creation, a new relationship between all created signs. John signals this dramatic trinitarian transaction earlier in his narrative when he comments "for as yet the Spirit had not been given because Jesus was not yet glorified" (7:49). It is in the event of the resurrection that history and creation are turned inside out. Only *after* the story of Jesus is told (the hour of glory—12.23) can the story of creation be properly narrated, including the depths of disfigurement, and the new re-creation inaugurated in Jesus Christ, a story that is still being enacted primarily in the community also designated a "new creation," the Marian church, the body of Christ. Quite literally, for John, all creation revolves around the resurrection, the constitutive event from which all creation takes its meaning, an event which is made ever anew in the practices of the church.[26] Hence, if we are to enquire about the Spirit in John, we must equally ask about the resurrection, and in John's logic, this is a question about the disciples who form the church: yesterday and today's Christians. The resurrection is a story of the formation of Christian community, just as for Luke, pentecost marks the beginning of that same story. As I shall suggest later, John's apparent "idealization" of the church does not in fact mitigate his ecclesiology, but rather it raises a question about the reality of the church today, as it did of John's church.[27]

If a central theme of John's theology of resurrection is the resurrected Jesus breathing upon the disciples with the words "Receive the Holy Spirit," (Jn 20:23) our question is: what is understood by the Holy Spirit? One major clue lies in the preceding chapters (The Farewell Discourse: Jn 13:31-17:26) where Jesus teaches his disciples about the Holy Spirit. Within this section there are four main Paraclete passages: 14:15-18; 14:25-27; 15:26-27; 16:7-15 (the final one often being treated as two), and the last of which contains the citation from *Redemptoris Missio* which steered my exploration back to John. As I cannot enter into a detailed exegetical defense of my reading, I draw the reader's attention to my main secondary sources.[28] It is also clear that the question of the Holy Spirit's role could have been addressed from very different angles, both within John and from within other gospels.

One important context for these four passages, which positions the Discourse section, is the new commandment to love one another *as Jesus has loved his disciples,* which is founded on the Father's love for his Son, and is reciprocated in Jesus' love for the world (Jn 13:34). This love is no abstract idea or general theory of theism, but a specific set of practices found in the person of Jesus. The commandment to love is therefore not an ideological egalitarian principle which can be translated without this particular narrative, in the way that nineteenth-century liberal Christianity exegeted its moral gospel, and continues to so do as we have seen in chapter one. Rather, this love has both its source and shape in the "person" of Jesus, God's gift to the world—apart from whom God's love is not known.[29] Such are the implications of a constitutive Christology. How, after Jesus' death, can the disciples enact such a commandment: to love one another as God has loved them, except in the form of a creative imitation of Christ? In being the church, the body of Christ, Christians are called to be Christ to the world. John Milbank highlights the constitutive, yet dynamic and unpredictable nature of tradition in so much as Christianity is not a dull imitation of a positive original, but a structured transformation in which the church is called to be as Christ to the world, proclaiming both judgment, mercy, and salvation, while always also being subject itself to the gospel. What is most significant about the quotation (see below), which harmonizes with my Johannine exegesis, is the way in which Christology and pneumatology are understood as primarily ecclesiologically structuring doctrines.

This loving as God loves is only possible by the indwelling of God's love by the power of the Holy Spirit, and by sharing the reality of love. Hence, the section preceding John 14:15-18 astoundingly suggests that the disciples will continue Jesus' work, and even "greater works than these" (v. 12), so that the reality of God's presence in the world is committed to a faithful community, whose witness to God's action is found in their structured and embodied form of life that should, as with Jesus' life, be both a judgment upon the world and a healing offer of forgiveness and redemption. Hence, for John, the disciples are called to re-enact the presence of God, first known in their encounter with the risen Jesus, and to then repeat and imitate Jesus, not as a recalling of a past event, but in a constant "repetition," although a non-identical repetition, of this judgment and promise, this saving transformation. As Milbank puts it:

> Christianity is not Platonism. It is not founded upon the vision of a transcendent original which we must imitate. Instead it makes affirmations about the real, and about "meaning," through the constant *repetition* of a historically emergent practice which has no real point of origination, but only acquires identity and relative stability *through* this repetition. And what is repeated is not an insight, not an idea (which is properly *imitated*), but a formal becoming, a structured transformation. The . . . forms of the gospel are therefore indispensable, not because they record and point us to a vision which is still available in its eternal "presence," but rather because they enshrine and constitute the event of a transformation which is to be non-identically repeated, and therefore still made to happen.[30]

To return to the Johannine text, the first Paraclete passage throws light on the source of the awesome new creation promised and inaugurated in the resurrection, the church, and made present through the power of the Spirit. Jesus speaks to his church:

> "If you love me, you will keep my commandments. And I will pray the Father, and he will give you another Counselor, to be with you for ever, even the Spirit of truth, whom the world cannot receive,

because it neither sees him nor knows him; you know him, for he dwells with you, and will be in you" (14:15-18).

The passage does not evoke an idea, a program, or transcendental, which will keep the church faithful to Christ, but rather, it evokes a practice ("if you love me, you will keep my commandments") sustained by a personal relationship: the indwelling of the Spirit. The theme of the Spirit's perichoretic indwelling of the disciples is predicated upon the indwelling of the Son and Father introduced right at the very beginning of the gospel (Jn 1:1,18), such that the Spirit's indwelling the disciples will be enacted in their keeping the commandment of love—learning to love as Jesus had loved. The later historical development of the trinitarian term "perichoresis" is vitally located within the dynamic of this Johannine ecclesiological trinity. For John, love for Jesus and learning to love as Jesus loved is central to the meaning of the new church, for otherwise Christians cannot learn to properly enter and enact the relationships within God's love which they are called to share, a series of relationships that actually configure the very being of the triune God. Furthermore, Christians cannot learn to love without the Counselor, the Spirit, who enables this practice of redeeming forgiveness and love. Some elements of later tradition freeze this particular role of the Spirit such that the person of the Spirit is purely understood as the go-between between the two major actors of the drama of salvation: the Father and Son. However, John's dramatic cast is fully trinitarian, and John also opens the drama such that his readers are now part of the cast, and the drama is an invitation to all creation to enact and participate in this story of redemption. But this does not mean that the Spirit is intelligible apart from the Son, just as Jesus remains unintelligible apart from the Spirit. Raymond Brown comments on this relationship when he argues that in the phrase "the Spirit of truth," the genitive is objective, indicating the relation of the Spirit to "the" truth who *is* Jesus. Hence, the rendering "Spirit of truth" is more accurate than the "Spirit *is* truth" (Jn 14:17).[31]

To conclude, the first Paraclete passage indicates that one role of the Spirit is in facilitating human participation in God's inner love, or intratrinitarian love. To respond to this gift, a form of life and practice is required and a constant attentiveness to the relationship in which this gift is recognized, nurtured, and received. What we have emerging in John is an intrinsic connection between trinity and ecclesiology and between doctrine and practice.

The second Paraclete passage develops this theme:

"These things I have spoken to you, while I am still with you. But the Counselor, the Holy Spirit, whom the Father will send in my name, he will teach you all things, and bring to your remembrance all that I have said to you" (Jn 14:25-27).

Compared to the first passage where the pronoun denoting the Spirit is neuter even though usually translated as "he," we have here the personalization of the Spirit with *ekeinos* (he, v. 26), which is also used of the Spirit in 15:26; 16:7, 8, 13, 14. While one cannot simply read into this term later controversies regarding "person" and "nature," it can be said that God, who is love (1 Jn 4:8), cannot be other than personal. Whether God is metaphorically best represented in solely masculine terms is a contentious point, but here I will remain with John's personalization of the Spirit, as "he." Indwelling relationships of love are central to this section, because they are central to John's trinitarian God. In predicating the presence of the Spirit, one is speaking of a personal indwelling presence of God, inseparable from Jesus Christ, but distinct from him, which in this passage means that the Holy Spirit functions as teacher and rememberer.

Once again, the Spirit testifies to Jesus, so that the phrase "he will teach you *all things*" (my emphasis) contrasts with the opening section, "These things I have spoken to you." This is supported by Jn 16:13, to which we will turn shortly, which certainly does not suggest that the contrast with "all" things is to be understood as implying various new truths, or new revelations, but rather a deepening appreciation, and therefore possibly differing practices and articulations, of the faith; or to put it differently, a non-identical repetition of the revelation which is given. This was the burden of *Lumen Gentium* 44, which I highlighted earlier regarding the implication of the Spirit's presence. This sense of the Spirit's presence, neither invokes a new revelation (as if the Spirit could be intelligible without Jesus), nor does it simply recall a past and finished story (as if Jesus was not a living and present reality). Regarding the phrase in this second passage, that the Spirit will "bring to remembrance," C. K. Barrett rightly comments on the word "remembrance":

> There is no independent revelation through the Paraclete, but only an application of the revelation in Jesus. The Paraclete recalls . . . and thereby recreates and perpetuates the situation of judgment and decision that marked the ministry of Jesus.[32]

Barrett's idea of "recreates" and "perpetuates" nicely focuses on the point that I am making, that the Holy Spirit helps us see the person of Christ as the inauguration of a transforming revelatory practice entrusted to the church, and called "church." Hence, if the Spirit's presence is predicated within other religions (or wherever), it does not denote a new revelation, but rather indicates the power of God working to disclose, further deepen, and enact the reality of his presence in his new creation, inaugurated in Jesus' resurrection. This is deeply significant and I shall return to this point in the next section of the present chapter.

The third Paraclete passage develops the theme of the Spirit as witness to Jesus in two related directions. First, the theme is presented in terms of the Spirit's strength and support to the disciples in persecution (a theme further developed in Jn 16:7ff). The passage comes immediately after a section (Jn 15:18-25) concerned with the hatred of the world toward Jesus, and the confirmation that if the world hates the disciples (who continue the new creation), it is because the world first hated Jesus. Second, the theme of witness is elaborated in terms of the Spirit's co-activity as witnessing to the new creation inaugurated in Jesus and unfolding within the church's practice. The third Paraclete passage reads as follows:

> "But when the Counselor comes, whom I shall send to you from the Father, even the Spirit of truth, who proceeds from the Father, he will bear witness to me; and you also are witnesses, because you have been with me from the beginning" (Jn 15:26-27).

The opposition to the world, and the Spirit's function in forensically affirming the disciples against the world, is usually rightly the focus of this passage, but sometimes at the cost of the simultaneously startling claim being made about the church. To a faithful church, which bears witness to the nuptial love that sustains it, it is the Spirit who co-constitutes this fidelity of witness, such that the structure of these two verses actually shows that the witness of the Spirit and that of the disciples "are not two separate witnesses," as noted by Brown—but are the same.[33] It is precisely because of this that John so daringly equates, as do Paul and Luke, the persecution of Jesus and the persecution of the church.[34] If this exegesis is correct, then the Spirit's testifying and teaching activity is to be understood as the *enabling practice* of the imitation of Christ's love in his risen body, the church. In his closing comments on vv. 26-7, Brown confirms Barrett's remarks, cited above, regarding the Spirit as the exegesis of Jesus: "Jesus is the supreme revelation of God to men: there can be no witness to the world other than the witness he bore. All other witness by the Paraclete through the disciples simply interprets that."[35] Hence, in predicating the activity of the Spirit one is already predicating a transformative practice that is inaugurated in Jesus, that witnesses to him, and in so doing, is thus an act of praise. It is and must therefore be a cause of both scandal to the world and persecution from the world; the practice of both judgment and redemption. This judgment is precipitated because of Jesus' "*inauguration* of the 'political' practice of forgiveness; forgiveness as a mode of 'government' and social being," and this in contrast to a "world of violence and suffering in which human words and conventions—'the law'—are powerless over structures of human egotism and over physical death."[36] Such is the dark unveiling of salvation. Hence, there is no salvation without judgment, no rejoicing without unmasking the forms of violence that structure our society and our desires.

The final two parts of the last of our four Paraclete passages, resume, develop, and confirm these themes. The first section, John 16:7-11, overturns the synoptic stress on the Spirit as advocate defending the disciples (e.g., Mt 10:20, "for it is not you who speak, but the Spirit of your Father"; and parallels in Mk 13:11; Lk 21:15) into that of the Spirit's prosecuting or convicting the world of its sin. It is, in Brown's words, a "reversal of the trial of Jesus, the world is found guilty of *sin* in that it has not acknowledged the *justice* of God in the glorified Jesus."[37] This inversion is typical of John's dramatic insight and timing:

> "Nevertheless I tell you the truth: it is to your advantage that I go away, for if I do not go away, the Counselor will not come to you; but if I go, I will send him to you. And when he comes, he will convince the world concerning sin and righteousness and judgment; concerning sin, because they do not believe in me; concerning righteousness, because I go to the Father, and you will see me no more; concerning judgment, because the ruler of this world is judged" (Jn 16:7-11).[38]

Here the Spirit enables the continuing ministry of Jesus to be exercised in the non-identical repetition of his transformative love through his body, the church. Those who rightly find in John an unrelenting opposition to the world should be profoundly questioned by the text. The commandment to love is unbearable. It quite literally leads to the cross, the tearing apart of the fabric of civility, decency, and self-righteousness that clothe our human cultural and religious projects. The cross unmasks them for what they so often are: a saying "no" to God's "yes" to us in his invitation to self-abandonment and participation in his weak, defenseless, forgiving practice of love. The threefold conviction of the world of sin, unrighteousness and false judgment are related to this body that is "raised" and "lifted up" (Jn 3:14), not only on the cross, but as a sign of the world's self-condemnation. This is why the resurrected Jesus, after breathing upon his disciples and giving them the gift of the Spirit, adds: "If you forgive the sins of any, they are forgiven; if you retain the sins of any, they are retained" (Jn 20:23). This ecclesiological body must now continue as Christ's body. The Spirit, through women and men, continues the work of Jesus, and even "greater works" (Jn 14:12). Any predication of the Spirit's presence in the world thereby involves the presence both of the condemnation of the world's sin and unrighteousness which will also include the church's sin and unrighteousness, just as the Spirit-filled body of Jesus called into question the earliest male disciples of Jesus who abandoned him. But the Spirit also evokes the forgiving love that is greater than this violence and destruction, the words of forgiveness on the cross. In so much as the church is called analogically to continue the incarnation, it also means that atonement must be historically received and enacted; it is a continuing event, not a finished story.

The second part of the passage returns to the teaching and guiding activity of the Spirit and reaches a crescendo in stating a key paradox: that

Jesus brings us God's life in himself, but this life is not a past gift, but a present invitation to die to ourselves, to live as if the future were joy; the madness of hope amidst real, unresolved tragedy, violence, and destruction. The paradox centers around the very figures of Jesus and Mary, through whom we have the fullness of God's self-gift, but through whom we enter into a process of constant receiving, sharing, and reciprocating this gift such that its full reception will only be a story capable of being told at the end of the story. This is traditionally designated as the tension between realized and future eschatology, the "between" being the site of the church's location. This gift of Jesus' life is constitutive of the "imitation of Christ," the non-identical repetition of forgiving practice and redeeming love. How this present gift is granted, and how it engages with the world, is for John a matter of yet another gift, that of the Holy Spirit:

> "I have yet many things to say to you, but you cannot bear them now. When the Spirit of truth comes, he will guide you into all the truth; for he will not speak on his own authority, but whatever he hears he will speak, and he will declare to you the things that are to come. He will glorify me, for he will take what is mine and declare it to you. All that the Father has is mine; therefore I said that he will take what is mine and declare it to you" (Jn 16:12-15).

The participation in the life of God, and nothing less, is promised to the disciples. Divinization through participation is a familiar theme in Orthodox theology. John indicates that the life of the disciples cannot therefore be anything other than a constant movement of dying into this new life, to bring forth a new creation. Participating in God's life is a matter of learning to practice the virtues that form a body of Christ characterized by faith, hope, and charity, and this can only be done within a community focused together upon worship of the triune God. The Spirit, as in the previous passages, helps to unfold the "glory" of Jesus, whose glory is that of the Father's, who shares this glory with both the Spirit and Son. The circulation of the gift of love within the triune life cannot be frozen, such that it be seen, as it sometimes has been, as originating from the Father alone (in a causally generative sense), but is the gift by virtue of its "constituting" the triune reality.

The Spirit's activity is not therefore a matter of disclosing new revelations and, as Brown says, is "more than a deeper intellectual understanding of what Jesus has said—it involves a way of life in conformity with Jesus' teaching."[39] This is why the later church was to affirm as "sacramental" the practices of love which conformed the community to Christ: conversion, through repentance (baptism), the constant repentance and forgiveness that is required on this pilgrimage (confession), the confirmation as adults of a choice possibly made on the child's behalf by parents or guardians (confirmation), a new communal sharing in God's life, the structured becoming of Christ's body and limbs (eucharist); the specific roles within the body (marriage, holy orders, none of which Jesus enacted); and the final healing reconciliation with death (holy unction). It recognized that in these practices, but not only in these, that new life was made possible, for living and participating in the life of the triune God requires the practice of forgiveness and vulnerable love. And yet to freeze any set of practices without attention to context is to make non-identical repetition a matter of imitation, a mechanized and depersonalized, ineffective "transmission" of grace. This was the danger that was generated by Trent's understanding of the sacraments as *ex opere operatis*, but balanced and contextualized in Vatican II.

To return to John 16:12-15, and the function of the Spirit's guiding and declaring, Bultmann rightly saw that the Spirit is the power of proclaiming Jesus' Word ever anew. In commenting on verse 14, "he will take what is mine and declare it to you," Bultmann writes:

> This is an express statement that the Spirit's word does not displace or surpass the word of Jesus, as if it were something new. . . . The word of Jesus is not a collection of doctrines that is in need of supplementation, nor is it a developing principle that will only be unfolded in the history of ideas; as the Spirit's proclamation it always remains the word spoken into the world from beyond. . . .the Spirit is not the "inner light" that brings new knowledge on its own authority; it is the ever new power of Jesus' word; it retains the old in the continual newness that arises from the speaking of the word in the present.[40]

Bultmann's point underscores my argument concerning exclusivism's retaining the "old" in a "continual newness," such that "continuity" is properly framed within "discontinuity." Hence, all truth, goodness and grace wherever they are found outside the church can never in any sense contradict the reality of God's transformative life inaugurated in Jesus, and when they are incorporated into the practice and articulation of the church, their new context will transform them radically—as well as transform the church. The gifts that the Spirit brings, which the disciples cannot bear now, are only authentic if they maintain "continuity," but not identical repetition, with what has been already given as gift in Jesus.[41] This is of course difficult to specify without examples of how the church has been transformed by, and in turn may have transformed, the Other, in its many historical engagements.

It is possible to summarize some of the biblical themes I have inspected by saying that in John the miracle of the resurrection is the beginning of a new creation, a new pentecost, whereby the life of the triune God is made present in Jesus' disciples' practice of keeping Jesus' commandments through the power of the Spirit. Crucifixion, resurrection, ascension, and pentecost are the single "hour" of glory. In the same way that the Father, Son, and Spirit indwell each other, and subsequently the disciples, so does the church structure the liturgical calender. Hence, after the celebration of Easter, we have Pentecost, then the feast of the Trinity, and then on the Thursday after Trinity Sunday, the feast of the Body and Blood of Christ and the founding of the church. The church's liturgical calender helps to structure our theological reading of John's gospel, which itself is generative of such a reading and practice. The trinitarian foundation of the church that is profoundly developed and clarified in John, is reiterated in Vatican II.[42] This is why one might say, in conclusion, that for John, Jesus' resurrection is the disturbing gift of the Spirit, who in the communal testimony and witness of the church forms the likeness of Jesus, both as a bountiful gift of new life to the world, and as a condemnation of sin, violence, and greed. For John, the Spirit's activity only takes place in indwelling those who follow Jesus' commandment to love as Jesus has loved.

THE TRINITY AND OPENNESS TO OTHER RELIGIONS

Having briefly examined one of the main themes related to John's understanding of the Holy Spirit, we might now see how this bears upon recent Conciliar and post-Conciliar pronouncements that the Holy Spirit is present in the world religions. However, before we proceed, there is a glaring problem raised by the exegesis offered above: the church so often falls desperately short of its grand descriptions such as the "body of Christ," a "transformative atoning community," a "new creation." And this dark and broken reality of unfaithful ecclesial practice throughout history should always stand alarmingly before us, lest we be seduced into the temptation to divinize the church and its practices. Even despite the many teachings that try to account for and properly explain that this "imperfection" is not in contradiction to the basic doctrines about the church; that it is a church of sinners, as well as saints; that we are saved by grace, and not works; that we are but a pilgrim church; there is always the danger that these teachings, profound as they are, will obscure the reality of the unbearable darkness of the cross, and the depths of our own sinfulness, stupidity, and self-deception. Does all this negate John's ecclesiology? Does the human history of the church simply serve to show that John unrealistically idealized and reified the notion of ecclesial community? I think not, for in part, John's grammar is both historical and eschatological: that is, his church is what the church *should be*, and always dimly *is*, for its light cannot be extinguished by human hands and it subsists in the church's charismatic, sacramental, and hierarchic structures despite the self-abuse that is constantly enacted by the church. Without recourse to its own traditions and prayer life, and without the gift of the Holy Spirit promised by Jesus to his disciples, the church would be incapable of realizing the extent to which it might stray and be unfaithful to its mission. Furthermore, John's context also allowed his writing to strike a deep and realistic note, for a persecuted church might often know and practice more profoundly what it is called to be, than will a church that has become accommodated to its surrounding culture and has become part of the status quo. Writing in the west, from a tenured academic position, and in a society allegedly Christian, there is a temptation to think that John was somewhat extreme due to his experience of deep persecution, rather than to turn the tables round and ask whether it is my/our own complacent context of Christian practice that makes his church sound so idealized.

To return to my question about the implications of affirming the presence of the Holy Spirit in the world, something that the church does see fit to do, without denying John's rightful caution, we might well bring some of the threads together regarding the church and its trinitarian self-understanding. One might even turn the question round and ask, what does it mean to the church to say that the Spirit is present outside itself—within the world religions? There are at least seven important points that follow.

First, it is clear from our exegesis, that all talk of the Spirit is only properly related to the ecclesial set of events in which the church's discernment of the Spirit actually generates new forms of practice and articulation in its non-identical repetition and reception of Christ's gift of redeeming love. This means that we must be *extremely reticent* about any abstract talk of the "Spirit in other religions," for this bears little Johannine rhetorical sense. If it is to bear any Johannine sense, then it can only be generated in the context of *specific* Christian engagements with non-Christian cultures and practices, for the claim that the Spirit is at work in the world can only be part of the church's discernment (not ownership) of the hidden depths of God's trinitarian action of love, struggling to be born into creation and culture. Hence, any claim about the Spirit in other religions should be taken neither as a phenomenological sociohistorical description of a religion, nor as a claim that will necessarily be well-received by a non-Christian (although such usage will always be meant positively). Rather it constitutes a theological evaluation that must spring from and lead to fresh practices *within the church* if the claim is to have any credence. The claims of the Holy Spirit's presence is therefore an *intra-Christian claim* and does not at all mitigate the challenges and questions that Christians might put to such alternative practices. It indicates that in such engagements with non-Christian cultures, the church is called to be a sign of judgment and forgiving redemption, like Christ. It may also receive the "gift" of God from the Other, in a way that is only retrospectively discerned by the church, and might well be denied, or not so interpreted and understood, by that Other.

Second, John helps us to make clear from the outset that a bogus question has haunted much of the contemporary discussion on other religions regarding whether "revelation" takes place within the religions of the world.[43] For John, the resurrection means that the question of new, different, and alternative "revelations" is a non-question, for it posits a false understanding of time and history. All creation, all time and history, all the irreducible particularities of each person, are now taken up into the new creation inaugurated by Jesus. This is why allegorical and typological readings of Israel's history and world history were permissible in the early and medieval church: for all history, especially Israel's, both prefigures and participates in this single new creation inaugurated in Jesus Christ. There can be no question of "other revelations" in so much as this might be understood as other "gods," or a cancellation of how God has chosen to reveal God's-self in trinitarian form. However, by saying *a priori* that there is no new revelation apart from Christ, one is neither circumscribing nor restricting the reality of the Holy Spirit's universal and particular activity, or limiting it exclusively to previous practices and understandings within the living tradition. The statement that there is no new revelation is a claim that all truth, in whatever form, will serve to make Christ known more fully to Christians—(and to the world?), *without understanding* what this will mean in advance in practice and theory. Milbank puts the matter well regarding the corporate "person" of Jesus as including reference to all other "persons":

> Jesus is perfectly identified only as the source, goal and context of all our lives: the *esse* of his personality is, in Thomist terms, *esse ipsum*, or the infinite totality of actualized being which is "eminently" contained in God. If this is the case, then it cannot be true that we have a metaphysically "initial" perfect vision of Jesus . . . which we later approximate through our imitations. On the contrary, only through such imitations, and through observing the likeness of Jesus in others, will a full sense of Jesus's personality be approximated to.[44]

Third, this "observing" the likeness of Jesus in others is precisely part of what it also means to say that the Holy Spirit is present in the world, in the "Other," and requires an ecclesial act of discernment, as it is here that the possible use of "Christ" language takes shape. The Spirit in the church allows for the possible (and extremely complex and difficult) discernment of Christ-like practice in the Other, and in so much as Christ-like activity takes place, then this can also only be through the enabling power of the Spirit.[45] It must be clear from this that other religions, in keeping with their own self-understanding, may generate profoundly Christ-like behavior. It may also be that such Christ-likeness is in resistance to elements within their own tradition. It may also be that the church fails entirely to recognize this Christ-likeness, as it has done in its own history (when persecuting those who are eventually declared saints, like Joan of Arc). Either way, this point facilitates an open and generous enjoyment of "good lives" found within other religions; indeed, to such an extent that Christians might even colloquially use the word "saint" of a non-Christian. However, I am extremely reticent about technically calling non-Christians saints, not because of any lack of holiness and sanctity within those who are not Christians, but because "saints" is a public term of recognition by the church of its own mission being incarnate in the life of a person.[46] However, the experience of holy lives outside the church is extremely significant for the church. It is here that the distinction and relationship of Spirit and Son language takes on one possible meaning in the context of other religions. This never-ending process of non-identical repetition involves reading *all creation* in Christ through the guidance of the Holy Spirit, in each and every moment of the church's life, such that Milbank adds immediately to the statement just cited:

> To some extent, the observation of *every* human "person" follows this pattern, but only in the case of Jesus does an accurate rendering of his personhood involve an ultimate attention to everyone, in so far as their "truth" lies in Christ.[47]

Fourth, this brings out the dynamic of John's theology, for it properly means that in so much as the Spirit is present in the world, then the world can be challenged on account of the elements of truth it might already hold, and these elements, when incorporated into Christian articulations and practice, serve to once more give praise to the triune God—even though such incorporation may rightly involve radical discontinuity. This understanding certainly precludes any triumphalist understanding of the Spirit's presence, for it does not elevate to an Archimedian point either the practices or articulations of the church, but shows the constant need to re-engage and re-present the gospel under the guidance of the Spirit.

Fifth, in the light of John, saying that the Spirit is present in the lives of non-Christians as do the Conciliar and post-Conciliar documents, is both a *judgment* upon the church and a sign of *promise* to the church. It is a judgment, for John has told us that the Spirit's presence in bringing to form a new Christ-like creation is always a condemnation on the powers of darkness, "the ruler of the world is judged" (Jn 16:11). For the church, it may be that through the actions of non-Christians it comes to recognize how it is itself ensnared by the powers of darkness. Through the witness that non-Christians give through their lives and teachings, Christians have often been called into more faithful discipleship. The Spirit's presence in other religions is also the source of promise and great joy to the church, for in being open and attentive to the Holy Spirit, it grows in its own relationship to God and those from other religions. This first movement (relationship to God) will mean inculturation and transformation. Dom Henri Le Saux (Abhishiktananda) at least in his early days, experienced precisely this in his meeting and learning from Hindu gurus, as did Thomas Merton in his meetings with Buddhist monks. Both "returned" to generate richer forms of Christian discipleship. There are countless other important testimonies, including one of the most famous: Jesus' exaltation of the Samaritan as an example of real love of neighbor (Lk 10:25-37).[48]

Sixth, despite the above, one should certainly not say that every event that prompts new practices of non-identical repetition is of the Spirit, for this would simply be an uncritical baptism with the Spirit of all creation and culture. Rather, it is to say that when the church's encounter with religions generates this type of Spirit language from the Christian (since it is language that belongs within the Christian context), then we must remain radically open to its implications which are deeply ecclesiological and trinitarian.

Seventh, John's theology of the Spirit drives us even further to explore any such affirmation of the Spirit's presence in other religions, for the new practice enjoined of the church in the making of such statements requires also the issues of indigenization and mission to be further clarified and developed for they are intrinsically interrelated. In the context of the present chapter, I would only like to make one general point. I would like to suggest that the often cited distinctions between mission, dialogue, and inculturation are fluid and unhelpful. This is because if the church must learn another language as its first language, if it is to engage in dialogue and mission, then both activities are intrinsically related. In any engagement, even the act of understanding, questions and criticism as well as affirmation will surface. In this sense, mission is impossible without dialogue, and vice versa. Furthermore, in so much as learning this second language will eventually alter our first language, especially when the second language users convert to Christianity, then a process of inculturation will follow, which will both possibly enrich Christian self-understanding and practice (see GS 44) or/and transform it so that radical discontinuity sets in (how modernity determines Christian discourse in Hick, Knitter, and Cohn-Sherbok).

Proper and legitimate inculturation or indigenization is always an act of continuity within a greater discontinuity: a taking up of what disciples from different cultures and religions may bring to the church, but in this taking up, this being raised, the configuration of new life that emerges can never be predicted or even fully assessed except retrospectively.[49] So while inculturation is always a process of transforming that which may have already been enlivened by the Spirit, it cannot but recreate and reconfigure elements within the church's new practice. Vatican II expresses this precisely and starkly concerning growth in indigenous churches:

> Whatever good is in the minds and hearts of men, whatever good lies latent in the religious practices and cultures of diverse peoples, is not only saved from destruction but is also healed, ennobled, and perfected unto the glory of God, the confusion of the devil, and the happiness of man (LG 17).

That which is Christ-like by the power of the Spirit outside the visible church is called into a greater completion, its most profound fulfillment which may, nevertheless, signal its destruction (viz. its loss of original context). "Healed," "ennobled," and "perfected" all express this sense of the emergence of the new creation, but a creation which is only finally consummated eschatologically. Here the church is always in great danger of obscuring the cross from itself in any premature identification of consummation and fulfillment with its present form—and we saw *Redemptoris Missio* 20 explicitly refusing such a strict identification. Stating that the church is in any sense a "fulfillment" must always require it to be an enacted fulfillment of that which is fulfilled, a new coming into being, if the notion of fulfillment is to have any credence at all. Hence, the word fulfillment must be constantly specified historically, if it is to be restored and used.

Finally, it is right and fitting that we end where Christ began, and from where John's theology of the resurrection unfolds: mission. The Holy Spirit given to the church is always a call to follow the commandment of love, as Jesus has loved us, with the love of the Father, through the power of the Spirit. And this is an invitation to respond to a gift which is so freely given that nothing can contain it, neither the heavens nor the earth, as Paul expresses it (Col 1:20). It is nothing short of the gift of new life, participating in a love that never ends and a love that is powerful in its weakness and vulnerability, as on the cross. It is inconceivable that witnessing to the gospel can ever be less than the meaning of living this new creation, so that John reminds us that in effect there can be no real dialogue (as it is often called today) between religions, without mission, for Christians have nothing to share with others, other than what has been given so bountifully to them.

WHOSE "OPENNESS," WHICH "TOLERANCE"?

To conclude this chapter, I want to take the terms so valued by pluralists and appropriate them but in so doing, transform them. This rhetorical strategy suggests that my trinitarian orientation may better attain the real goals of pluralists, "openness," "tolerance," and "equality," even if these goals are so changed as to be unrecognizable to pluralists. In this sense, they are not the same goals at all. However, since my dialectical arguments were deployed to show that the pluralist goals, as they themselves understood them, were unattainable, then this strategy allows us to see coherent and sustainable ways in which openness, tolerance, and equality might be displayed—and even be proposed as attractive to pluralists. There may be a clearer relationship between dialectics and rhetorics for my engagement with Christian pluralists, but obviously less so for those from other religions.

Regarding openness, I tried to show that a certain *a priorism* operated negatively regarding other religions within our Christian, Jewish, Hindu, and Buddhist thinkers. In varying ways, they all knew what they would find within other religions prior to any real historical engagement. In varying ways they also all knew what they would value and prize within other religions, prior to their meeting them. In varying ways they were all actually left untouched by the different engagements with others, with the exception of the Dalai Lama who felt, for example, that Christianity's social engagement helped him understand compassion more fully. In contrast, there are at least three important ways in which openness can be genuinely said to exist within my trinitarian orientation. First, I have been arguing above that since the trinitarian doctrine of God is only eschatologically "closed," and is always also a doctrine about the shape of the church, it means that the very doctrine of a trinitarian God within Christianity allows Christianity to maintain a real openness to God *in history*. Since God acts historically, as we have seen in the incarnation, and the doctrine of the church is such that we see this action continuing in history, although through a "glass darkly," and this very church acknowledges God's continuous activity outside its visible confines, we therefore have a strong theological basis for such an openness. Since we have seen that the Holy Spirit may be active within other religions, if the church is closed to other religions, then the church will be guilty of being inattentive to the promptings of God which may lead it into greater holiness, truth, and goodness. Being inattentive to other religions is a form of idolatry.

Second, there can be no *a priori* knowledge of what other religions may disclose: the surprises, beauty, terror, truth, holiness, deformity, cruelty, and goodness that they might display. The history of religions is still in the making and it is therefore necessary for the church to be attentive to the auto-interpretation of the religions if it is to be open to history. Of course, there is an *a priori* set of commitments within this process, that of commitment to the Roman Catholic church, but what I want to suggest is that this commitment cannot *a priori* negate or affirm other religions apart from the context of detailed historical engagement with those traditions. Any such positive or negative judgments are then *a posteriori* and must be accounted for.

Third, taking the reality of other religions seriously, either in their auto-interpretation or within Christianity's hetero-interpretation (which may or may not overlap in part), means that the church is laying itself open to genuine change, challenge, and questioning. I tried to show learning from other religions is not simply a matter of looking at the Other to see Christianity's already attained mirror image (as the undialectical notion of fulfillment tended to suggest), but in meeting the Other, there may be a real challenge to Christian identity in the radical manner expressed in *Gaudium et Spes* 44. Hence, Christian practice and reflection may change in ways that are not *a priori* predictable in the light of encountering other religions.

This is certainly a greater "openness" than found within our varying pluralists, with the possible exception of the Dalai Lama.

It has to be acknowledged that the type of picture I am drawing of Christianity, at least within Roman Catholicism, has only been possible within the last forty years and is still open to debate and challenge. This emphasis on history allied with a positive appreciation (in terms of auto and hetero-interpretation) of other religions is quite novel. None of the above mitigates either the sense that this is an authentic development of the tradition, nor does it mitigate the significance of mission: both as apologetics and rhetoric. In fact, the very way in which my argument has been constructed is evidence of this.

When we turn to "tolerance" and "equality," some very interesting features emerge about the intrasystematic debate within Roman Catholicism—which is far from resolved. I hope by now to have established that the various types of pluralism that we have looked at are neither tolerant (by their own criteria), nor do they grant equality of truth to the religions—which in varying ways they claim to do. This latter is manifestly impossible, for all truth is tradition-specifically narrated. Hence, it should be clear from the outset that the terms "tolerance" and "equality" cannot be narrated from a trinitarian context such that they bear on the truth claims of other religions. But in what sense can tolerance and equality be narrated within the church in regard to other religions? This was precisely the question that eventually grew out of the Schema of chapter IX of *De Ecclesia*, which started life as the question of the relation between state and church, transformed into a question of religious freedom to be treated in chapter V in *Unitatis Redintegratio*, and eventually finished as an entirely separate document, *Dignitatis Humanae* (1965)—after six Schema (draft documents), and some of the most contentious and passionate debate in the Council's history.[50]

I will briefly outline the major points of the document and show how it offered a serious reinterpretation of earlier teachings, such that some Roman Catholics still view it as "corruption" rather than development. To explain why some Roman Catholics have questioned its authority, and even imputed error to it, it is important to note three interrelated tenets that were established, more or less on papal teachings, prior to Vatican II. The first tenet regarded the relation between state and church. If a country was mainly and overwhelmingly Catholic, then it was right for the state to be Catholic. In such a state, those citizens who were not Catholics do not have the right, formally speaking, to practice their religion, just as those who hold erroneous views do not have a right, formally speaking, to profess those errors publicly. However, both for the sake of the common good of that community, and for all men and women, it may be that allowing such an alternative profession might be legitimate. Historically the Catholic church was too often painfully consistent in practicing this former teaching. Second, it is always the duty of the state to follow the objective natural law, and thus if Catholics are in a minority, it is still the duty of the state to allow Catholics freely to profess and practice their own religion. Third, and relatedly, error and falsity have no rights since it can never be the duty of anyone to choose error and falsity. Put together, as they often were, and for example in Pius IX, they amounted to a clear social teaching regarding religious pluralism and Christian tolerance. In *Quanta cura* (1864), which accompanied the *Syllabus of Errors*, Pius IX condemned the following propositions that were becoming established within liberal secular governments:

> Contrary to the teaching of the Holy Scriptures, of the Church, and of the holy Fathers, these persons do not hesitate to assert, that "the best condition of human society is that wherein no duty is recognized by the government of correcting, by enacted penalties, the violators of the Catholic Religion, except when the maintenance of the public peace requires it." From this totally false notion of social government, they fear not to uphold that erroneous opinion most pernicious to the Catholic Church, and to the salvation of souls, which was called by Our Predecessor, Gregory XVI (lately quoted) the insanity (*deliramentum*): namely, "that the liberty of conscience and of worship is the peculiar (or inalienable) right of every man, which should be proclaimed by law, and that citizens have the right to all kinds of liberty, to be restrained by no law, whether ecclesiastical or civil, but which they may be enabled to manifest openly and publicly their ideas, by word of mouth, through the press, or by any other means."[51]

If we remove "all" from the phrase "all kinds of liberty" in Pius IX's citing of Gregory XVI's passage, we find that just such a liberty as is condemned in 1864 (and earlier[52]) is now proclaimed by the Fathers of Vatican II in *Dignitatis Humanae* 2:

> This Vatican Synod declares that the human person has a right to religious freedom. This freedom means that all men are to be immune from coercion on the part of the individuals or of social groups and of any human power, in such wise that in matters religious no one is to be forced to act in a manner contrary to his own beliefs. Nor is anyone to be restrained from acting in accordance with his own beliefs, whether privately or publicly, whether alone or in association, within due limits.
>
> The Synod further declares that the right to religious freedom has its foundation in the very dignity of the human person, as this dignity is known through the revealed Word of God and by reason itself. This right of the human person to religious freedom is to be recognized in the constitutional law whereby society is governed. Thus it is to become a civil right.

If I have labored to show elsewhere that Vatican II on other religions was not a reversal, in any way, of the "no salvation outside the church" axiom, but a clear contextualized application and development of that teaching, it is clear that here we have what seems nothing short of a "U-turn." Just after the Declaration, in 1966, John Courtney Murray, S.J., one of the American architects of *Dignitatis Humanae* notes precisely this point:

> The notion of development, not the notion of religious freedom, was the real sticking-point for many of those who opposed the Declaration even to the end. The course of the development between the *Syllabus of Errors* (1864) and *Dignitatis Humanae Personae* (1965) still remains to be explained by theologians. But the Council formally sanctioned the validity of the development itself; and this was a doctrinal event of high importance for theological thought in many other areas.[53]

This is not the place to argue for *Dignitatis Humanae* against its critics, as I would wish to, although I do think it raises some difficult questions both regarding the notion of legitimate development within the tradition, as well as raising questions about the extent of modernity's understanding of freedom replacing that of Christian attention to truth, which determines all freedom.

However, in regard to my overall argument in this book there are three points that I would like to make. First, given my own criticisms of the notion of freedom within modernity, it is important to note that *Dignitatis Humanae* founds its position on "the revealed Word of God and by reason itself." We should not read this last phrase as endorsing modernity's notion of pure reason, but in contrast, it endorses the notion of the objective natural law, or "objective moral order" (DH 7). It is positioned in the argument, and in the text, because it was the single text of the Council which was addressed to all men and women. The first chapter of the document is attempting to address all persons who follow the objective natural law. The way in which it is founded in revelation takes up sections 9-12, and forms chapter II of the document. This is an apologetic strategy which is perfectly legitimate. My only reservation is that while the biblical-Christological justification is persuasive, it is a shame that it never begins to be a trinitarian justification. But then the Council cannot be comprehensive, nor is it a systematic theological treatise, so it leaves this task open, as it does in terms of developing Christological arguments to support its position.[54] Hence, my first point is that while the notion of freedom, duties, and rights in *Dignitatis Humanae* shares some overlap with themes in modernity (focused on freedom), and clearly reflects the church engaging more critically with modernity, it is shaped and orientated by Christological and theological concerns.

Second, the document does not encourage a theological-religious indifferentism—which was one major factor (rightly) resisted by previous popes.[55] None of what it says pertains to the question of whether other religions are true, or that one has any duties or rights to error. It affirms only that other religions have a "civil right" (DH 2) based not on what they teach, but on the dignity of all persons created in the image of God. Hence, this right should be safeguarded by the state. While *Dignitatis Humanae* is in fact unequivocally clear on this point, it is interesting to find the 1994 *Catechism of the Catholic Church* reiterating this point with reference to Leo XIII and Pius XII, and further invoking *Quanta cura* (Pius IX) and Pius VI's *Quod aliquantum* (1791) to show that there is actually no shift on the question of religious indifferentism, or rights, but rather a question of the right to be free from coercion. This would seem to be in response to precisely the sort of criticisms that I have advanced, with MacIntyre, against modernity's notion of freedom. Paragraph 2108 of the *Catechism* says:

> The right to religious liberty is neither a moral license to adhere to error, nor a supposed right to error, but rather a natural right of the human person to civil liberty, i.e., immunity, within just limits, from external constraint in religious matters by political authorities. . . . The right to religious liberty can of itself be neither unlimited nor limited only by a "public order" conceived in a positivist or naturalist manner. The "due limits" which are inherent in it must be determined for each social situation by political prudence, according to the requirements of the common good, and ratified by the civil authority in accordance with "legal principles which are in conformity with the objective moral order" (DH 7.3).

Hence, the notion of tolerance, or more precisely the right to be free from civic coercion in the practice of one's religion, is stated only negatively within *Dignitatis Humanae*, thereby safeguarding the important principle that error has no rights. The object of the right in the document is freedom from coercion, and is not at all connected with the contents of religious faith.

Third, it is interesting that it is precisely this document that contains just such an example of the type of change and transformation that is possible within Catholicism when engaging with the Other. In grappling with the question of other religions and civic society, we find a doctrinal development regarding the emergence of negative universal rights based on the revealed dignity of the human person and found in the objective moral order. That this point created one of the most protracted struggles within the Council is evidence of precisely the fact that the church's sense of truth can grow more deeply in history. Furthermore, it is also interesting that it is in this document that we find the most forthright acknowledgment that the church is sometimes actually guilty of obscuring the gospel, a point that I have been trying to develop via *Gaudium et Spes* 44. In the church's life "there have at times appeared ways of acting which were less in accord with the spirit of the gospel and even opposed to it." It is a complex admission of error, which should not be read anachronistically, but clearly indicates that the church learns and grows in wisdom, even if it sometimes obscures and obstructs it.[56]

In conclusion, I have tried to show that the type of openness (taking history seriously), tolerance (or negative civic religious rights) and equality (in terms of human dignity) capable of being advanced from my trinitarian orientation is more dialectically sustainable, has realistic limits, and while having unresolved difficulties, nevertheless takes religions seriously, facilitating their freedom such that genuine dialogue with Otherness and difference might be possible. My position does not side-step the difficult questions of whether and why Christians should resist Islamic theocracy; or the civic legitimation of caste Hinduism; or democratic free choices to legalize abortion or euthanasia on demand. It does not side-step the genuine possibilities of effective interreligious co-operation and social action on many questions regarding justice and peace. With integrity, and with less self-contradiction than we have seen within positions examined in Part I, my position is able to offer an account of openness, tolerance, and equality which are doctrinally plausible, socially realistic, and rhetorically attractive. In so doing, I hope I have been able to establish a trinitarian orientation to the question of other religions which is neither pluralist nor inclusivist, but both open and faithfully committed to its tradition-specific way of narrating the world.

I now want to test my trinitarian orientation with a particular pastoral problem: that of interreligious prayer. This will help to evaluate the effectiveness of my approach and show the ways in which it could be developed in relation to a host of problems and difficulties. Needless to say, this does not in any way obscure the complex intrasystematic questions that must be faced in professing the trinity.[57]

Notes

1. For close commentary and a good background on the documents see especially H. Vorgrimler, ed., *Commentary on the Documents of Vatican II*, Burns & Oates, London, 1967-9; Miikka Ruokanen, *The Catholic Doctrine of Non-Christian Religions according to the Second Vatican Council*, E. J. Brill, Leiden, 1992, 33-45.

2. See my " 'Extra ecclesiam nulla salus' revisited," in Ian Hamnett, ed., *Religious Pluralism and Unbelief: Studies Critical and Comparative*, Routledge, London, 1990, 130-47; and for a full background to this question in church history: Francis A. Sullivan, *Salvation Outside the Church?*, Geoffrey Chapman, London, 1992, and Jacques Dupuis, *Toward a Christian Theology of Religious Pluralism*, Orbis, Maryknoll, N.Y., 1997.

3. Cited by Claud Nelson, "A Response to Nostra Aetate" in Walter M. Abbott, ed., *The Documents of Vatican II*, Guild Press, New York, 1966, 669-70; original source not cited. For the most recent and strong statement, see the Commission for Religious Relations with the Jews document: *We Remember: A Reflection on the* Shoah, March 1998, esp. ch. v., 13 (CTS English translation).

4. See "Dei Filius," (1870), esp. ch. 2; and the anathema DZ 3026. Natural knowledge of God is also affirmed in *Dei Verbum* 3, but carefully related in its function as a *preparatio evangelica* and therefore of being fulfilled in Christ (4).

5. Augustine's *City of God*, 1917 (PL 41, 646) and the *Instruction of the Sacred Congregation for the Propagation of the Faith*, Collectenea 1, no. 35, 42, is also referred to. Augustine makes the important point that the truth may very well not be known to those who hold it when held by a non-Christian!

6. I have explored this yes/no dialectic in "Revelation and 'revelations': Beyond a Static Valuation of Other Religions" in *Modern Theology*, 10, 2, 1994, 165-84.

7. Paul Knitter, "Roman Catholic Approaches to Other Religions: Developments and Tensions," *International Bulletin of Missionary Research*, 1984, 50, my emphasis.

8. Karl Rahner, "On the Importance of the Non-Christian Religions for Salvation," *Theological Investigations*, Darton, Longman & Todd, London, Vol. 18, 1983, ch. 17, 290-1. Rahner is wrong to suggest that the Council established the premises for a conclusion it did not draw (290), for Rahner polarizes the possible answers regarding the status of non-Christian religions: "Are they (as institutions and doctrines) merely 'religion' as opposed to 'faith'?" I have argued elsewhere (see note 6 above) that the answer must be both at the same time. Rahner fails to be dialectical enough.

9. Miikka Ruokanen, *The Catholic Doctrine*, 11-34, 115-120, notes that the major issue concerns the relationship between nature and grace; as does Rowan Williams, but in a more nuanced fashion than Ruokanen who tends to put De Lubac and Rahner on one side of a very clearly drawn line (without recognizing significant differences). See Rowan Williams, "Balthasar and Rahner," in John Riches, ed., *The Analogy of Beauty*, T. & T. Clark, Edinburgh, 1986, 11-34, who brilliantly shows the complexity of the problem and that the nature-grace relationship is at the heart of the matter.

10. Jonathan Cape, London, 1994.

11. Glasgow, 1980, 130.

12. See Knitter and Ruokanen in debate in Ruokanen, *The Catholic Doctrine*, and further critiques of those who have gone too far in Joe DiNoia, *The Diversity of Religions: A Christian Perspective*, Catholic University of America Press, Washington, D.C., 1992, and H. van Straelen, *L'Eglise et les religions non chréstiennes au seuil du XXe siècle*, Beauchesne, Paris, 1994.

13. See chapter one, notes 15 & 16, for bibliographical details on Knitter's work. His most relevant article on this precise point is "A New Pentecost? A Pneumatological Theology of Religions," *Current Dialogue*, 19, 1992, 418-37.

14. See Panikkar, *The Trinity and the Religious Experience of Man*, Darton, Longman & Todd, London, 1973, 71-2, and 53-4, where Panikkar explicitly prioritizes the idea of the Logos, prior to its instantiation in Jesus Christ. See also the helpful Christological and trinitarian criticisms of Panikkar in *Cross Currents*, Summer, 1979, by Harold Coward and Ewert Cousins; and Ewert Cousins' excel-

lent overview of the strengths and weaknesses of Panikkar's position in "The Trinity and World Religions," *Journal of Ecumenical Studies*, 7, 1990, 476-98.

15. See Jacques Dupuis, *Toward a Christian Theology of Religious Pluralism*, 330-57; and my detailed review of the book in *The Journal of Theological Studies*, 49, 2, 1998, 910-4.

16. See my account of Rahner in *Theology and Religious Pluralism*, Blackwell, Oxford, 1986, ch. 4.

17. See, for example, my discussion in "Theology of Religions," in David F. Ford, ed., *The Modern Theologians*, Blackwell, Oxford, 1997, 626-44, and the secondary bibliography included there.

18. For the *preparatio* tradition, see Sullivan, *Salvation*, chs. 2, 3, for pre-Vatican II sources, and chs. 8-10, for Conciliar and post-Conciliar trajectories.

19. In H. Vorgrimler, ed., *Commentary on the Documents of Vatican II*, Vol. 5, Burns & Oates, 1967-9, 219-20.

20. Within national and continent-based synods this has already taken place, see for example the Asian Synod of 1998, and previous documents in G. Rosales and C. G. Arévalo, eds., *For All the Peoples of Asia: Federation of Asian Bishops' Conferences Documents from 1970 to 1991*, Orbis, Maryknoll, N.Y., 1992. In some sections of the Roman curia, this can also be seen. See the interesting cross-currents that work in the joint curial document: *Dialogue and Mission*, 1991, and for commentary on this document, see William Burrows, ed., *Redemption and Dialogue*, Orbis, Maryknoll, N.Y., 1993, especially the chapter by Jacques Dupuis, "A Theological Commentary: Dialogue and Proclamation," 119-58.

21. Regarding this identification, reference is made to the International Theological Commission, *Select Themes of Ecclesiology on the Twentieth Anniversary of the Closing of the Second Vatican Council*, Rome, 1985, ch. 10, which clearly refuses a strict identification between church and kingdom, but equally affirms an indissoluble bond between the two by virtue of Christ's presence.

22. John Paul II is rightly more suspicious of liberal modernity, the "culture of death," than some of the more "progressive" elements within the Council. See *Evangelium Vitae*, 1995. And in contrast, he is more open to some religious cultures, although not uncritically. See above in main text.

23. In reading accounts of converts to Christianity one can find stressed elements of continuity (Brahmabandhab Upadhyay; see Animanda, *The Blade: The Life and Work of Brahmabandhab Upadhyay*, Roy & Son, Calcutta, n.d.), sheer discontinuity (see Rubindranath R. Maharaj, *Death of a Guru* [with Dave Hunt], Hodder & Stoughton, London, 1977), or both (Steven Masood, *Into the Light*, STL Books, Bromiley Kent, 1986, and the works of the Jewish Christian writer, Michelle Guiness). Some see that there are unresolved tensions, such as the "Jews for Jesus" and "Hebrew Christians."

24. Raymond E. Brown, *The Gospel according to John*, Geoffrey Chapman, London, 1971, vol. 2, 1013.

25. See Rudolf Bultmann, *The Gospel of John: A Commentary*, Blackwell, Oxford, 1971, especially 681-99.

26. See Oscar Cullmann's not dissimilar reading of Luke in *Christ and Time: The Christian Conception of Time and History*, SCM, London, 1952.

27. For John's possible church reconstructed, see Raymond E. Brown, *The Community of the Beloved Disciple*, Geoffrey Chapman, London, 1979.

28. See Brown, *John*; Bultmann, *John*; C. K. Barrett, *The Gospel According*

to John, 2nd ed., SPCK, London, 1978; Barnabas Lindars, *The Gospel of John*, Oliphants, London, 1972; George Johnston, *The Spirit-Paraclete in the Gospel of John*, Cambridge University Press, Cambridge, 1970; C. F. D. Moule, *The Holy Spirit*, Mowbrays, London, 1978.

29. *Redemptoris Missio* 18, also insists on the kingdom as centered around the "person" of Christ, not an idea, program of action, or transcendental. For an extremely interesting reading of "person" as narrative relationship rather than enduring substance, see Bruce Marshall, *Christology in Conflict*, Blackwell, Oxford, 1987, 176-89 and related notes.

30. See John Milbank's essay, "The Name of Jesus: Incarnation, Atonement, Ecclesiology," *Modern Theology*, 7, 4, 1991, 311-33: 319. I am indebted to Milbank's articulation of an ecclesiological practice as the required site of revelation. Milbank, however, is in danger of playing down the problem of authority involved in such new practices.

31. Brown, *John*, 639; see also Bultmann, *John*, 615. 1 Jn 5:7 does use "is," but the context there does not affect this reading.

32. Barrett, *John*, 467.

33. Brown, *John*, 700; also Bultmann, *John*, 554; Barrett, *John*, 482-3.

34. See for example Luke's account of Paul's conversion in Acts 9:4ff; 22:7ff; 26:15ff, where the voice from heaven replies to Paul's questioning of its identity, "I am Jesus, whom you are persecuting," when in fact Paul has clearly been persecuting the church. And see Paul's own account of the church's relation to Christ, as "body" in 1 Corinthians 12-13.

35. Brown, *John*, 701.

36. Milbank, "Name" 327, the second quotation cited in the sentence is from 319.

37. Brown, *John*, 705.

38. See Pope John Paul II's excellent meditative exegesis on this passage in *Dominum et Vivificantem* (*On the Holy Spirit in the Life of the Church*), 1986, Pt. II.

39. Brown, *John*, 715.

40. Bultmann, *John*, 576. See also Moule's illuminating comment about the Spirit in the New Testament as a whole: *Spirit*, 38.

41. See Lindars, *John*, 506.

42. Chapter one of *Lumen Gentium* is devoted to the trinitarian foundations of Vatican II's ecclesiology. See the commentary on this by Aloys Grillmeier in Herbert Vorgrimler, *Commentary on the Documents of Vatican II*, Vol. 3, Burns & Oates, London, 1967-9, 138-52, esp. 142 summarizing art. 4 of the document.

43. See my "Revelation and 'revelations'," 165-84.

44. Milbank, "Name," 325. He uses "imitation" here in contrast to the earlier citation (note 20) to mean non-identical repetition as the imitation of Christ.

45. See *Redemptoris Missio*, esp. 17-20; 28-30.

46. See discussion of non-Christian saints in chapter 5, pp. 152-3, and see also David McCarthy Matzko, "Christ's Body in Its Fullness: Resurrection and the Lives of the Saints," in Gavin D'Costa, ed., *Resurrection Reconsidered*, Oneworld, Oxford, 1996, 102-17. See also Jean Daniélou's beautiful treatment of pre-Christian saints: *Holy Pagans of the Old Testament*, Longman, Green & Co., London, 1957. All easy talk about saintly lives avoids the complex question of identifying saintliness, which is still one good reason for the cumbersome process of

canonization employed by the Roman Catholic church. Countless unsung saints are also praised in the Roman Missal.

47. Milbank, "Name," 325, my emphasis.

48. The Samaritans were seen at best as heretical and schismatic Jews, and at worse, as "pagans." See Joseph A Fitzmeyer, *The Gospel According to Luke: X-XXIV*, The Anchor Bible, Doubleday, New York, 1985, 887. One should also recall the earlier rejection of Jesus by the Samaritans in Lk 9:51; and Jesus' exchange with the Samaritan women at the well in Jn 4:1-42. These other passages make the story in Lk 10:25-37 even more remarkable.

49. See D'Costa, "Nostra Aetate" on Indian examples, and also "Inculturation, India, and Other Religions," *Studia Missionalia*, 44, 1995, 121-47.

50. See Pietro Pavan's historical and theological commentary, "Declaration of Human Freedom," in Vorgrimler, ed., *Commentary on the Documents*, Vol. 5, 49-86; and for a strong critique of Pavan and an alternative reading of the history and theology of the document see Michael Davies, *The Second Vatican Council and Religious Liberty*, Neumann Press, Minnesota, 1992.

51. Davies, *Vatican Council*, 60.

52. In *Mirari vos* (1832) Gregory XVI warns against indifferentism: "that widespread and dangerous opinion sown by the perfidy of the wicked, according to which it is possible, by the profession of some sort of faith, to procure the soul's salvation, provided that one's morals conform to the norms of justice and probity"; or earlier in 1814, with Pius VII's outrage at Article 22 of King Louis XVIII's new Constitution regarding religious liberty: "This law does more than establish liberty for all cultures without distinction, it mingles truth with error and places heretical sects and even Judaism on equal terms with the holy and immaculate Bride of Christ . . . in promising favor and support to heretical sects and their ministers it is not simply their persons but their errors which are favored and deplored" (cited in Davies, *Vatican Council*, 56).

53. John Courtney Murray, "Religious Freedom," in Walter M. Abbot, ed., *The Documents of Vatican II*, Guild Press, New York, 1966, 672-4, 673.

54. See Pavan, "Freedom," 79: "The Council fathers were deeply divided in their views of scriptural arguments in favor of religious freedom. Some thought it useless to quote texts for the simple reason that religious freedom in the sense of the Declaration was never mentioned in Scripture."

55. This is certainly a major charge advanced by Davies, *Vatican Council*. However, he offers no arguments against the revelational basis of the document establishing universal human dignity.

56. See Pavan, "Freedom," 80-3, for some helpful contextualizations of this admission, and also for his inadvertent highlighting of the problem that rights have been disassociated with *telos* at points in the document (82).

57. For that task, see my forthcoming book, *The Trinity and the Murder of the Mother*, SCM, London, 2000.

5

Praying Together to the Triune God? Is Interreligious Prayer Like Marital Infidelity?

INTERRELIGIOUS PRAYER: MARITAL INFIDELITY OR LOVING RISK?

> For all who are led by the Spirit of God are sons of God. For you did not receive the spirit of slavery to fall back into fear, but you have received the spirit of sonship. When we cry, "Abba! Father!" it is the Spirit himself bearing witness with our spirit that we are children of God. . . . Likewise the Spirit helps us in our weakness; for we do not know how to pray as we ought, but the Spirit himself intercedes for us with sighs too deep for words. And he who searches the hearts of men knows what is the mind of the Spirit, because the Spirit intercedes for the saints according to the will of God (Rom 8:14-16; 26-27).

If prayer leads us into perichoretic communion with the saints, with Mary, and all those who have received the spirit of adoption, by leading us into communion with the triune God, then prayer is clearly vital to the future of trinitarian theology. But perichoretic relations do not stop at the boundaries of the church, nor does love and subsistent relations, for one major aspect of contemporary culture is the fact that many Christians in large cities live with those from other religions. There is intermarriage and there is persecution, there is the sharing of places of "prayer" at international airports, and there is the burning of each other's places of prayer. One particular question from this new situation in the last half century is that of interreligious prayer. For the Christian, all prayer, as with all life, is directed toward the trinitarian God—or at least that is the "theory." In practice all sorts of idolatries may be masked in the Christian life. I want to look at what is often seen as the practice of idolatry in other religions: praying to false gods, and ask the difficult question—is interreligious prayer possible? Does interreligious prayer not require Christian participation in idolatry, for surely only the triune God is worthy of worship? I think it right to frame this question in nuptial terms, for that is what prayer constitutes for the Christian: a deepening of the life of covenanted love, through sickness and death, and through happiness and despair. But I want to turn the question around to suggest that a refusal to even consider encountering the mystery of God within the other in shared prayer runs the risk of idolatry: worshiping only the god of our own construction. Admittedly, this is to put the case far too strongly. However, I want to suggest that there is a case to be made that the prayers of others might be reconfigured in the act of shared prayer, such that the Christian might discover the mystery of the triune God more fully, and also share with the other the "gift" that prayer always is: an invitation to communion with the triune God. If Paul is confident that the "Spirit helps us in our weakness; for we do not know to pray as we ought, but the Spirit himself intercedes for us with sighs too deep for words," and we can also be confident that the same Spirit is possibly at work in other religions, then their prayers may tell us (and them) more than we (or they) can predict.

In this chapter I will focus on the question of interreligious prayer by first reflecting on the various practices of interreligious prayer that have taken place, and introduce some terminological distinctions so as to focus the question more precisely. I will then consider the question within a very narrow context of definition, suggesting only the outlines of an argument that would require much more development.

NUPTIAL PRAYER AND INTERRELIGIOUS PRAYER

> Love breeds love; and mine, Jesus, for you, keeps on thrusting out towards you, as if to fill up that chasm which your love has made—but it is no good; mine is something less than a drop of dew lost in the ocean. Love you as you love me? The only way to do that is to come to you for the loan of your own love; I couldn't content myself with less (Thérèse of Lisieux).[1]

Thérèse's comment on prayer makes at least two things clear. First, prayer is part of our communal love affair with God, our discovery that his love and graciousness invite us into a love that ceaselessly overflows. This love, like married love, takes place through banal everyday events, as well as dark barren times of desolation, and even brutal suffering, that may shape our lives. All this characterized Thérèse's life. The intensity of her love affair with Jesus also illustrates a second point: that the only way to participate in this trinitarian love is to "make a loan" from this love, to engage in "a sharing in this unique source" (LG 62). Imagine asking your lover to teach you to love, to loan some of his or her love to facilitate your own. Of course, all but the proud will have done this at some time, and all of us will have learned to love (or hate, deny, and envy) by complex imitation.[2] Thérèse's writings and life of prayer are an embodied commentary on *The Catechism of the Catholic Church*'s (subsequently *Catechism*) threefold characterization of prayer as gift, covenant, and communion. Prayer is understood as gift, because "*humility* is the foundation of prayer. Only when we humbly acknowledge that "we do not know how to pray as we ought" [Rom 8:26] are we ready to receive freely the gift of prayer." It is understood as covenant, for prayer is the "place of encounter, because as image of God we live in relation: it is the place of covenant." Prayer is *communion*, for "the life of prayer is the habit of being in the presence of the thrice-holy God and in communion with him."[3]

In this light interreligious prayer may well be seen as marital infidelity: praying with communities that are not our own explicitly covenanted communities; communities which do not profess the same *credo*; and praying to gods that do not bear the name of Father, Son and Spirit—and thus communing one knows not where and with whom; and in so doing, causing public scandal. Even if one were to argue that this may not in fact be the case, as I shall do to a very limited extent, it is not always easy to assess the importance of scandal that can be given in this sensitive area. Even scandalizing those who are weak or unlearned should not be minimized as Paul reminds the community at Corinth in a not dissimilar context, when arguing that while eating the food offered to idols cannot be defiling, for "we know that an idol has no real existence," he nevertheless is keenly sensitive to the scandal this might cause among those who do not understand the issues properly. "Thus, sinning against your brethren and wounding their conscience when it is weak, you sin against Christ" (1 Cor 8:4-13). Furthermore, many who oppose interreligious prayer are neither weak nor unlearned but deeply committed to good interreligious relations and social practices. They argue that one does not have to sleep with another man's wife to practice real love and respect toward her. Likewise, one need not worship with other religions to show love and respect toward them.

It will be helpful to look at some examples of interreligious prayer to focus on what is at stake, and in what situations the most acute scandal is caused. The situation in England has grown critical, to the point that both the (now renamed and reformed) British Council of Churches and the state Anglican church have produced studies and guidelines on the issue.[4] The Roman Catholic bishops have not published anything similar, but the late Cardinal Hume was represented at the controversial Commonwealth Day Observance which has been held at Westminster Abbey every March.[5] Here religious representatives from the Commonwealth countries pray together with the Queen, who is head of the Anglican church and the

Commonwealth, and publicly read from their own scriptures to show how the "five common Affirmations" that form the heart of the Observance are "endorsed by the religious tradition of us all" as the 1994 program states. The five common affirmations concern the stewardship of the earth, human worth, justice and peace, love in relationships, service, and sacrifice.[6] The Observance has fueled bitter controversy in the Church of England against the "worship of other gods" within Anglican churches. This is how the matter was construed in the "Open Letter" of October 1991 which was publicly signed by seventy key church persons and later by two thousand additional supporters.[7] However, some of the signatories were not *per se* opposing prayer with people of other faiths in every circumstance. For example, some apparently supported interreligious prayer by a hospital chaplain at a sick bed in times of crisis. That is, they allow for an Anglican chaplain to pray with a person from another faith who makes such a request to a chaplain and who might be in distress. This might include quiet shared prayer (where each person prayed their own prayers together, but in silence), or/and the Christian praying Christian prayers with the other, who may verbally or silently join in with them. What in fact such people opposed was the public use of Anglican churches for worship other than Christian, for this seems to place Christianity on a par with other religions "as far as salvation is concerned."[8]

Interreligious prayer on the international scene forms a complex picture. One of the most high-profile meetings was the Day of Prayer for Peace in Assisi, October 1986 (inaugurated by Pope John Paul II), and there are a number of institutionally constructed events centering around the United Nations, the World Congress of Faiths, and, as we have seen, the Commonwealth. However, equally important are those events generated out of long-term personal friendships and out of crises such as the citizenship action against hunger and misery in Rio, Brazil; the prayers during the aftermath of the Oklahoma bombing in the USA; the interfaith center of Aloysius Pieris in Sri Lanka relating to the conflicts in that troubled country; the Ribat es Salam (the Bond of Peace), a Muslim-Christian prayer group around the Trappist monks of Tibhirine (Algeria) which was brutally destroyed with the murder of seven monks.[9] Furthermore, the dynamics of interreligious prayer will be characterized by many different factors, such as the power of the different groups involved, the sites of their meeting, the intentions behind such practices, the gender of participants, their professional status and representative authorization—and so on.

This complexity gives rise to the need to at least roughly define different types of event that go under the name of "interreligious prayer" in which a Roman Catholic might take part, so as to focus on the problem of alleged infidelity more carefully. These types are nothing more than categories and reality rarely fits into such models with any strict correspondence. First, in terms of Catholic theology, we should resist any fundamental theological distinction between *private* and *communal* prayer for whether in the desert alone or in a modern cathedral packed to capacity, when we pray we pray with the "communion of saints," the whole church, living and dead. The *Catechism* points out that *the* prayer of the church begins " 'Our' Father," even when we pray it alone, for the "Our" leaves

> individualism behind, because the love that we receive frees us from it. The "our" at the beginning of the Lord's prayer, like the "us" of the last four petitions, excludes no one. If we are to say it truthfully, our divisions and oppositions have to be overcome (cf. Mt 5:23-24; 6:14-15).[10]

The biblical references to Matthew chapters 5 and 6 show that forgiveness between lovers—and even between enemies—is the *only* requisite for Christian prayer. Hence, although an interreligious prayer event may be very public and high-profile, and proportionately give more scandal and thereby demand more rigorous accountability, even were it private and unknown to any but those who took part in it, the same theological issues are at stake for a Christian. For every Christian is accountable to the community of believers of which they are part.

However, while all prayer may be communal, it might be legitimate to distinguish between prayer used in formal public *cultic* acts, such as baptism, confession, and mass for example, and prayer used in *spontaneous private prayer* or composed for various *ad hoc* occasions such as a blessing on a meal, or shared prayer with a sick friend.[11] Cultic prayer cannot really be shared by those outside the cult, as such prayers form part of public self-identification within the cult. The lack of resolution in these cultic matters even between different Christian denominations regarding the extent of participation and sharing in the eucharist, for example, is indicative that cultic worship and practice is intentionally exclusive to those who are not Christian. However, even having said that, mixed-faith marriages and other civic and public occasions present important exceptions to this general rule. Christmas mass is an obvious example, or the funerals of those in a public tragedy. Nevertheless, this distinction between cultic and non-cultic worship accounts for the following guidelines in a document from the Vatican Secretariat for Non-Christians published in 1969 (under Cardinal Marella):

> Some people ask if we can pray with Muslims. Although it is evident that we must not take part actively in the cult of another religion, we can be associated with spontaneous prayer. Nevertheless, apart from special and very rare occasions, when certain prayers drawn from one or other religious heritage could be said in common, it would seem preferable to compose, or better still to get others to compose, special prayers, which can express the religious sentiment of all those taking part, whether Christian or Muslim prayers based on common

> beliefs. Certain psalms carefully chosen or some of the texts from Muslim mystics, can express these things very well.[12]

In the light of the above distinctions, in what follows I shall exclude cultic prayer as a site of interreligious prayer, although the implications of my exploration of non-cultic interreligious prayer upon cultic prayer cannot be predicted.

Non-cultic prayer can take on the form of organized scripts that are used by all participants or can be spontaneous, or a mixture of both. I would also like to suggest two, admittedly fluid, distinctions. First, there are meetings that I shall call *multireligious prayer* events, whereby each religious community has a slot where some representative or representatives makes a contribution, usually related to some agreed theme.[13] The scale and representative nature of such meetings can greatly vary, as can their aims. The site on which they are performed is extremely important—as in the case with Westminster Abbey for the Commonwealth Observance, or Ayodhyā for a multireligious prayer meeting between Muslim, Hindu, and Christians after the destruction of the Ayodhyā mosque in India. For the purpose of definition, in multireligious prayer, there is *no* public united praying together, rather a respectful witnessing of each other at prayer. Nevertheless, this witnessing can often lead toward inner participation with prayers from another tradition in different ways and at different levels of intensity. This indicates the inadequacy of tight labeling. The second part of the Day of Prayer for Peace in Assisi, October 1986, is a typical example of multireligious prayer.[14] In the first part of the day, each religious group met on its own to fast and pray/mediate for peace. In the afternoon, the second part of the day, the "leaders" of different religious groups met together in the Basilica of St. Francis in a semi-circle at the head of the nave. Each of their five-minute contributions, lasting two and a half hours, was separated by silence. The Commonwealth "Observance" is more difficult to classify, for it seems to place an act of multireligious prayer within an act of Christian worship. The program notes for the Observance state: "it will be clear to all present that the Observance has a Christian orientation that is appropriate to this place [Westminster Abbey]."[15] It is not entirely clear to me that a Hindu saying Hindu prayers, and likewise a Muslim saying Muslim prayers, can be described as acting with a "Christian orientation" without substantial theological commentary to justify or explain this. Furthermore, this kind of arrangement always allows for the criticism that what is supposed to be a joint meeting is in fact being controlled and managed by one group—in this instance, Christians.

However, multireligious prayer, as loosely defined above, and carefully carried out, can often be appropriate for civic and social occasions where different faiths want to come together to make some common cause, be it peace, as in Assisi; or the five Affirmations that supposedly bind all Commonwealth citizens together; or at times of national or international tragedies or celebrations. The advantage of multireligious prayer, according to a recent Vatican and WCC Consultation, "is that the integrity and rich variety of each tradition is honored. The disadvantage is that one may remain a mere bystander without entering into the spirituality of the other."[16] Of course it is precisely this "entering into another's spirituality" that is seen as problematic by many. A further disadvantage of such meetings is the possibility of a concoction of bland lowest common denominator prayers chosen to cause no offense to any of the other traditions present but which subsequently reflects no tradition adequately.

In contrast to multireligious prayer, there are acts of what I shall call *interreligious prayer* which is "an occasion when people of different faith traditions plan, prepare, and participate in a prayer which all those who come can or may claim as their prayer."[17] The level of planning and preparation will vary, but the key point here is a real *praying together*, whatever that might mean, although it is precisely that which it might mean that is most controversial. The WCC/RC Consultation just referred to says of this type of interreligious prayer: "The advantage is that it allows all present to pray together. The disadvantage is that it can at times reduce prayer to the lowest common denominator and it can take away the uniqueness of each religion."[18] The disadvantages of interreligious prayer are somewhat stacked against the advantages, leaving aside the question of biblical support for interreligious prayer—which is extremely thin.[19] However, in what follows I want to explore "advantages," and for the rest of this chapter, only the category of non-cultic interreligious prayer as defined above is addressed, as I take this to be the most difficult test case: i.e., if interreligious prayer can be justified in some circumstances, then multireligious prayer can be justified in some circumstances, but not vice versa.

I shall also take for granted four presuppositions when discussing this question. First, that a Roman Catholic so involved in interreligious prayer is not intending to create a new syncretistic religion, although his or her own form of Christian worship may as a result of interreligious prayer be changed, sometimes to a scandalous or prophetic degree, such as when Swami Abhishiktananda (the French Benedictine, Henri Le Saux) reportedly said mass using only the word "Om"! There are other instances, for example, when Benedictine monks have utilized *zazen* meditational practices and technique to deepen their own contemplation and prayer as Christian monks. This question is clearly not unconnected with that of inculturation. Second, that a Roman Catholic so involved does not hold to any form of theological pluralism or "indifferentism,"[20] whereby interreligious prayer might signify a release from the obligation to preach Christ crucified and the church as the means to salvation, although the way in which these obligations come to be understood and practiced cannot be decided in advance.[21] Third, during interreligious prayer we must remember that, in the words of the *Catechism*, "the Tempter who does all he can to turn man away from prayer" (2725) can do so, not simply by making us turn away from prayer, but also possibly by drawing people into interreligious prayer. Interreligious prayer can make people neglectful of their own particular tradition, and can cause people to seek interreligious prayer when they have failed to find genuine nourishment within their own prayer tradition. Finally, we assume that a Roman Catholic involved in interreligious prayer is doing so with a firm commitment to the teaching that all authentic prayer (and therefore even interreligious prayer) must be characterized in the threefold manner stated in the *Catechism*: as gift, covenant, and communion with the triune God. But is such a characterization possible of interreligious prayer? In the light of much of the argument of this book, it hardly seems so.

ON SEEKING FIDELITY THROUGH LOVING RISK

In the Name of God, the Merciful, the Compassionate.
Praise belongs to God, the Lord of all Being,
the All-Merciful, the All-compassionate,
The Master of the Day of Doom.
Thee only we serve; to Thee alone we pray for succor.
Guide us in the straight path,
the path of those whom Thou hast blessed,
not of those against whom Thou art wrathful,
nor of those who are astray (Qur'an 1:1-7).

I shall explore positive theological support for interreligious prayer within the framework of the *Catechism*'s teaching on prayer, and the church's official teaching regarding other religions to be found in and since Vatican II.[22] I want to suggest that interreligious prayer, within certain parameters, might not after all be like marital infidelity, but rather an act of loving risk, somewhat like Jacob's wrestling with the mysterious figure, whose identity is unknown and who refuses to be named, but names or rather renames "Jacob" as "Israel." Interreligious prayer, to some extent, is not unlike "wrestling" in the dark, an abandonment of control in an ambiguous act of love and trust, even when we are not sure who God is, crying out to God: "I will not let you go, unless you bless me" (Gen 32:26). For those who have found blessings from interreligious prayer and who, as a result, have become even closer to their church, Jacob's renaming is highly significant, for their apparent "infidelity" may also be renamed "loving risk," a "striving with God."[23]

A word on the word "God." There are significant distinctions between theistic and other traditions, and *Nostra Aetate* makes it clear that there is a *sui generis* relationship with Judaism, and a special relation with Islam through the "sharing" of scriptures and history, in varying ways, as in the common monotheism of the three Semitic faiths.[24] However, it is clear from *Nostra Aetate* that non-theistic religions are not excluded from relationship with "God." One cannot simply conclude that prayers and meditation within non-theistic religions are valueless, and such a negative view is nowhere to be found in official church teachings. For the purpose of some clarity, I shall simply use Islam in the examples that follow and comment on some special difficulties when non-theistic traditions are being considered.

To explore the issues, I want artificially to freeze three moments that can occur within any act of interreligious prayer, and I shall do so under the headings given in the *Catechism* when outlining what constitutes Christian prayer: gift, covenant, and communion. If interreligious prayer is in the least acceptable, it must, for the Christian, bear these three marks if it is to keep fidelity to the triune God and the community of the church—even if in this case "keeping faithful" requires the risk of "infidelity."

> *Gift*: *humility* is the foundation of prayer. Only when we humbly acknowledge that "we do not know how to pray as we ought" are we ready to receive freely the gift of prayer. "Man is a beggar before God."[25]

Both St. Paul and St. Augustine knew that the ability to pray is a gift from the Holy Spirit, nothing which we can command and control, a gift given out of God's thirst for us, for "God thirsts that we may thirst for him."[26] The gift of the Holy Spirit helps us to be conformed to Christ, to become co-redeemers, and to share in the love of God within the covenant drama of salvation, a drama that continues through every Christian community's life and embraces all creation. As we saw in chapter four, Catholic teaching shows no reservation in acknowledging the presence of the Holy Spirit throughout creation and in all cultures and religions, although specifying the manner of this presence is left an open question—while always affirming its intrinsic relation to Christ.[27] It is only within this context of humble receptivity that we might "receive freely the gift of prayer." It is precisely why Pope John Paul II explained the significance of the Assisi event in terms of the Holy Spirit, for

> every authentic prayer is called forth by the Holy Spirit, who is mysteriously present in the heart of every person. This too was seen at Assisi: the unity that comes from the fact that every man and woman is capable of praying, that is, of submitting oneself totally to God and of recognizing oneself to be poor in front of him.[28]

While this position makes John Paul II an advocate of multireligious prayer, not interreligious prayer, the point he is making regarding the action of the Holy Spirit as inspiring and moving all genuine prayer, be it Christian or otherwise, is extremely significant to my argument.[29] It supports the point I am making: prayers from other religious traditions can be moved by and be authentic promptings by the Holy Spirit. Hence, in interreligious prayer we may be genuinely waiting upon God, knowing that the Holy Spirit may move the hearts of men and women in their prayer and meditation, and in such events we are offered the "gift" of seeing others truly pray and of learning how to pray, in ways we cannot foresee, predict, or control.

This "gift" can be discerned in two particular areas. First, we might note that the semiotic configurations of prayer and meditation can challenge Christians to consider their own practice. For example, one might learn the benefits of breathing techniques and posture for prayer and meditation used by Hindus and Buddhists. The careful incorporation of such techniques into Christian practice can sometimes help to cultivate prayer and meditation centered around the triune God. This is not a simple matter, for one cannot simply detach various practices and skills from the world view within which they operate, and a careful vigilance is required in such cross-fertilization. The Congregation for the Doctrine of the Faith issued a warning against such easy and uncritical appropriations of the practices and techniques used in other religions (in *Some Aspects of Christian Meditation: A Few Reflections*), precisely because some practices cannot be divorced from the philosophical frameworks and assumptions that inform them.[30] Furthermore, it might often be the case, as with the founder of the Christian meditation movement, John Main, that such meditative practices lead us to discover areas of the Christian tradition that have been long neglected. Main first learned meditation in the East and through this discovered the Ninth Conference of John Cassian, a fourth-century spiritual writer, upon whom he now relies so heavily.[31] It should be stressed that all techniques, skills, disciplines, and preparations cannot in any way replace the centrality of personal relationship that constitutes prayer. And on this, there should be no ambiguity.

The second area where this discernment is important is at the level of the "heart," as the *Catechism* puts it, the center and source of all prayer. To state it bluntly, there are "saints" within other religions whose lives can be seen to be "temples of the Spirit." This is already true of "Judaism" in, say, the figures of St. Anne and St. Joachim, Mary's mother and father. From being in the presence of such people, we might find an ethos in which prayer and meditation are encouraged. Learning to pray with those who are virtuosos in prayer is the intuition that underlies the call to pray with the saints, living and dead, within the church—for the Spirit resides within human hearts. Hence, learning from the saints in their practices and teachings is enhanced through prayer, for in prayer we genuinely pray with them in so much as we know they are temples of the Spirit. St. Basil says: "The Spirit is truly the dwelling of the saints and the saints are for the Spirit a place where he dwells as in his own home, since they offer themselves as a dwelling place for God and are called his temple."[32] This is why the *Cate-*

chism suggests of the saints and their various spiritualities, that in "their rich diversity they are refractions of the one pure light of the Holy Spirit."[33] I do not want to suggest that we start calling "holy" Muslim and Hindu men and women "saints," for this term is clearly construed as a Christian emblem within a cultic perspective. Rather, in so much as we do experience the presence of God within people from other religions, then we best attend upon this presence with reverence and openness.[34] Such men and women may be, in various and different ways, "refractions of the one pure light of the Holy Spirit," and they, like the saints and our ordinary Christian congregation, may help us pray more deeply and together give glory to God. And through our praying together, we may also learn to love each other more fully through prayerful cohabitation in the Spirit.

Hence, while this point regarding the *gift* of the Holy Spirit may relate to techniques, such as breathing, posture, use of chants, images, and so on, the pulsing life of the gift is witnessing the Spirit's action upon a "humble and contrite heart" (Ps 130:1), and being moved to pray with, and in, this movement of the Spirit.[35] Being open to the gift of the Holy Spirit in the person and prayers of a Muslim is a risk, as it would be in any real situation of vulnerability. Judging such risks is only possible within specific situations and in consultation with others within the church. However, when interreligious prayer is generated organically through crisis, suffering and pain, and through friendship and love, the risk may well be different from sometimes institutionally high-profile interreligious "productions." However, in interreligious prayer, we must recall that prayer, just straightforward Christian ecclesial prayer is always a "battle" against "ourselves and against the wiles of the Tempter who does all he can to turn man away from prayer, away from union with God"—and interreligious prayer is certainly no exception.[36] Our desire for interreligious prayer can mask our jaded or non-existent prayer life and our slow movement away from the difficult wrestling of Jacob with God. On the other hand, as I have begun to suggest, it might be the possible site for a mutual sharing of the gift of the Spirit that might be present in the praying and prayers of the other. The presence of the Spirit calls for attentive discernment, such that our own practices, doctrines, and liturgies might well be called into constructive questioning—leading to greater purification. To see whether this suggestion is plausible, let me turn to the second mark of prayer, covenant relationship:

Covenant: The heart is the place of decision, deeper than our psychic drives. It is the place of truth, where we choose life or death. It is the place of encounter because as image of God we live in relation: it is the place of covenant.

Christian prayer is a covenant relationship between God and man in Christ. It is the action of God and of man, springing forth from both the Holy Spirit and ourselves,

> wholly directed to the Father, in union with the human will of the Son of God made man.[37]

Relationship is key to the covenant, and not accidentally central in the technical vocabulary when speaking of trinitarian love. Created in the image of God, we were created for loving relationship, both for God and for each other—such was the practice of the Son, through the power of the Holy Spirit, who reveals the Father's love so that we could continue to be the "body of Christ." This definition of authentic prayer, as part of covenant relationship, calls for two particular areas of clarification: whether the word "covenant" can be properly applied to other religions (apart from Judaism); and secondly, if it can, does it imply sufficient accord such that interreligious prayer might be justified.

The Christian (and Jewish) tradition has always recognized the beginnings of the covenant as a covenant of cosmic dimensions, made with all humanity represented by Noah (Gen 9:8-16).[38] This means that all creation is in covenant with God, without negating the specific and particular covenants later made with Abraham, Moses and eventually Jesus. What is particularly pertinent to our concern here is the way in which the *Catechism* uses the category of covenant to highlight the value of prayer, and the good and righteous lives found in non-Christian peoples. First, there is a stress on the Noahcite covenant to affirm that an upright and undivided heart constitutes "walking with God." Of this walking, it says: "This kind of prayer is lived by many righteous people in all religions." And it continues: "In his indefectible *covenant* with every living creature (Gen 9:8-16), God has always called people to prayer."[39] This of course does not guarantee that their prayer is genuine, but what the Christian may glimpse in the act of interreligious prayer is the fragmented relationality and perichoresis that can exist between different religions when they come together in love, in the actual process of prayer. This may be a glimpse of a unity that will be enjoyed eschatologically when together, all creation, transformed and redeemed, gives praise to God. This may be a glimpse of the transformation of all signs that will take place in the end days—such that our sense of meaning and significations now are either called into question or reconfigured in fruitful and refreshing ways. To be sure, authentic trinitarian transfiguration has only one outcome: loving communion. Hence, we may conclude that there is a covenant relationship between God and all creatures and therefore, in a very specific and unique sense, possibly between God and all religions.

If there is a shared covenant, can there be sufficient "accord" (Acts 1:14) of heart to justify interreligious prayer? Is interreligious prayer directed toward the same God?[40] And here one is usually impaled upon the horns of a dilemma: if one replies "yes, interreligious prayer is done with one accord," then one is in danger of upholding pluralism or indifferentism as a consequence. However, if one answers "no, interreligious prayer is not done with one accord," then it cannot possibly be justified, whatever the circumstances. If the latter was true, it would certainly not be appropriate to participate in interreligious prayer so as to avoid offending the other who might make this invitation, nor could it be undertaken as a gesture of solidarity during a difficult time. If it is idolatry, it must be resisted. The only reason for undertaking interreligious prayer must be praise and worship of the triune God, not the use of prayer to other social ends.

There are two aspects to this question: what is the relation of formal doctrines and practices within other religions to that spoken of as God within Christianity; and what is the intentionality of those undertaking prayer in another tradition? I need to clarify what might be meant by "intentionality," as there is a long philosophical history to this question. I am using "intentionality" here in three different and related senses, none of which is straight-forwardly transparent to an outsider looking on at the actions of another. The three senses relate to what I will call the intentionality of the heart, the mind, and the will/action. Regarding the heart, the *Catechism* rightly teaches that prayer takes place primarily in the heart:

> The heart is our hidden center, beyond the grasp of our reason and of others; only the Spirit of God can fathom the human heart and know it fully. The heart is the place of decision, deeper than our psychic drives. It is the place of truth, where we choose life or death. It is the place of encounter, because as image of God we live in relation; it is the place of covenant.[41]

At this level, one's intentions might not be explicitly known or finely articulated, yet, nevertheless, the "decisions" of the heart are vital. I would not wish to equate the subconscious with the heart, and the *Catechism* clearly indicates that the heart is "deeper than our psychic drives," but locating intention at this level is helpful in illuminating two features of prayer. First, that those without sophisticated conceptualities, might genuinely participate in prayer without the requirement that they need to be able to articulate conceptually what is going on, or share a complex level of reflexivity regarding doctrinal matters. The Aristotelian emphasis on the priority of knowledge over love has often led to a down-playing of the heart's role. A further effect of this has been that for most of Christian history, the participation of children and the mentally handicapped in prayer has been down-played.[42] The point I want to make is that by highlighting the intentionality of the heart, one must recognize a form of intentionality that cannot be measured by propositional correctness alone regarding the true "object" of our prayers. In commenting on Paul's passage, "likewise the Spirit helps us in our weakness; for we do not know how to pray as we might, but that very Spirit intercedes with sighs too deep for words," Sarah Coakley insightfully suggests that this involves "a certain loss of noetic control to the leading experiential force of the Spirit in the face of our weakness."[43] I would not want to push this so as to bypass the importance of the propositional, but only to contextualize the propositional in a more holistic manner.

The second level of intentionality concerns that of the mind and explicit conceptual knowledge. It is here that the horns of the dilemma are most clearly seen, and in some sense represents two misleading polarities. One misleading polarity can be found in Peter Geach's exclusive stress on propositional knowledge as the sole criterion to authentic worship and prayer.[44] On this criterion, interreligious prayer cannot be done with one accord, as all parties could not say together the Apostle's Creed. For Geach, the matter is thus settled. I think Geach's argument is important. We cannot avoid the fact that different religions are different: in their conceptual, ritual, and ethical dimensions. Each tradition-specific form of enquiry must be taken seriously on its own terms—and none profess a trinitarian God, other than Christianity. However, three qualifications are in order.

First, different traditions are different and are, therefore, not *a priori* commensurate or incommensurate. Positively one can say that while no other tradition affirms the trinity, it is not *a priori* clear that they deny the trinity. Negatively, one might say that in so much as there is a formal denial of the trinity in various historical moments within Judaism and Islam, it is not *a priori* clear that these denials necessarily correspond to what Christians may profess as God's triune reality. This is not to skirt the conceptual problems, but simply to register the complex hermeneutical task in gauging the significance of what is propositionally held within different traditions. Second, propositional contents cannot be decoded apart from the context of their practice. The medieval Christian who proclaims "Jesus is Lord" as he slices off the head of an infidel may understand this statement very differently from a pacifist Mennonite. Likewise, *śūnyata* need not be understood as emptiness in a nihilistic sense, if connected with its realization is the practice of perfect compassion and concern for all sentient beings. The third qualification to Geach's argument would be that he perhaps overestimates the continuity and homogeny within a religious tradition by virtue of a common conceptual creed. As the example above indicates, one cannot *a priori* assume that Christians actually mean the same thing when they recite the creed, both in comparing different periods of Christian history and in comparing contemporary Christians with each other. In conclusion, while the propositional element must be considered carefully, I think Geach comes to a premature ahistorical conclusion.

However, if Geach errs in one direction, the other extreme is perhaps more insidious. There are those who wish to promote interreligious prayer by avoiding the question of common intentionality, and to do so is unpersuasive, for they propose a solution which fails entirely to address the problem. To propose interreligious prayer on subjective grounds, such as common friendship, trust and respect, is to devalue prayer. For instance, Glifford G. Hospital writes movingly of his visit to the South Indian temple of Śrī Padmanābha in Trivandram where he was able to partake in joint worship, given the (shared) sincerity of the Hindu priest in his devotions and reverence. While Hospital's account is moving and important, I think he is rightly questioned by William P. Zion who argues that one cannot base shared prayer on a subjectivist-experiential communality. Zion argues that "intentionality" is the "terminus ad quem" of the prayer, and the subject who prays cannot be divorced from the object of prayer.[45]

One interesting attempt to steer a middle path on this issue is found in a promising article by John Daniels.[46] Daniels makes out an interesting argument that takes intentionality very seriously. He first shows, based on field work in Leeds, England, that if intentionality is an important criterion for shared prayer, then Hindu *pūjā* and Christian prayer are two very different events. However, Daniels then singles out a possible co-intentionality based on the *Bhagavad Gītā*'s notion of acting "without intention" and the Christian Heidegerrian Charles Scott's understanding of prayer as an action "not to intend." This is defined as

> that state of being in which people are united not by allegiance to a common ideology or provenance within a common heritage, but by a shared release into a place of disclosures which are no one's to program.[47]

Hence, in this instance, Daniels argues for co-intentionality when a Hindu and Christian pray "without intention," a possibility that he has found within these particular stands in both traditions.[48] I think that Daniels's argument goes in the right direction, but I have two serious reservations. First, his solution circumvents the tradition-locatedness of each person. Daniels abstracts non-intentional prayer within Hinduism, and non-intentional prayer within Christianity into an identity by robbing this intentioned non-intention of its differing teleological contexts. He seems to acknowledge this when stating this possible objection: that Hindu non-intention viz. the *Gītā* is shaped by Sāṃkhya philosophy, which is quite different from any metaphysical context within Christianity. However, he responds to this problem in an unconvincing manner. He argues that "this does not establish that the condition of non-willing, once attained" is actually different, even if differently arrived at.[49] But it must be, for the very notion of "attainment" is entirely defined by Sāṃkhya philosophy, whereby attainment is freedom from *prakriti*, freedom from matter into pure consciousness and pure being. What Daniels must show for his argument to work is whether there is any overlap with Christianity in this specific attainment in Sāṃkhya/*Gītā* terms. For example, R. C. Zaehner far more plausibly argues that this "attainment" within Sāṃkhya is best understood as the contemplation of the eternal soul, but it certainly cannot be easily equated with relational love regarding a trinitarian "object" of worship and participation.[50] I do not think that Daniels and I are in fundamental disagreement, but I think he reaches a clean resolution a little too quickly.

The second problem takes us a step back to Daniels's discussion of *pūjā* in Leeds, which he sees as incompatible with Christianity on three counts.[51] While there may indeed be an incompatibility, Daniels again makes the case too quickly. I take just one of his examples. In contrast to Hindu *pūjā*, he suggests that Christians cannot accept that worship is crucial to the well-being of the world.[52] In one sense this is correct, for true worship does not ensure the well-being of the world. If no one prayed, the world would carry on. However, all Christian prayer is oriented toward the redemption of all creation, and therefore in one very important sense, is for the well-being of the world. The liturgy is full of such prayers, and the intercessory prayers are often directed toward these issues. Indeed, one might pursue the difference in terms of the ontological status of this "well-being," given the Sāṃkhya denigration of *prakriti*, although admittedly, Christianity's denigration of matter, the flesh, also has a long and complex history. It would be unfair to criticize Daniels's excellent entry into this knotty problem, given the brief compass of his article. I would summarize our main difference as being that I hold that since Christianity and Hinduism are different religions, there is never any pure co-intentionality. If there is any co-intentionality, it will always exist within non-co-intentionality and one should not seek for more, even though one shouldn't set limits to the possibilities that might arise. The question would then be: how much shared co-intentionality justifies the possibility of shared prayer?

I shall be shortly suggesting a more fluid manner in which to relate propositional claims, as I shall be contending that if there is a real engagement with the other, then the meaning of our prayers, or that of the other's, cannot have a fixed and static sense; and if genuine prayer is an openness to the Holy Spirit, then we cannot predefine the meaning that words, gestures, and signs may take within prayer. Furthermore, while this takes propositional intentionality with full seriousness, it also recognizes that meaning is always contexts-determined and therefore, never static.

Finally, the third level of intentionality can be that disclosed in action. The *Catechism* makes it clear that prayer is not a pure interiority that is separable from other aspects of life. It puts the matter strongly: "Prayer and *Christian life* are *inseparable*, for they concern the same love and the same renunciation, proceeding from love."[53] Hence, in the loving action of persons, given that these are not transparent actions, it may well be that there is already a praying together.

The most obvious example is to be found in interreligious marriages, where the shared love of husband and wife, while being of different faiths, is already a testimony (in Christian terms) of their praying together—the prayer of their lives lived. Hence, we need to recognize that praying with "one accord" isn't exclusively a doctrinal matter, but a complex interrelationship between head, heart, and practice—without in any sense wanting to push the three distinctions strongly or to prioritize one over the other.

To attempt to answer our question, let us return to "gift," for in interreligious prayer we speak of the possibility of a double gift: the gift of God's self-presence; and secondly, what each participant brings and shares, our human effort, which may well facilitate God's presence. God's presence, which is pure gift, is always mediated in signs, and signs are constructed by us, even if we have no control over their significatory power. There are then (at least) two dimensions within the dynamics of gift exchange that are pertinent to our question: do we pray with one accord? First, for the Christian, interreligious prayer is an invitation to the Muslim to a real sharing, via Christian prayer, of the most precious gift that we have been given, and one over which we have no control: the presence of the triune God. In this sense the profound missionary dimension and witness afforded in prayer within interreligious prayer cannot be denied or minimized—at least for Christians. This is not to suggest that interreligious prayer be *used* as a strategy for mission. Rather, it is to suggest that prayer with others can be nothing other than a sharing in the gift we have been given, the Spirit's moving within our hearts and praying with us, such that we enter into an ever deepening relationship with the triune God. This also means a similar kind of vulnerability to what the other may have to bring in their prayer. Both parties may be self-deceptive and even be led by the "tempter." This cannot be known without careful discernment and maturity, for we are never free of the temptation to idolatry.

But this leads to the second point: the very notion of "gift" means that we no longer control that which is given and shared. In one sense, every prayer inspired by the Spirit is not under anyone's control, but prayed *with* the Spirit. This has potentially alarming consequences which are not often explored in the literature and closely relate to our question: do we pray with "one accord"? The answer to this question, I shall suggest, must be a resolute "no" *and* "yes," without knowing in advance the weight of such a "no" and "yes," and to some extent not knowing how rigorously we might be able to make such judgments. If the "no" was decisive in a particular situation, then interreligious prayer would be inappropriate.

To focus on this yes/no dialectic, let us imagine an interfaith prayer group of Christians and Muslims, who have met to discuss issues and take common action over events in their community and who have come to know each other quite well. They then begin to pray informally together sometimes using various texts. They pray for good religious relations after difficult social circumstances which have caused mistrust and suspicion between the different religious communities. The *Fātiḥa* (the opening verses of the Qur'an—cited at the beginning of this section) is prayed at the start of one such meeting. When Muslims pray this prayer, it has a rich tapestry of associations and resonances which will inform its meaning and practice. Christians praying this prayer with their Muslim friends will not be doing so "as Muslims" in the sense that they do not share the fabric of beliefs and practices within which their Muslim friends pray this prayer. The requirement that the partners have exactly the same relationship to the prayer is both unrealistic and deeply objectionable.[54] Hence, when Christians pray the *Fātiḥa* with Muslims, while sharing a number of common overlapping senses, Christians may also have in mind that much of the Muslim tradition has identified the final line as referring to Christians ("those who are astray"). Many Muslim authorities read this line as castigating Christians for their belief that Jesus was the Son of God. This is just one of a myriad of difficulties that Christians may sense, and one which may be shared or will be shared with Muslim friends if this is to be a real friendship.[55]

Hence, if a Christian prays this prayer with a Muslim, it will be with Muslim resonances in mind, but a Christian will pray the *Fātiḥa* in so much as he can affirm only *some* of these resonances; and by the fact of praying it as a Christian, he also introduces *novel resonances* to the prayer, echoes emanating from the Christian tradition. Through saying the *Fātiḥa*, the gift of words that has been given and shared in an act of interreligious prayer, differing meanings and significations can be generated for both Muslim and Christian praying this together, without necessarily denying the association that the prayer has in its complex historical contexts. These further significations, which to the Christian may be interpreted as the Holy Spirit's inspiration, can be generated in a number of ways: for instance, by the juxtaposition of prayers: the *Fātiḥa* followed by the "Our Father," in the same way in which the antiphons from the New Testament or spiritual writers are juxtaposed with Psalms in the *Divine Office*, which generate multiple meanings, many of which would not have been present in those texts if taken in isolation, but are generated by a new semantic field created by bringing together these different texts. Saying the *Divine Office* shows this clearly. One might say the same psalm over a year with very different antiphons, and on very different feast days and ceremonies. During each occasion, the various juxtapositions will generate numerous open-ended significations. This of course may also mean that the Christian might have very different insights into his *own* Christian prayers via the process of uncontrolled juxtapositions with Muslim prayers. This is part of the "loving risk" that interreligious prayer entails. Of course, there is a danger of eisegesis (simply reading out of the text whatever we wish) rather than allowing new forms of possibly inspired praying exegesis, whereby the praying of the text itself, through the Spirit, moves our heart and shapes our mind and practice in an unpredictable fashion toward deeper communion with God.

In this risky process, and in a way that cannot be predetermined, it may then be that both Muslim and Christian are praying, however *imperfectly* and *fragmentarily*, with "one accord." This accord can never be more than that, while the Christian remains a faithful Christian and the Muslim remains a faithful Muslim. In one sense, if the heart is the seat of prayer, the judgment upon my claim here will lie only with God—which does not of course relieve us of the complex and difficult task of this discussion. However, this accord is not just in terms of the subjective good feelings that co-worshipers may well have, or in terms of the heart alone, but also in relation to explicit intentionality regarding the "object" of prayer, for there would have to be some overlap in beliefs, or just enough to sustain praying together for interreligious prayer to be considered; but certainly not enough to warrant the Muslim becoming a Christian, or vice versa, and certainly not enough to endorse indifferentism or pluralism. Hence, despite the profound differences, the Christian may therefore share with the Muslim, as Vatican II puts it, the adoration of "one God, living and enduring, merciful and all powerful, Maker of heaven and earth and Speaker to men."[56] And in sharing this adoration through prayer, a Christian may be all the more sensitive to the workings of the Holy Spirit within Islam, and be able to understand Islam more sympathetically—and critically—for praying together allows us uniquely to sense the heart of the people we pray with. Hence, there may be a real sharing of the Islamic reverence for the "majesty" and "compassion" of God—even if strictly speaking, this sense of majesty and compassion might not accord fully with a Muslim's sense of these terms. Consequently, there is in a *fragmentary* and *imperfect* manner, a praying with "one accord," a shared reverence for the one God, not only in some sense of doctrinal and practical overlap—although when taken as organic wholes there is none—but also through the common concern that brings such people together, a concern which is itself shaped by desiring to follow God's will. If no such overlap, no such moments of co-intentionality were at all possible, then the church's teaching about other religions would be utter projection, rather than bearing some real relation to the religions in question.[57] Equally, if there were not sufficient overlap and sufficient co-intentionality in the manner defined above, then it would not be proper to take part in interreligious prayer in such circumstances. Such decisions would be required by local churches in fraternity with the wider church.

In speaking, as I have, of "overlaps" and a measure of "one accord," Christian participation in interreligious prayer should not rest easy with finding lowest common denominators, for if abstracted from the whole they become artificial, lifeless, and uninteresting; and the "whole" for the Christian faith is formed through the trinitarian God who calls his people into loving communion in the church. This takes us to the final mark of Christian prayer: communion.

> *Communion:* Thus, the life of prayer is the habit of being in the presence of the thrice-holy God and in communion with him. This communion of life is always possible because, through Baptism, we have already been united with Christ (Cf. Rom 6:5). Prayer is *Christian*

> insofar as it is communion with Christ and extends throughout the Church, which is his Body. Its dimensions are those of Christ's love (Cf. Eph 3:18-21).[58]

While I have been arguing that interreligious prayer may be done imperfectly and fragmentarily with one accord and in this sense might be legitimate, we must now confront a further dimension of the same question, perhaps the greatest stumbling block to interreligious prayer: the uniqueness of Christ and the centrality of the trinity. Is it right to take part in interreligious prayer if trinitarian and specifically Jesus-centered prayers are omitted for fear of alienating Muslims, or for offending their beliefs? For example, we might turn to Kenneth Cragg's inspiring and important collection of Christian and Muslim prayers for interreligious contexts, *Alive to God*. Cragg studiously avoids *Tasliyah* (salutation of Muhammad, greetings of his "Companions" and petitions about "dying as a Muslim") in his choice of Muslim prayers. He also omits trinitarian prayers or prayers containing the phrase "through Jesus Christ our Lord" in his choice of Christian prayers. Cragg tries to justify these omissions with two arguments. First, he argues that in the context of interreligious prayer, "these questions are in suspension—not in indifference or neglect, but in suspension, in the sense that they do not have to be answered within the terms of the enterprise in hand."[59] Second, that the "name" of Christ, following Philippians 2:5-11, need not be understood as always having explicitly to use the "name" Christ, but the point of Paul's passage is that the Christ status is borne through suffering and kenotic love: "the Messiah will energize Messianic community to perpetuate his saving secret and to follow the pattern of his humility."[60] I find Cragg's second argument convincing on exegetical grounds and it also coheres with the ecclesiocentric grounding that I have been trying to give both trinitarian and Christological doctrines. However, the first argument, despite Cragg's intentions, implies that we may also have to suspend our hearts and minds and body in prayer, for the real achievement of "one accord" is praying together *despite* these differences, rather than by means of suspending them. Precisely, some of these problems and differences may be addressed through shared prayer—and their exclusion from such prayer is oddly artificial.

Cragg's intentions are noble, but I wonder whether the highly selective use of Christian prayers obscures the intention of genuine Christian prayer: communion with "the thrice-holy God." In one sense, it is surely disrespectful to share anything but the most profound heart of our faith—communion with Father, Son, and Spirit—in interreligious prayer. Furthermore, even if we could get around the problem of the explicit naming of Christ or trinity such as when the "Our Father" is used in interreligious prayer, we cannot sidestep the issue that when we pray to God, we are speaking of God as trinitarian, revealed through the particularity of Jesus

Christ, and the Muslim is not—and non-theists are probably not even speaking of "God" at all.

The *Catechism* makes it absolutely clear that praying *to* Jesus, *through* him, and *with* him, constitutes the centrality of Christian prayer, be it communal, personal, vocal, or interior.[61] But this Christological focus is not a matter of linguistic correctness, for as Cragg properly understands, invoking the name of Jesus by itself means nothing, for "No one can say 'Jesus is Lord,' except by the Holy Spirit."[62] This also makes it clear that Christological problems are always properly trinitarian—and ecclesial. Hence, in one very important sense, just as when we say the "Our Father" we do not use the name of Jesus explicitly even though this very prayer is considered *the* Christian prayer,[63] there is no necessary scandal if explicitly Christological or trinitarian prayers are omitted in interreligious prayer, where, for example, the Prayer of St. Francis might well be the most apt, or a Psalm, or the "Our Father." If the "Our Father" were to be used in interreligious prayer, then a whole range of meanings will inform the co-praying of it, just as with a Psalm or St. Francis's prayer. There will be both continuity and discontinuity, overlap and difference between the Muslim and Christian in praying together—and such tensions are unlikely to be resolved. As I have suggested, depending on the balance of these tensions, praying with "one accord" may be possible, in however fragmentary and imperfect a manner.

However, there is something to be said for keeping these very profound differences *explicit* within interreligious prayer, as part of our real sharing—contrary to Cragg's well-intentioned strategy of shedding all such difficult references. In the context of interreligious prayer, those who come together may well be acutely aware of the differences between them such as trinitarian representation, or claims regarding Muhammed, but nevertheless may still wish to pray together, knowing too that they have much to share, without suspending or denying these differences and difficulties. Such praying together bears the marks of Jacob's wrestling with the living God, rather than a comfortable interreligious prayer meeting where we might all feel a warm euphoria, but at the cost of a cold or tepid heart toward God and neighbor. In both instances, when the explicit name of Jesus is used, or not, in interreligious prayer, we must still face the question: can we pray with one accord when the triune God is not the explicit "object" of worship of our partner? If Jesus Christ is not affirmed as Lord, can there finally be any real accord?

This is a difficult and complex question and I will gesture toward two avenues for further positive exploration without attempting a resolution. One avenue lies in the fact that since Vatican II, relentlessly reiterated by John Paul II, there has been a clear teaching that "we are obliged to hold that the Holy Spirit offers everyone the possibility of sharing in the Paschal Mystery in a manner known to God."[64] This was developed and defended in the previous chapter. This means that the presence of the Holy Spirit must in *some manner* entail the reality of Christ's presence, and therefore the Father's presence, within a person's life and within the semiotic configurations that form their religious culture. There have been numerous theories proposed by Catholic theologians to explain this claim, ranging from Rahner's anonymous Christianity, to the old nature-grace explanation found in van Straelen, to that of de Lubac, Congar's and von Balthasar's affirmation of supernatural "presence" without the entailments of Rahner's theory.[65] For the moment it is not necessary to attend to these different theories, for all I am concerned to do here is suggest that if relations and perichoresis are taken seriously, then it is impossible to claim that the Spirit is present, without at the same time claiming that Christ, the kingdom, and the Father are also present, even if "inchoately," as is maintained in *Redemptoris Missio* 17-20; 28-9.[66]

If this much is acknowledged regarding relations and perichoresis, even if we are not here able to elaborate the details of these connections, then there may be grounds for supporting interreligious prayer on the basis that there is at least an inchoate intentionality toward the triune God, or in other words, what I have been calling an "imperfect" and "fragmentary" possibility of common desire, generated and nourished by God's desire for us. Clearly, this line of argument would need very careful development.

A second avenue requiring further exploration, which is not unconnected to the above, focuses on the mode of trinitarian presence within acts of real love and charity. This is not to reduce doctrine to praxis, as has been done by some strands of liberation theology in the theology of religions, nor to replace prayer with action.[67] All forms of action are always part of tradition narratives such that actions cannot be divorced from their narrative context. The *Catechism* is clear that:

> Prayer and *Christian life* are *inseparable* for they concern the same love and the same renunciation, proceeding from love; the same filial and loving conformity with the Father's plan of love; the same transforming union in the Holy Spirit who conforms us more and more to Christ Jesus; the same love for all men, the love with which Jesus loved us.[68]

If prayer and life are rightly inseparable for the Christian, then it may also be true for others. Hence, when we are confronted with the life stories and prayers from other traditions which, however imperfectly, but often so much more perfectly than us Christians, reflect charity, compassion, and suffering love—we are called to humble attentiveness. Unless we wish to remain hard-hearted, it is quite possible that we will glimpse and share the secret of such love within other traditions only when we pray together, and thereby be given more fully the gift of the source and goal of all love: the triune God. In an important sense then, through being co-involved in acts of justice, charity, and compassion, interreligious prayer may seem an entirely appropriate site where the meeting of hearts can join together, and the common cause of such action may then justify interreligious prayer as praying with "one accord"—however fragmentarily and imperfectly.

There is something very disturbing about the reality of love refusing to be controlled by our theorizing. Aquinas properly saw that charity, *caritas,* was a participation in divine love, and unlike faith and hope, which are always mediated here, love would remain unchanged within the beatific state.[69] Aquinas was speaking of love within a Christian context, but many will have met God's love through friendship (and often marriage) with those from other religions, so that a qualified extension of Aquinas's point is not entirely inappropriate. This is not to obscure the fact that for Aquinas, as well as contemporary Catholicism, we still retain the belief that it is the trinitarianly narrated God who most properly teaches us to love, and true charity is impossible without this proper *telos* and formation. However, if we are not open to finding the reality of redeeming love outside the church, then we have *a priori* limited God's freedom to act with love. What one can remain sure of is that such free acting by God will never involve revoking his covenant with us. Perhaps an analogy will help. The Catholic church only used to permit interreligious marriage if the non-Catholic partner suspended their identity during the marriage service. Now, it allows that an interreligious marriage within the Church may properly reflect the covenant of suffering and passionate love between the triune God and the two partners without requiring the partners to hide their real identity. And if this is possible with the integrity of the non-Catholic partner being respected, then is it not possible that interreligious prayer may be analogous to extending our celebration of the covenant which is principally celebrated through the church, to those outside the church, for the "dimensions" of Christ's love are greater than we can ever know?[70] Hence, when interreligious prayer is done with a reverence and devotion to God in real love of God, with the consequent thirst for greater love between people, which always stems from and is nourished by a greater love of God, then in love's celebration of love by the lovers, we glimpse the reality of the trinity in human community—even if not by common accord in name, but by one accord in the heart of love.

ON FINISHING WITHOUT CONCLUSIONS

God rebuked Moses, saying: "I am God, I fell sick; thou camest not."
Moses said: "O transcendent One, thou art clear of defect, what mystery is this? Explain, O Lord."
God said unto him again: "Wherefore didst thou not kindly ask after me when I was sick?"
He answered: "O Lord, thou never ailest. My understanding is lost: unfold the meaning of these words."

> God said: "Yea, a favorite and chosen slave of mine fell sick. I am he. Consider well: his infirmity is my infirmity, his sickness is my sickness" (Jalal Al-Din Rūmī).[71]

Thérèse of Lisieux, with whom we started, saw that her relationships with those around her, even if it was within the fixed environment of a Carmel, constituted the arena whereby that love that was poured upon her might be shared, and freshly discovered, even if she did not always like those who shared the arena! She writes: "Your love, Jesus, is an ocean with no shore to bound it; and if I plunge into it, I carry with me all the possessions I have. You know, Lord, what those possessions are—the souls you have seen fit to link with mine; nothing else."[72]

I have been suggesting that plunging into the love of the triune God may well call us to risk finding an even greater love of God through interreligious prayer, and into discovering the darkness and mystery of God afresh. Our marriage to our Lord, may itself suffer infidelity in an absolute resistance to the promptings of suffering love which might entail interreligious prayer. But equally, interreligious prayer may also be an act of irreverent infidelity. The church is called to pray fervently for those who engage in interreligious prayer for the sake of Christ. All I have sought to suggest is that under certain conditions such a risk in some circumstances is more than worthwhile, indeed it is a risk that Jesus' reckless love calls us to take. Discerning those situations where interreligious prayer should be encouraged is first the task for the local church and its bishops, and then the universal church, for the blessings that may come through such participation are blessings for the whole church, or they are not blessings at all.

None of the above either attempts to erase difference or otherness, nor obscure the ways in which prayer is always related to the social formation of religions which are fundamentally different. Neither does the above attempt to offer a grand theory of the religions, either affirming all of them positively or criticizing them all negatively. We are, thankfully, not God and cannot know the prudential meaning of religious diversity, if indeed there is any such meaning, but we do know that God's trinity calls Christians to seek to serve and worship this God in sometimes quite unpredictable ways.

Notes

1. Thérèse of Lisieux, *Autobiography of a Saint*, trans. Ronald Knox, Fontana, London, 1958, 244.

2. This is perhaps why the doctrine of original sin requires the doctrine of the immaculate conception, for only a sinless Mary could have raised a sinless son. Augustine, in his close and complex watching of the interaction of infants and mothers makes some insightful and perplexing observations: *Confessions*, trans. R. S. Pine-Coffin, Penguin, London, 1961, Book 1, 6.

3. *Catechism of the Catholic Church*, Geoffrey Chapman, London, 1994: 2559, 2563, and 2565 respectively.

4. *A Statement on Inter-Faith Services*, British Council of Churches (subsequently BCC), 1968; *Can we Pray Together? Guidelines on Worship in a Multi-Faith Society*, BCC, 1983. For the Anglican communion, the most important documents are: *Report of a Working Group on Interfaith Service and Worship*, in *Ends and Odds*, No. 22, March, 1980; *Multi-Faith Worship?*, Church House Publishing, London, 1992, and the subsequent response by the house of bishops: *Multi-Faith Worship? Guidance on the Situations which Arise*, GS Misc. 411, Church House, London, 1993. For the English history and background see: *Multi-Faith Worship?*, 11-7; Marcus Braybrooke, ed., *Inter-Faith Worship*, Galliard, London, 1974, 3-7.

5. Readers should consult *Bulletin*, 64, 1987, and subsequent issues of the journal to see how the question of interreligious prayer keeps resurfacing.

6. *An Observance for Commonwealth Day*, Monday, 14 March, 1994, preface.

7. See Christopher Lamb, "The Experience of Interfaith Prayer," *The Way Supplement: Interfaith Spirituality*, 78, 1993, 81-8 for a helpful commentary on the Open Letter. See also, *Interfaith Update*, the occasional bulletin of the Open Letter Group, and *Prophecy Today*, 8, 5, 1992, which is published with the heading: "Anglican Church turns to Other Gods" (an odd use of capital G?), and *Prophecy Today*, 9, 1, 1993, which also includes Archbishop Carey's reply to Clifford Hill's criticisms of the Westminster Observance and Archbishop Carey's support of the event.

8. Lamb, "The Experience," 83. Lamb's phrase "praying with Muslim, Sikh, or Hindu patients in hospital" (83) does not necessarily mean interreligious prayer (as defined below by me). This is akin to atheists or agnostics becoming members of a choir to sing Handel's *Messiah*. This could hardly count as interreligious prayer.

9. See *Findings of an Exploratory Consultation on Interreligious Prayer*, jointly arranged by the Pontifical Council for Interreligious Dialogue and the Office on Inter-Religious Relations of the WCC, 1966, 1; Paul Knitter, *One Earth Many Religions*, Orbis, Maryknoll, N.Y., 1995, 167-81; *Pro Mundi Vita Bulletin*, January 1982, contains an account of interreligious prayer in India, esp. 8-10; and Braybrooke, ed., *Worship*, 2-3, 6-7.

10. *Catechism* 2792.

11. See Mariasusai Dhavamony, *Christian Theology of Religions*, Peter Lang, Berlin, 1998, 238-40 on this distinction. One should also be sensitive to the fact that these distinctions may or may not have parallels in, say, the Muslim difference between *ṣalāt* (ritual prayer) and *dua'* (non-ritual prayer), or the Hindu practice of *pūjā* which need not require a priest and can be carried out at home in a wide manner of practices. For Islam, see Cragg's interesting discussion and his use of prayers from Islam from the context of *dua'*: *Alive to God*, Oxford University Press, London, 1970; also Michael L. Fitzgerald & Robert Caspar, *Signs of Dialogue: Christian Encounters with Muslims*, Silsilch Publishers, Samboanga City, 1992, ch. 5, "Christian Liturgy and Islamic Texts," 105-28. For Hindu prayer/*pūjā* in Britain, see Kim Knott, *Hinduism in Leeds*, University of Leeds, Leeds, 1986; and Judith Law, *The Religious Beliefs and Practices of Hindus in Derby*, University of Leeds, Leeds, 1990. For a general survey, see Geoffrey Parrinder, *Worship in the World Religions*, Faber & Faber, London, 1961; and the classic study by Friedrich

Heiler, *Prayer: A Study in the History and Psychology of Religion*, Oxford University Press, Oxford, 1932. While dated in many ways, this is still a remarkable and pioneering work. However, Heiler operates with pluralist (theistic pietist) assumptions that often run against his alleged scientific objectivity. Nevertheless, I would agree with him, as with Von Hügel whom he quotes in this regard, that real prayer in the world religions testifies to the " 'prevenience and givenness' of the grace of God" (iv).

12. Secretariat pro Non-Christianis, *Guidelines for a Dialogue between Muslims and Christians*, Edizion Ancora, Rome, 1971 (1st ed. 1969), 140.

13. Much of the literature cited in note 4, re UK churches, calls such events "serial interfaith worship"; for example *Multi-Faith Worship?*, 49ff.

14. See *Bulletin*, 64, 1987, which contains all the texts from the Assisi meeting; and the account of two Buddhists who were present at Assisi in *Bulletin*, 93, 1996, 350-3.

15. Program for 1994, preface.

16. *Findings*, 1. Forthcoming: *Bulletin*, 98, 2, 1998.

17. *Findings*, 1.

18. *Findings*, 1-2.

19. This would be my main criticism of *Can We Pray Together?* and *Multi-Faith Worship?*: In *Multi-Faith Worship?*, paragraph 38, for example, it is surely illegitimate to use Naaman, Jethro, Nebuchadnezzar, and the people of Nineveh to suggest any support for interreligious prayer, as in all instances they actually acknowledge Israel's God as the true God—a dynamic which has no analogy within interreligious prayer. While Malachi 1:11 might well bear the interpretation suggested in the document, it is difficult to see it as anything other than Malachi's contrasting the depths to which Israel has fallen—and the remaining extremely exclusivist book of Malachi certainly runs against placing overmuch weight upon 1:1 as is too often done.

20. "Indifferentism" was first officially used by Leo XII in *Ubi Primum* (1824) [DZ 2720], and then by subsequent popes up to the present day to condemn what I have been calling "pluralism" in Part I. See also pp. 132-8 above.

21. I have been cautiously critical of Aloysius Pieris (Sri Lanka) and Felix Wilfred (India) on this account, even though I am sympathetic to many of their conclusions. See "*Nostra Aetate*—Telling God's Story in Asia: Promises and Pitfalls," in Leo Kenis, ed., *Vatican II*, Leuven, forthcoming; and in more detail on Wilfred in "Inculturation, India, and Other Religions," in *Studia Missionalia*, 44, 1995, 121-47.

22. I have drawn so heavily from the *Catechism* simply because the section on prayer is so good.

23. *Catechism* 2573 indicates that from Genesis 32:36 "the spiritual tradition of the Church has retained the symbol of prayer as a battle of faith and as the triumph of perseverance."

24. *Nostra Aetate* 3-4.

25. *Catechism* 2559, citing Romans 8:26 and Augustine, *Sermo* 56, 6, 9, respectively.

26. *Catechism* 2560, citing Augustine, *De diversis quaestionibus octoginta tribus* 64, 4.

27. *Findings*, 4, lines 1-3 fail to make this relation clear, which in the context of interreligious relations is problematic. See *Redemptoris Missio* 17-18, criti-

cizing the uncoupling of the church and trinity to the "kingdom," while acknowledging the kingdom's presence outside the visible church. Even more significantly, *Redemptoris Missio* 29 insists on the incomprehensibility of detaching the Spirit from Christ, esp., "Whatever the Spirit brings about in human hearts and in the history of peoples, in cultures and religions serves as a preparation for the Gospel, and can only be understood in reference to Christ." This is said while clearly acknowledging the presence of the Holy Spirit outside the church, even from before the time of Christ. I have discussed this in "The Kingdom and a Trinitarian Ecclesiology," in Paul Mojzes and Leonard Swidler, ed., *Christian Mission and Interreligious Dialogue*, Edwin Mellen Press, New York, 1991, 51-61. See also Kevin Vanhoozer's perceptive criticisms of such a tendency in "Does the Trinity Belong in a Theology of Religions? On Angling in the Rubicon and the 'Identity' of God," in Kevin Vanhoozer, ed., *The Trinity in a Pluralistic Age*, W. B. Eerdmans, Grand Rapids, 1997, 41-71; although his Lutheran position has difficulty explaining how the Spirit could be at all operative before the coming of Christ.

28. John Paul II, "Address to the Roman Curia," 22 December 1986, *Bulletin*, 64, 1987, 60. There had been some criticisms of interpretations of the Assisi meeting within Vatican circles.

29. Regarding Assisi it is clear that John Paul II did not see this event as interreligious prayer: "For this reason the formula chosen for the gathering at Assisi is: being together in order to pray. Certainly we cannot 'pray together,' namely to make a common prayer, but we can be present whilst others pray." *Bulletin*, 64, 1987, 22.

30. See *Bulletin*, 75, 1990, 262-6 for a helpful contextualization of this Congregation for the Doctrine of Faith document by Bishop Michael Fitzgerald of the Pontifical Council for Interreligious Dialogue.

31. See as an introduction, *Silence and Stillness in Every Season: Daily Readings with John Main*, Paul Harris, ed., Darton, Longman & Todd, London, 1998.

32. Cited in *Catechism* 2684, from *De Spiritu Sancto*, 26, 62.

33. *Catechism* 2684.

34. See David Matzko's critique of calling Gandhi a "saint" in "Postmodernity, Saints and Scoundrels," *Modern Theology*, 9, 1, 1993, 19-36, esp. 33-6.

35. Ps 130:1 is cited in *Catechism* 2559 as the prerequisite to prayer.

36. *Catechism* 2725.

37. *Catechism* 2563, 2564.

38. This is curiously overlooked in the entry on "Covenant" in *Sacramentum Mundi*, Vol. 2, by Henri Cazelles. For the Noachite covenant, see David Novak, *The Image of the Non-Jew in Judaism*, Toronto Studies in Theology, Edwin Mellen Press, New York, 1983, ch. 1.

39. *Catechism* 2569.

40. See Paul's usage of the phrase "one accord" in Philippians 2:2, and St. John Chrysostom's usage that is found in the Anglican Book of Common Prayer: "Almighty God, who hast given us grace at this time with one accord to make our common supplications unto thee."

41. *Catechism* 2563.

42. Christianity, in fact, redeemed children from their inferior status within Greek society, especially with the introduction of infant baptism. See Thomas Wiedemann, *Adults and Children in the Roman Empire*, Yale University

Press, London/New Haven, 1989. However, the Enlightenment began to erode this tradition; see David Cunningham, *These Three Are One: The Practice of Trinitarian Theology*, Blackwell, Oxford, 1998, 288-97. Cunningham's book is one of the very few to attend to children within the context of systematic theology. For another very helpful treatment, see Stanley Hauerwas, *Naming the Silence: God, Medicine and the Problem of Suffering*, T. & T. Clark, Edinburgh, 1993, 1-39.

43. See Sarah Coakley, "Living into the Mystery of the Holy Trinity: Trinity, Prayer, and Sexuality," *Anglican Theological Review*, LXXX, 2, 1998, 223-232, 227.

44. Peter Geach, "On Worshipping the Right God," in Peter Geach, *God and the Soul*, Routledge & Kegan Paul, London, 1969, ch. 8.

45. William P. Zion, "Response to Hospital" (93-7; 93) in response to Clifford G. Hospital, "Christian *Pūjā*?" *Toronto Journal of Theology*, Spring 1985, 1, 1, 80-92.

46. John Daniels, "With One Accord? Some Reflections on Multi-faith Worship," *Theology*, August, 1997, 252-9.

47. Daniels, "Accord?" 258.

48. Daniels, "Accord?" 258.

49. Daniels, "Accord?" 257.

50. R. C. Zaehner, *Mysticism Sacred and Profane*, Clarendon Press, Oxford, 1957, chs. 6, 7, esp. 124-8.

51. Daniels, "Accord?" 255-6.

52. Daniels, "Accord?" 256.

53. *Catechism* 2745.

54. See John Paul II's commentary on Assisi regarding the prayers of others: "We respect this prayer even though we do not intend to make our own formulae that express other views of faith. Nor would the others on their part wish to adopt our prayers" (*Bulletin*, 64, 1987, 22). This must be balanced by another statement of his regarding the sharing of the spiritual resources within prayer: "When circumstances permit, it means a sharing of spiritual experiences and insights. This sharing can take the form of coming together as brothers and sisters to pray to God in ways which safeguard the uniqueness of each religious tradition" (*Bulletin*, 64, 1987, 24).

55. Other difficulties may include the reference to Judaism in this same last line of the prayer; the fact that the *Fātiḥa* marks the beginning of *ṣalāt* prayers in the mosque; the authority of the Qur'an from which the prayer is said, and its interpretation and injunctions upon a whole range of theological and practical issues. See further, William Montgomery Watt, *Muslim-Christian Encounters: Perceptions and Misperceptions*, Routledge, London, 1991. I use "he" in what follows to indicate that many Christian-Muslim meetings are marked, more than usually, by the presence of men.

56. *Nostra Aetate* 3.

57. Clearly religions cannot be treated as static entities, so that one can automatically be assured of finding "goodness" and "truth" within a religion *per se*, for this presence is always dependent on the free initiative of God.

58. *Catechism* 2565.

59. Cragg, *Alive*, 21.

60. Cragg, *Alive*, 26.

61. *Catechism* 2663-2669.

62. *Catechism* 2670, citing 1 Cor 12:3.

63. *Catechism* 2761.

64. *Gaudium et Spes* 10, 15, 22; *Redemptoris Missio* 28.

65. See bibliographical references and my outline of these positions in David F. Ford, ed., *The Modern Theologians*, (2nd ed.), Blackwell, Oxford, 1997, 626-45.

66. See my discussion in chapter 4 above; and my article, "Revelation and 'revelations'," *Modern Theology*, 1994, 165-84.

67. See my critique of Knitter in chapter 1 above, and also see Hans urs von Balthasar's engaging critique of the move to view prayer as action in Medard Kehl and Werner Löser, eds. *The von Balthasar Reader*, T. & T. Clark, Edinburgh, 1982, 326-47; the latter part of these reflections are especially pertinent to our concerns here.

68. *Catechism* 2745.

69. Thomas Aquinas, *Summa Theologia*, 2a2ae. 27,4 and 26, 1 & 2.

70. *Catechism* 2565.

71. From *Mathnawi*, cited in Kenneth Cragg, *Alive*, 99.

72. *Autobiography*, 242.

Bibliography

Abbott, Walter M., ed. *The Documents of Vatican II*, Guild Press, New York, 1966.

Abe, Masao. *Buddhism and Interfaith Dialogue*, Steven Heine, ed., University of Hawaii Press, Honolulu, 1995.

Allen, Prudence. *The Concept of Woman: The Aristotelian Revolution 750 BC - AD 1250*, Eden Press, Quebec, 1985.

Animanda. *The Blade: The Life and Work of Brahmabandhab Upadhyay*, Roy & Son, Calcutta, n.d.

Aquinas, Thomas. *Summa Theologiae*, Blackfriars/Eyre & Spottiswoode, London/ McGraw-Hill Book Co., New York, 1976.

Arapura, J. G. *Radhakrishnan and Integral Experience*, Asia Publishing House, London, 1966.

Augustine, St. *Confessions*, trans. R. S. Pine-Coffin, Penguin, London, 1961.

Barnes, Philip. "Continuity and Development in John Hick's Theology," *Studies in Religion*, 21, 4, 1992, 395-402.

Barrett, C. K. *The Gospel According to John*, SPCK, London, 1978, 2nd ed.

Barthes, Roland. *Mythologies*, Paladin, London, 1983.

Braybrooke, Marcus. *Inter-faith Worship*, Galliard, London, 1974.

British Council of Churches. *A Statement on Inter-Faith Services*, British Council of Churches, London, 1968.

——— *Can we Pray Together? Guidelines on Worship in a Multi-Faith Society*, British Council of Churches, London, 1983.

Brockington, J. L. *The Sacred Thread*, University Press of Edinburgh, Edinburgh, 1981.

Brown, Raymond E. *The Gospel according to John. I-XII*, Geoffrey Chapman, London, 1971.

——— *The Gospel according to John. XIII-XXI*, Geoffrey Chapman, London, 1971.

——— *The Community of the Beloved Disciple*, Geoffrey Chapman, London, 1979.

Browning, R. "Reasons and Intuition in Radhakrishnan's Philosophy" in P. A. Schilpp, ed., *Radhakrishnan*, 1952, 173-279.

Buckley, Michael J. *At the Origins of Modern Atheism*, Yale University Press, New Haven, Connecticut, 1987.

Bulletin, Pontifical Consilium pro Dialogo Inter Religiones, 64, 1987, Assisi texts.

Bulletin, Pontifical Consilium pro Dialogo Inter Religiones, 98, 1998, "Interreligious Prayer."

Bultmann, Rudolf. *The Gospel of John. A Commentary*, Blackwell, Oxford, 1971.

Burrows, William, ed. *Redemption and Dialogue*, Orbis, Maryknoll, N.Y., 1993.
Cabezón, José Ignacio. *Buddhism and Language. A Study of Indo-Tibetan Scholasticism*, State University of New York, Albany, 1994.
Catechism of the Catholic Church, Geoffrey Chapman, London, 1994.
Church of England. *Multi-Faith Worship?* Church House Publishing, London, 1992.
——— *Multi-Faith Worship? Guidance on the Situations which Arise*, GS Misc. 411, Church House, London, 1993.
Coakley, Sarah. "Living into the Mystery of the Holy Trinity: Trinity, Prayer and Sexuality," *Anglican Theological Review*, LXXX, 2, 1998, 223-32.
Cohn-Sherbok, Dan. *Issues in Contemporary Judaism*, Macmillan, London, 1991.
——— *The Future of Judaism*, T. & T. Clark, Edinburgh, 1994.
——— *Judaism and Other Faiths*, Macmillan, London, 1994.
——— *Modern Judaism*, Macmillan, London, 1996.
Commission for Monastic Interfaith Dialogue (MID). *Contemplation and Interfaith Dialogue*, MID, 1995.
Commission for Religious Relations with the Jews. *We Remember: A Reflection on the Shoah*, Vatican City, Vatican, 1998.
Compson, Jane. "The Dalai Lama and the World Religions," *Religious Studies*, 32, 1996, 271-9.
Conze, Edward. "Buddhism: The Mahāyāna" in R. C. Zaehner, ed., *The Concise Encyclopedia of Living Faiths*, Hutchinson, London, 1971, 2nd ed., 293-317.
Cousins, Ewert. "The Trinity and World Religions," *Journal of Ecumenical Studies*, 7, 1990, 476-98.
Coward, Harold. *Pluralism: Challenge to World Religions*, Orbis, Maryknoll, N.Y., 1985.
Cragg, Kenneth. *Alive to God*, Oxford University Press, London, 1970.
Cullmann, Oscar. *Christ and Time: The Christian Conception of Time and History*, SCM, London, 1952.
Cunningham, David. *These Three Are One: The Practice of Trinitarian Theology*, Blackwell, Oxford, 1998.
Dalai Lama, His Holiness, the Fourteenth / Tenzin Gyatso. *Universal Responsibility and the Good Heart*, Library of Tibetan Works and Archives, Dharamsala, 1980.
——— *An Interview with the Dalai Lama*, John F. Avedon, ed., Littlebird Publications, New York, 1980.
——— *Kindness, Clarity and Insight*, Snow Lion, New York, 1984.
——— *The Bodhgaya Interviews*, José Ignacio Cabezón, ed., Snow Lion, New York, 1988.
——— *The Good Heart: A Buddhist Perspective on the Teachings of Jesus*, Wisdom, New York, 1996.
Daniélou, Jean. *Holy Pagans of the Old Testament*, Longman, Green & Co., London, 1957.
Daniels, John. "With One Accord? Some Reflections on Multi-faith Worship," *Theology*, August, 1997, 252-9.
Davies, Michael. *The Second Vatican Council and Religious Liberty*, Neumann Press, Minnesota, 1992.
D'Costa, Gavin. *Theology and Religious Pluralism*, Blackwell, Oxford, 1986.

——— *John Hick's Theology of Religions*, University Press of America, London/New York, 1987.

——— "The Kingdom and a Trinitarian Ecclesiology: An Analysis of Soteriocentrism," in Paul Mojzes and Leonard Swidler, eds., *Christian Mission and Interreligious Dialogue*, Edwin Mellen Press, New York, 1990, 51-61.

——— " 'Extra ecclesiam nulla salus' revisited" in Ian Hamnett, ed., *Religious Pluralism and Unbelief: Studies Critical and Comparative*, Routledge, London, 1990, 130-47.

——— "Christian Theology of Religions: An Evaluation of John Hick and Paul Knitter," *Studia Missionalia*, 42, 1993, 161-78.

——— "Whose Objectivity? Which Neutrality? The Doomed Quest for a Neutral Vantage Point from which to Judge Religions," *Religious Studies*, 29, 1993, 79-95.

——— "Revelation and Revelations: The Role and Value of Different Religious Traditions," *Bulletin*, 85-86, 1994, 145-64.

——— "Revelation and 'Revelations': Beyond a Static Valuation of Other Religions," *Modern Theology*, 10, 2, 1994, 165-84.

——— "Inculturation, India and Other Religions," in *Studia Missionalia*, 44, 1995, 121-47.

——— "The Impossibility of a Pluralist View of Religions," *Religious Studies*, 32, 1996, 223-32.

——— "Theology of Religions," in David F. Ford, ed., *The Modern Theologians*, Blackwell, Oxford, 1997, 2nd ed., 626-44.

——— "On cultivating the disciplined habits of a love affair, *or* on how to do theology on your knees," *New Blackfriars*, 79, 925, 1998, 116-36.

——— "Trinitarian Différance and World Religions: Postmodernity and the 'Other,' " in Ursula King, ed., *Faith and Praxis in a Postmodern Age*, Cassell, London, 1998, 28-46.

——— "Review of Dupuis, *Towards a Christian Theology of Religious Pluralism*," *The Journal of Theological Studies*, 49, 2, 1998, 910-14.

——— "*Nostra Aetate*—Telling God's Story in Asia: Promises and Pitfalls," in Leo Kenis, ed., *Vatican II*, Leuven, forthcoming.

——— *The Trinity and the Murder of the Mother*, SCM, London, 2000.

D'Costa, Gavin, ed. *Christian Uniqueness Reconsidered*, Orbis, Maryknoll, N.Y., 1990.

——— *Resurrection Reconsidered*, Oneworld, Oxford, 1996.

De Smet, R. and J. Neuner, et al., eds. *Religious Hinduism: A Presentation and Appraisal*, St. Paul's Press, Allahbad, 1964.

Denzinger, H. and A. Schönmetzer, eds. *Enchiridon Symbolorum Definitionum et Declarationum de Rebus et Morum*, 36th ed., Herder, Freiburg, 1976 (DZ).

Deutsch, Eliot, ed. *Culture and Modernity: East-West Philosophical Perspectives*, University of Hawaii Press, Honolulu, 1991.

Dhavamony, Mariasusai. *Christian Theology of Religions*, Peter Lang, Berlin, 1998.

DiNoia, Joe. "Pluralist Theology of Religions: Pluralistic or Non-Pluralistic?" in D'Costa, ed., *Christian Uniqueness Reconsidered*, 1990, 119-34.

——— *The Diversity of Religions: A Christian Perspective*, Catholic University of America Press, Washington, D.C., 1992.

The Divine Office (*Liturgia Horarum*), Collins, London, 1974.

Dupuis, Jacques. *Toward a Christian Theology of Religious Pluralism*, Orbis, Maryknoll, N.Y., 1997.

——— "A Theological Commentary: Dialogue and Proclamation," in William Burrows, ed., *Redemption and Dialogue*, 1993, 119-58.

Fallon, P. "Rāmakrishna, Vivekananda, and Radhakrishnan," in R. De Smet & J. Neuner, et. al., eds., *Religious Hinduism*, 1964, 288-91.

Ferm, V., ed. *Religion in Transition*, George, Allen & Unwin, London, 1937.

Findings of an Exploratory Consultation on Interreligious Prayer, jointly arranged by the Pontifical Council for Interreligious Dialogue and the Office on Inter-Religious Relations of the WCC, 1966, in *Bulletin*, 98, 1998, 231-37.

Fitzgerald, Michael. "IV East-West Spiritual Exchange: Appendix—Some Aspects of Christian Meditation: A Few Reflections," *Bulletin*, 75, 1990, 262-66.

Fitzgerald, Michael L. and Robert Caspar. *Signs of Dialogue: Christian Encounters with Muslims*, Silsilch Publishers, Samboanga City, 1992.

Fitzmeyer, Joseph A. *The Gospel According to Luke: X-XXIV*, The Anchor Bible, Doubleday, New York, 1985.

Ford, David F., ed. *The Modern Theologians*, Blackwell, Oxford, 1997, 2nd ed.

Forman, Robert K. C., ed. *The Problems of Pure Consciousness: Mysticism and Philosophy*, Oxford University Press, New York, 1990.

Forrester, Duncan. "Professor Hick and the Universe of Faiths," *Scottish Journal of Theology*, 29, 1, 1976, 65-72.

Frei, Hans W. *The Eclipse of Biblical Narrative: A Study in Eighteenth and Nineteenth Century Hermeneutics*, Yale University Press, New Haven, Connecticut, 1974.

Geach, Peter. *God and the Soul*, Routledge & Kegan Paul, London, 1969.

Gellner, Ernst. *Postmodernism, Reason and Religion*, Routledge, London, 1992.

Gnanapragasam, Ignatius. *Dr. Radhakrishnan and Jnana: An Essay on the Metaphysical Aspects of a Spiritual Wisdom*, Ph.D., Gregorian University, Rome, 1956.

Griffiths, Paul J., ed. *Christianity through Non-Christian Eyes*, Orbis, Maryknoll, N.Y., 1990.

Gyatso, Tenzin. *See* Dalai Lama.

Hacker, Paul. "Aspects of New-Hinduism as Contrasted with Surviving Traditional Hinduism" in Lambert Schmithausen, ed., *Writings of Paul Hacker: Kleine Schriften*, Harrassowitz, Wiesbaden, 1978, private trans. by Dr. Dermott Killingley.

Halbfass, Wilhelm. *India and Europe: An Essay in Understanding*, State University of New York, Albany, 1988.

Hallencreutz, Carl F. *New Approaches to Men of Other Faith*, World Council of Churches, Geneva, 1970.

Hamnett, Ian, ed. *Religious Pluralism and Unbelief: Studies Critical and Comparative*, Routledge, London, 1990.

Harris, Ishwar C. *An Exposition of the Concept of Universalism in S. Radhakrishnan's Thought*, Ph.D., Claremont Graduate School, Claremont, California, 1974.

Hartman, David. *Conflicting Visions: Spiritual Possibilities of Modern Israel*, Schocken Books, New York, 1990.

Hauerwas, Stanley. "Some Theological Reflections on Gutierrez's Use of 'Liberation' as a Theological Concept," *Modern Theology*, 3, 1, 1986, 67-76.

——— *Naming the Silence: God, Medicine and the Problem of Suffering*, T. & T. Clark, Edinburgh, 1993.

Hauerwas, Stanley and Charles Pinches. *Christians among the Virtues: Theological Conversations with Ancient and Modern Ethics*, University of Notre Dame Press, Indiana, 1997.

Haynes, Richard. "Gotama Buddha and Religious Pluralism," *Journal of Religious Pluralism*, 1, 1991, 65-95.

Heelas, Paul. *The New Age Movement: The Celebration of the Self and the Sacralization of Modernity*, Blackwell, Oxford, 1996.

Heiler, Friedrich. *Prayer: A Study in the History and Psychology of Religion*, Oxford University Press, Oxford, 1932.

Heschel, Abraham Joshua. "No Religion is an Island," in Paul J. Griffiths, ed., *Christianity through Non-Christian Eyes*, 1990, 26-40.

Hick, John. *Faith and Knowledge*, Cornell University Press, New York, 1957.

——— *God and the Universe of Faiths*, Fount/Collins, London, 1977.

——— *God Has Many Names*, Macmillan, London, 1980.

——— "On Grading Religions," *Religious Studies*, 17, 4, 1981, 451-67.

——— *Problems in Religious Pluralism*, Macmillan, London, 1985.

——— "The Non-Absoluteness of Christianity," in Hick and Knitter, eds., *The Myth of Christian Uniqueness*, Orbis, Maryknoll, N.Y., 1987, 16-36.

——— *An Interpretation of Religion*, Macmillan, London, 1989.

——— "The Possibility of Religious Pluralism: A Reply to Gavin D'Costa," *Religious Studies*, 33, 1997, 161-6.

Hick, John and Hasan Askari, eds. *Religious Diversity*, Gower, Aldershot, 1985.

Hick, John and Paul F. Knitter, eds., *The Myth of Christian Uniqueness: Toward a Pluralistic Theology of Religions*, Orbis, Maryknoll, N.Y., 1987.

Horton, John and Susan Mendus, eds. *After MacIntyre: Critical Perspectives on the Work of Alasdair MacIntyre*, Polity Press, Oxford, 1994.

Hospital, Clifford G. "Christian *Pūjā*?" *Toronto Journal of Theology*, Spring 1985, 1, 1, 80-92.

Inge, W. R., et al., eds. *Radhakrishnan: Comparative Studies in Philosophy in Honour of his Sixtieth Birthday*, George Allen & Unwin, London, 1951.

International Theological Commission. *Select Themes of Ecclesiology on the Twentieth Anniversary of the Closing of the Second Vatican Council*, Rome, 1985.

Jacobs, Louis. *A Jewish Theology*, Darton, Longman & Todd, London, 1973.

John Paul II, His Holiness Pope. *On the Holy Spirit in the Life of the Church, Dominum et vivificantem*, 1986.

——— "Address to the Roman Curia," *Bulletin*, 64, 1987, 58-66.

——— *On the Permanent Validity of the Church's Missionary Mandate, Redemptoris Missio*, 1991.

——— *Crossing the Threshold of Hope*, Jonathan Cape, London, 1994.

——— *On the Value and Inviolability of Human Life, Evangelium vitae*, 1995.

Johnston, George. *The Spirit-Paraclete in the Gospel of John*, Cambridge University Press, Cambridge, 1970.

Jung, Moses, et al., eds. *Relations among Religions Today*, E. J. Brill, Leiden, 1963.

Kant, Immanuel. *Religion with the Limits of Reason Alone*, Harper & Row, New York, 1960.

Katz, Stephen. "Mysticism and Philosophical Analysis" in Katz, ed., *Mysticism and Philosophical Analysis*, Sheldon, London, 1978, ch. 9.

Katz, Stephen, ed. *Mysticism and Language*, Oxford University Press, New York, 1992.

——— *Mysticism and Philosophical Analysis*, Sheldon, London, 1978.

King, Ursula, ed. *Faith and Praxis in a Postmodern Age*, Cassell, London, 1998.

Klein, Anne. *Knowledge and Liberation: Tibetan Buddhist Epistemology in Support of Transformative Religious Experience*, Snow Lion, New York, 1986.

Knight, Kelvin, ed. *The MacIntyre Reader*, Polity Press, Oxford, 1998.

Knitter, Paul F. *No Other Name? A Critical Study of Christian Attitudes toward Other Religions*, Orbis, Maryknoll, N.Y., 1985.

——— "Roman Catholic Approaches to Other Religions," *International Bulletin of Missionary Research*, 1984, 44-51.

——— "Dialogue and Liberation," *Drew Gateway*, 58, 1, 1987, 1-53.

——— "Interpreting 'Silence': A Response to Miikka Ruokannen," *International Bulletin of Missionary Research*, 1, 14, 1990, 62-3.

——— "A New Pentecost? A Pneumatological Theology of Religions," *Current Dialogue*, 19, 1992, 418-37.

——— *One Earth Many Religions, Multifaith Dialogue and Global Responsibility*, Orbis, Maryknoll, N.Y., 1995.

——— *Jesus and the Other Names*, Orbis, Maryknoll, N.Y., 1996.

Knitter, Paul F., John Cobb Jr., Len Swidler, and Monika Hellwig. *Death or Dialogue*, SCM, London, 1990.

Knott, Kim. *Hinduism in Leeds*, University of Leeds, Leeds, 1986.

Kopf, David. *The Brahmo Samaj and the Shaping of the Modern Indian Mind*, Princeton University Press, Princeton, 1979.

Lamb, Christopher. "The Experience of Interfaith Prayer," *The Way Supplement: Interfaith Spirituality*, 78, 1993, 81-8.

Law, Judith. *The Religious Beliefs and Practices of Hindus in Derby*, University of Leeds, Leeds, 1990.

Lee, V. T. *The Concept of History in S. Radhakrishnan*, Ph.D., Northwestern University, Evanston, Illinois, 1977.

Legenhausen, Muhammad. Book review of *Whose Justice? Which Rationality?* in *Al-Tawhid*, 14, 2, 1997, 158-76.

Lindars, Barnabas. *The Gospel of John*, Oliphants, London, 1972.

Lindsell, Harold, ed. *The Church's Worldwide Mission: Proceedings of the Congress on the Church's Worldwide Mission*, World Books, Waco, Texas, 1966.

Lipner, Julius. "The Christian and Vedāntic theories of originative causality: A study in transcendence and immanence," *Philosophy East and West*, 28, 1, 1978, 53-68.

Lott, Eric. *Vedāntic Approaches to God*, Macmillan, London, 1980.

Loughlin, Gerard. "Myths, Signs and Significations," *Theology*, 730, 1986, 268-75.

——— "Prefacing Pluralism: John Hick and the Mastery of Religion," *Modern Theology*, 7, 1990, 29-55.

MacIntyre, Alasdair. *After Virtue*, Duckworth, London, 1985, 2nd ed.

——— *Whose Justice? Which Rationality?*, Duckworth, London, 1988.

——— *Three Rival Versions of Moral Enquiry*, Duckworth, London, 1990.

——— "How intellectual excellence in philosophy is to be understood by a

Catholic philosopher," *Current Issues in Catholic Higher Education*, 12, 1, 1991, 47-50.

——— "Incommensurability, truth, and the conversation between Confucians and Aristotelians about the virtues," in Deutsch, ed., *Culture and Modernity*, 1991, 104-22.

Maharaj, Rubindranath R. *Death of a Guru*, (with Dave Hunt), Hodder & Stoughton, London, 1977.

Main, John. *Silence and Stillness in Every Season: Daily Readings with John Main*, ed. Paul Harris, Darton, Longman & Todd, London, 1998.

Marshall, Bruce. *Christology in Conflict*, Blackwell, Oxford, 1987.

Masood, Steven. *Into the Light*, STL Books, Bromley Kent, 1986.

Matzko, David McCarthy. "Postmodernity, Saints and Scoundrels," *Modern Theology*, 9, 1993, 19-36.

——— "Christ's Body in its Fullness: Resurrection and the Lives of the Saints," in Gavin D'Costa, ed., *Resurrection Reconsidered*, Oneworld, Oxford, 1996, 102-117.

McKain, David W., ed. *Christianity: Some Non-Christian Approaches*, Greenwood Press, London, 1964.

Milbank, John. *Theology and Social Theory*, Blackwell, Oxford, 1990.

——— "The End of Dialogue," in Gavin D'Costa, ed., *Christian Uniqueness Reconsidered*, Orbis, Maryknoll, N.Y., 1990, 174-91.

——— "The Name of Jesus: Incarnation, Atonement, Ecclesiology," *Modern Theology*, 7, 4, 1991, 311-33.

——— *The Word Made Strange: Theology, Language, Culture*, Blackwell, Oxford, 1997.

Mojzes, Paul and Leonard Swidler, eds. *Christian Mission and Interreligious Dialogue*, Edwin Mellen Press, New York, 1991.

Moule, C. F. D. *The Holy Spirit*, Mowbrays, London, 1978.

Mukerji, A. C. "Reality and Ideality in the Western and the Indian Idealistic Thought," in W. R. Inge, et al., eds., *Radhakrishnan: Comparative Studies in Philosophy in Honour of his Sixtieth Birthday*, George Allen & Unwin, London, 1951, 216-31.

Mukerji, Chuni. *A Modern Hindu View of Life*, SPCK, London & Calcutta, 1930.

Nasr, Seyyed Hossein and Veena Das. "Special Issue: proceedings of the first meeting of the Harvard Divinity School's Jerome Hall Dialogue Series," *The Muslim World*, LXVII, 2, 1987, 96-105, 109, 116-36.

Neill, Stephen. *Christian Faiths and Other Faiths*, Oxford University Press, London, 1961.

Novak, David. *The Image of the Non-Jew in Judaism*, Toronto Studies in Theology, Vol. 9, Edwin Mellen Press, New York, 1983.

An Observance for Commonwealth Day, Monday, 14 March, 1994, London.

Ogden, Schubert. "Some Thoughts on a Christian Theology of Interreligious Dialogue," *Criterion*, 11, 1994, 5-10.

Panikkar, Raiumundo. *The Trinity and the Religious Experience of Man*, Darton, Longman & Todd, London, 1973.

Parrinder, Geoffrey. *Worship in the World Religions*, Faber & Faber, London, 1961.

Pontifical Council for Interreligious Dialogue & Congregation for the Evangelization of Peoples. *Dialogue and Mission*, 1991.

Pontifical Council for Interreligious Dialogue. See *Bulletin*.

Pye, Michael. *Skilful Means: A Concept in Mahāyāna Buddhism*, Duckworth, London, 1978.

Race, Alan. *Christians and Religious Pluralism*, SCM, London, 1983; 2nd ed.; SCM, London, 1994.

Radhakrishnan, Sarvapelli. *Indian Philosophy*, 2 Vols., George Allen & Unwin, London, 1923.

——— *The Hindu View of Life* (1926), Unwin, London, 1980.

——— *An Idealist View of Life* (1929), Unwin, London, 1980.

——— "My Search for Truth" in V. Ferm, ed., *Religion in Transition*, George Allen & Unwin, London, 1937.

——— *Eastern Religions and Western Thought*, Oxford University Press, Oxford, 1939.

——— *Recovery of Faith*, George Allen & Unwin, London, 1956.

Rahner, Karl. *Theological Investigations*, Vol. 1, Darton, Longman & Todd, London, 1965.

Rahner, Karl, et al., eds. *Sacramentum Mundi*, Burns & Oates, London, 1968.

——— *Theological Investigations*, Vol. 18, Darton, Longman & Todd, London, 1983.

Raju, P. T. "The Idealism of Sir S. Radhakrishnan," *Calcutta Review*, August 1940, 168-84.

——— "Radhakrishnan's Influence on Indian Thought," in Schilpp, ed., *Radhakrishnan*, 513-41.

Rasmusson, Arne. *The Church as Polis: From Political Theology to Theological Politics as Exemplified by Jürgen Moltmann and Stanley Hauerwas*, Lund University Press, Sweden, 1994.

Ratzinger, Joseph. *In the Beginning . . . A Catholic Interpretation of the Story of the Creation and Fall*, W. B. Eerdmans, Michigan, 1990.

——— "Central Problem for Faith," *Briefing*, Vol. 27, 1, 1997, 36-42.

Report of a Working Group on Interfaith Service and Worship, in *Ends and Odds*, No. 22, March, 1980.

Riches, John, ed. *The Analogy of Beauty*, T. & T. Clark, Edinburgh, 1986.

Rosales, G. and C. G. Arévalo, eds. *For All the Peoples of Asia: Federation of Asian Bishops' Conferences Documents from 1970 to 1991*, Orbis, Maryknoll, N.Y., 1992.

Rosenzweig, Franz. *The Star of Redemption*, trans. William B. Hallo, Routledge, Kegan & Paul, London, 1971.

Ruokanen, Miikka. *The Catholic Doctrine of Non-Christian Religions according to the Second Vatican Council*, E. J. Brill, Leiden, 1992.

Schillebeeckx, Edward. *Revelation and Theology*, Vol. 1, Sheed & Ward, London, 1967.

Schilpp, P. A., ed. *The Philosophy of Sarvapelli Radhakrishnan*, Tudor Publishing Co., New York, 1952.

Schmitt, K. Randall. *Death and After Life in the Theologies of Karl Barth and John Hick*, Rodopi, Amsterdam, 1986.

Secretariat pro Non-Christianis. *Guidelines for a Dialogue between Muslims and Christians*, Edizion Ancora, Rome, 1971.

Sharma, Arvind, ed. *Neo-Hindu Views of Christianity*, E J Brill, Leiden, 1988.

Sharpe, Eric. *Not to Destroy but to Fulfil*, Gleerups, Lund, 1965.

Sherwin, Byron L. and Harold Kasimow, eds. *John Paul II and Interreligious Dialogue*, Orbis, Maryknoll, N.Y., 1999.

Singer, Milton. *When a Great Tradition Modernizes*, Pacific Press Publications Association, Mount View, California, 1980.

Sinkinson, Christopher. *The Nature of Christian Apologetics in Response to Religious Pluralism: An Analysis of the Contribution of John Hick*, University of Bristol, Ph.D., 1997.

Solomon, Norman. *Judaism and World Religion*, Macmillan, London, 1991.

Spae, Joseph. *Buddhist-Christian Empathy*, The Chicago Institute of Theology and Culture, Illinois, 1980.

Spear, Percival. *A History of India*, Vol. 2, Penguin, London, 1965.

Suchocki, Marjorie Hewitt. "In Search of Justice," in Knitter and Hick, eds., *The Myth of Christian Uniqueness*, Orbis, Maryknoll, N.Y., 1987, 140-61.

Sullivan, Francis A. *Salvation Outside the Church?* Geoffrey Chapman, London, 1992.

Surin, Kenneth. "A Certain 'Politics of Speech': Towards an Understanding of the Relationships Between the Religions in the Age of the McDonald's Hamburger," in D'Costa, ed., *Christian Uniqueness Reconsidered*, Orbis, Maryknoll, N.Y., 1990, 192-212.

Suzuki, Beatrice Lane. *Mahāyāna Buddhism*, George Allen & Unwin, London, 1981.

Suzuki, D. T. *On Indian Mahāyāna Buddhism*, Harper Torchbooks, New York, 1968.

Therésè of Lisieux, *Autobiography of a Saint*, trans. Ronald Knox, Fontana Books, London, 1958.

Thomas, M. M. *The Acknowledged Christ of the Indian Renaissance*, SCM, London, 1969.

Tuck, D. R. *Māyā: Interpretative Principle for an Understanding of the Religious Thought of Śankara and Radhakrishnan*, Ph.D., School of Religion, Iowa University, 1970.

Urumpackal, Thomas. *Organized Religion According to Radhakrishnan*, Universita Gregoriana Editrice, Rome, 1972.

van Straelen, H. *L'Eglise et les religions non chréstiennes au seuil du XXe siècle*, Beauchesne, Paris, 1994.

Vanhoozer, Kevin. "Does the Trinity Belong in a Theology of Religions? On Angling in the Rubicon and the 'Identity' of God," in Kevin Vanhoozer, ed., *The Trinity in a Pluralistic Age*, 1997, 41-71.

Vanhoozer, Kevin, ed. *The Trinity in a Pluralistic Age*, W. B. Eerdmans, Grand Rapids, 1997.

Voll, J. O. *Islam: Continuity and Change in the Modern World*, Longman, London, 1982.

von Balthasar, Hans urs. Medard Kehl and Werner Löser, eds., *The von Balthasar Reader*, T. & T. Clark, Edinburgh, 1982.

Vorgrimler, H., ed. *Commentary on the Documents of Vatican II*, 5 Vols., Burns & Oates, London, 1967-9.

Wadia, A. R. "The Social Philosophy of Radhakrishnan" in Schilpp, ed., *Radhakrishnan*, Tudor Publishing Co., New York, 1952, 755-87.

Watt, William Montgomery. *Muslim-Christian Encounters: Perceptions and Misperceptions*, Routledge, London, 1991.

Wiedemann, Thomas. *Adults and Children in the Roman Empire*, Yale University Press, London/New Haven, 1989.

Williams, Paul. "rMa bya pa Byang chub brtson 'grus on Madhyamaka Method," *Journal of Indian Philosophy*, 13, 1985, 205-25.

——— *Mahāyāna Buddhism: The Doctrinal Foundations*, Routledge, London, 1989.

——— "Some Buddhist Reflections on Hans Küng's Treatment of Mahāyāna Buddhism in *Christianity and the World Religions*," *World Faiths Insight*, n.s. 22, 1989, 13-26.

——— "The Recent Work of Raimundo Panikkar," *Religious Studies*, 27, 1989, 511-21.

——— *Altruism and Reality: Studies in the Philosophy of the Bodhicaryāvatāra*, Curzon, London, 1998.

——— *Mahāyāna Buddhism in India: A Doctrinal Overview*, University of Bristol, ms. 1999, forthcoming: Routledge, London, 2000.

Williams, Rowan. "Balthasar and Rahner," in Riches, ed., *The Analogy of Beauty*, 1986, 11-34.

Yamaguchi, Susumu. *Mahāyāna Way to Buddhahood*, Buddhist Books International, Tokyo, 1982.

Young, Robert. *White Mythologies: Writing History and the West*, Routledge, London, 1990.

Zaehner, R. C. *Mysticism Sacred and Profane*, Clarendon Press, Oxford, 1957.

Zaehner, R. C., ed. *The Concise Encyclopedia of Living Faiths*, Hutchinson, London, 1971, 2nd ed.

Zion, William P. "Response to Hospital," *Toronto Journal of Theology*, Spring 1985, 1, 1, 93-7.

Index

Other Titles in the Faith Meets Faith Series

Toward a Universal Theology of Religion, Leonard Swidler, Editor
The Myth of Christian Uniqueness, John Hick and Paul F. Knitter, Editors
An Asian Theology of Liberation, Aloysius Pieris, S.J.
The Dialogical Imperative, David Lochhead
Love Meets Wisdom, Aloysius Pieris, S.J.
Many Paths, Eugene Hillman, C.S.Sp.
The Silence of God, Raimundo Panikkar
The Challenge of the Scriptures, Groupe de Recherches Islamo-Chrétien
The Meaning of Christ, John P, Keenan
Hindu-Christian Dialogue, Harold Coward, Editor
The Emptying God, John B. Cobb Jr. and Christopher Ives, Editors
Christianity through Non-Christian Eyes, Paul J. Griffiths, Editor
Christian Uniqueness Reconsidered, Gavin D'Costa, Editor
Women Speaking, Women Listening, Maura O'Neill
Bursting the Bonds?, Leonard Swidler, Lewis John Eron, Gerard Sloyan, and Lester Dean, Editors
One Christ—Many Religions, Stanley J. Samartha
The New Universalism, David J. Kreiger
Jesus Christ at the Encounter of World Religions, Jacques Dupuis, S.J.
After Patriarchy, Paula M. Cooey, William R. Eakin, and Jay B. McDaniel, Editors
An Apology for Apologetics, Paul J. Griffiths
World Religions and Human Liberation, Dan Cohn-Sherbok, Editor
Uniqueness, Gabriel Moran
Leave the Temple, Felix Wilfred, Editor
The Buddha and the Christ, Leo D. Lefebure
The Divine Matrix, Joseph A. Bracken, S.J.
The Gospel of Mark: A Mahāyāna Reading, John P. Keenan
Revelation, History, and the Dialogue of Religions, David A. Carpenter
Salvations, S. Mark Heim
The Intercultural Challenge of Raimon Panikkar, Joseph Prabhu, Editor
Fire and Water: Women, Society, and Spirituality in Buddhism and Christianity, Aloysius Pieris, S.J.
Piety and Power: Muslims and Christians in West Africa, Lamin Sanneh
Life after Death in World Religions, Harold Coward, Editor
The Uniqueness of Jesus, Paul Mojzes and Leonard Swidler, Editors
A Pilgrim in Chinese Culture, Judith A. Berling
West African Religious Traditions, Robert B. Fisher, S.V.D.
Hindu Wisdom for All God's Children, Francis X. Clooney, S.J.
Imagining the Sacred, Vernon Ruland, S.J.
Christian-Muslim Relations, Ovey N. Mohammed, S.J.